"A life recollected in vivid scenes, *Cells* is both brutal and tender in its depiction of the relationships that shape a self. Leading the reader through moments of darkness and of luminosity alike, this is a work of intellect and eloquence, but also a work of great heart. I was deeply moved as I read, and so grateful that this book found its way to me."

DOIREANN NÍ GHRÍOFA, AUTHOR OF *A GHOST IN THE THROAT*

"This is a book that brims with stored-up pain—and with a very particular kind of courage. For all its dark and sometimes brutal honesty, what the reader is going to remember here is the way that McCrea's prose fights on through his hurt to bring home pages that seem lit from within by love and beauty. A memoir that is as rewarding as it is undoubtedly challenging."

NEIL BARTLETT, AUTHOR OF *READY TO CATCH HIM SHOULD HE FALL* AND *ADDRESS BOOK*

"A brave, raw, visceral memoir told with such acuity, insight, and compassion, I could barely put it down. Gavin McCrea's unflinching mapping of his family's struggles, his own journey towards individuation and self-realisation, as well as his deep, conflicted love for his mother, is beautifully rendered, painful, and real. A stunning, memorable read."

LISA HARDING, AUTHOR OF *BRIGHT BURNING THINGS*

"Reading *Cells*, I was struck by McCrea's generosity in interrogating personal histories as they relate to wider familial and social systems. Contemplating devotion and loss with revolutionary sensitivity, what results is a stunning work of emotion-mapping. *Cells* is a dazzling exploration of nuance; pondering the formative threads that piece together the self, sewing a new lineage of interconnectedness towards acceptance."

PETER SCALPELLO, AUTHOR OF *L'*

T0035668

"Profound, intimate, and exquisitely written, *Cells* is staggeringly good. McCrea is a singular voice of contemporary Ireland."

HELEN CULLEN, AUTHOR OF *THE TRUTH MUST DAZZLE GRADUALLY*

"Gavin McCrea has written a succession of cells that open up a world of wonder. As smart as it is witty, this memoir grips in a journey that will make the reader feel, understand, and, on top of that, marvel at the cost of love and the things people need do to survive."

GILLIAN SLOVO, AUTHOR OF *EVERY SECRET THING*

"Gavin McCrea's wonderful memoir *Cells* is aptly named. His writing gets under the skin and drills through the bone and into the marrow of what pain and joy it is to be a mother and to be that very particular mother's child."

TISH DELANEY, AUTHOR OF *THE SAINT OF LOST THINGS*

CELLS

Gavin McCrea is the author of two critically acclaimed novels, *Mrs Engels* (2015) and *The Sisters Mao* (2021), both published by Scribe. His articles have appeared in *The Paris Review*, *The Guardian*, *The Irish Times*, *Catapult*, and *LitHub*.

CELLS

MEMORIES FOR MY MOTHER

GAVIN McCREA

SCRIBE
Melbourne • London

Scribe Publications
18–20 Edward St, Brunswick, Victoria 3056, Australia
2 John St, Clerkenwell, London, WC1N 2ES, United Kingdom
3754 Pleasant Ave, Suite 100, Minneapolis, Minnesota 55409, USA

Published by Scribe 2022

Typeset in Garamond Premier Pro 12/16 pt by the publishers

Printed and bound in the UK by CPI Group (UK) Ltd, Croydon CR0 4YY

Scribe Publications is committed to the sustainable use of natural resources
and the use of paper products made responsibly from those resources.

978 1 957363 34 9 (US edition)
978 1 922585 09 7 (Australian edition)
978 1 914484 04 9 (UK edition)
978 1 922586 60 5 (ebook)

Catalogue records for this book are available from the
National Library of Australia and the British Library.

scribepublications.com
scribepublications.co.uk
scribepublications.com.au

This book is for my mother, Breda

CONTENTS

PROLOGUE: DUBLIN, 2020

I am spending the quarantine in a small flat in south Dublin with my eighty-year-old mother, who, according to the emergency regulations, is not allowed outside at any time or for any reason, but who at ten o'clock every morning, having breakfasted and hoovered and watered the flowerpots and decided she can't spend another moment within these walls, insists on packing her coin purse and a bottle of water into her backpack—she leaves her mobile phone on the kitchen counter—and setting off on a route that takes her along the Dodder River, through Rathgar, then Milltown, then Clonskeagh, into Donnybrook, where, in the only place open, a SPAR supermarket, she buys a takeaway coffee and a pastry to be eaten as she makes her way through Herbert Park, Ballsbridge, Ringsend, reaching the River Liffey at Tom Clarke Bridge, in normal circumstances a busy toll link but now empty of traffic, which allows her to stand in the middle of the road as she looks across to the port on the other bank, and the moored boats, and the warehouses, and the cranes that seem to be holding up by thin threads the skeletons of new office blocks, and I wonder what comes to her mind then, at that spot, taking in this scene, which even devoid of people and cars and in this bright spring weather cannot, I imagine, be beautiful, is there something specific that touches her, the sight of a swallow returned from Africa perhaps, before she turns around and returns the way she came—eight kilometres each way, sixteen in total—and comes back through the door and takes off her shoes, and I say to her from the kitchen where I am preparing our lunch—vegetarian salads or soba noodles or pilaf or

1

roasted vegetables and, twice a week, fresh fish, for both of us are skinny and live in terror of weight gain—'Did you get arrested?' and she says, 'Pardon?' because she is almost deaf, and I say, 'Did they slap a fine on you at least?' and if she hears this, which she sometimes chooses to, she lets out a laugh before going into her bedroom to get changed into her indoor jumper and slacks, and, because she doesn't emerge for a while, I call in to her, 'This is ready, come in and sit down,' but she can never sit down immediately, she has to do something first, like put a wash into the machine, so I am always at the table before her, waiting, already irritated, and when finally she does come, she says, 'This is gorgeous,' before she has even tasted the food, and then, 'Are you going into town today?' which annoys me further because it is something she says all the time, having forgotten she said it before, and I say, 'Jesus, Mum, not this again,' and she says, 'What again?' and I say, 'Why would I be going into town? Town is shut down,' and while she can see I am upset and wants not to upset me like this, she is also wounded by my tone, and I am ashamed then and can only look at my plate, and I decide not to bring up what I intended to bring up, about the past, and about my need for her to apologise for it.

CELL I

Entrance is by a glass-fronted door on the east side of the building. Going through, I am in a vestibule about twice the size of an old telephone box. It is cold here, even on a warm day. Lights flash on an alarm box mounted on the wall, announcing its readiness for use. My mother is against alarms, the idea as much as the noise, and I would switch it off permanently to save the energy, but the required code has long been forgotten. Turning around to close the door behind me, my rucksack of groceries ruffles the leaves of a plant that sits on a low table. Placed in that particular spot, the plant does not get knocked over by the opening door or broken by things coming through the letter box, but it does obstruct access to the narrow flight of stairs, forcing me to mount the first step diagonally rather than straight-on.

There are fifteen steps up, covered in an old carpet of beige, mauve, burgundy, and blue stripes. When my mother bought this flat a decade ago, she was adamant that a stairlift be immediately installed in case she suddenly lost her mobility. She was coming from a semi-detached suburban house—with a big sitting room downstairs into which a bed could be put, if it ever came to that—and she wanted to be prepared. She had lived the first years of her life in a single room at the top of a house in the city centre, so she knew what it was like: the breath that was expended ascending and descending, the lugging up of water pails, the dragging down of ash. She also knew that people sometimes gave up and took to staying in, requiring others to do the up-and-down for them. She was frightened of that end for herself. The loss of independence. The shame of having to rely on others.

3

Really rather irrational, we thought.

'Not quite at the stairlift stage, Mum. We'll hold off on that.'

The legs, we were right to believe, would be the last thing to go.

Coming up the stairs, there is about a handspan of distance on either side between my shoulders and the walls. For two people to cross each other here, they would have to put their backs against the wall, and even then their torsos, their busts would rub against each other.

Que leurs torses, leurs bustes se frottent!

(A little command from my ego. A director in search of a cast.)

Through a second door and I am in the main living space. (I am arriving alone, in case there was any ambiguity.) A single room with an open kitchen, a dining table, and a seating area. A large window in the opposite wall, facing west. A smaller window in the kitchen. A glass door giving on to a tiny balcony. Bright enough, overall, not to require lights until late in the evening. And quiet. No flat overhead, and the one downstairs has been empty for some time. No car engines or horns because the main road is at a distance. No television set. No music player. There is a flashy internet radio—the internet itself I had installed only a couple of weeks ago—but it is only rarely turned on these days because, unless she sits right beside it and turns the volume right up, she can no longer make out the voices. For a while she missed them. Then she stopped mentioning them.

To the right, running along the north wall, are her bookshelves. Her collection was thinned out during the move from the family home, but what remains is by any standard impressive; that it belongs to a woman with only a bare-bones primary education, I think is extraordinary. The Irish, of course. But also the Russians. The French. The English. The Americans. A special section dedicated to Richard Ford, with whom she is in a sort of psychogenic relationship. She buys his books in hardback as soon as they come out, and cuts out his interviews, and talks about his professed devotion to his wife as something marvellous, if a bit weird. She met him once at a book signing in Dublin. While waiting for him to finish writing on her copy of *Lay of the Land*, she took a good look at his shoes.

4

'My goodness. They're exactly the sort I imagine Frank Bascombe to wear.'

Over which they shared a good old laugh.

Of all Ford's works, she holds a particular fondness for his memoir of his parents, *Between Them*. Ford's father had been a travelling salesman, a bit like my own father, and Ford's mother had been educated by nuns and then taken out of school without explanation, a bit like her.

'Just ordinary people. No great earthquakes.'

She finished the book, cried, then opened it at the beginning and went again.

Ford says of his relationship with his mother: 'We could always say "I love you" to clarify our complicated dealings without pausing. That seems perfect to me now and did then.'

It seems perfect to me, too. I admire it, as I think my mother does, though she would not tolerate much of it in reality. Sometimes, in our moments of intimacy, I do manage an *I-love-you*, but she does not return it. She is proficient in the other gestures. It is the words that are hard for her.

'I'm a doer, not a sayer.'

When I point out to her that that is a false division, that in fact saying is a form of doing, she looks put out. She enjoys hearing things that she herself could not say, reading things she could not write. She likes articulate people. But that does not mean she wants them in her kitchen, coming at her.

On the floor, just beyond the threshold, is a folded newspaper on which my hiking boots and her walking sandals are placed side by side. There being space for these two pairs only, I keep my runners on as I head for the big window opposite, which is closed and needs to be opened unless the heating is on, and sometimes even then: the place must be kept aired. After six steps, I am in the seating area, which consists of three ill-matching bits of furniture. One: a moss-green two-seater couch, too uncomfortable to settle into, but fine for perching on to get access to my mother's good ear. Two: a massive, and I mean *massive*, coffee table—the weight, I would wager, of one of those new Cinquecentos I see parked everywhere outside—on whose lower shelf she keeps her theatre and concert programmes, her art books, her poetry collections, her saved articles, her things to dip into. Three: an armchair in cream faux leather, pre-ergonomic. This is where my mother reads her novels and does her crosswords. Right now, it is empty, because she is out for her walk. Morning is for exercising, and the hour after lunch is for washing up and drying and organising, but after that, in the late afternoon and evening, her rest earned, she permits herself to sit, and this is her place. A nice part of the day, that. Both of us exercised and fed. Me in my room working. She in her chair reading and scribbling. The place hushed. Peaceful. My favourite time. My most productive. Unless:

'Do you know what *terpsichorean* means?'

'No.'

'No? And you a doctor of literature.'

A couple of more steps gets me to the window, which is framed by a pair of curtains decorated with horizontal bands of gold and coral. Outside on the grass, two heterosexual families, safely detached, are having picnics. Nearby, a pair of infants, girls, are playing house in a branded and highly gendered tent: pink, princess, turrets, *bleugh*. I open the window, which lets the voices in, though I am careful not to listen to the message they are carrying. The dwellings in this development are completely ordinary: what, situated in any other part of the city, any other part of Europe, would be working-class homes. Squat, uninspired blocks of red brick. Two and three storeys. Two-bed units, mostly. But the area, the so-called postcode—recently replaced by a more complex *Eircode* but persisting as a single digit in the national consciousness—has the highest property prices in the country. I am ashamed even to know this. It disgusts me that people get to live here, as I do, on these roads, by this river, with these shops, and town right there. My only reassurance is the certainty that the conversations happening around me are abysmal.

Headline: *The Perfect Pandemic Escape in Wicklow for €550,000.*

Possibly the picnickers are talking about that. As I am talking about it now. *The perfect escape: is that not death?* In the meantime, there is no getting way from ourselves. I look down at my neighbours on their blankets, picking from plastic tubs of olives, and it is painful because they could just as well be me.

Moving from the window towards the kitchen, I pass the dining table, another colossal structure. A rectangle long enough for six high-backed chairs in brown-and-beige faux leather. The surface divided into two parts. On one end, two place mats (more beige faux leather) that mark our meal-time positions: mine on the inside facing out, hers on the outside facing in. On the other end, her easel, along with a box of watercolour paints and some mixing trays, all now unused. She used to paint all the time. Well, a couple of times a week in the summer, anyway. At the dining table in the old family home. In the afternoon, after lunch, accompanied by a vinyl of classical music. Jars of water brought in from the kitchen tap. To begin with, her brushes glancing the surface of the water, just to moisten the bristles; then plunging deep and swirling around, turning everything brown. 'Change that water for me, can you, love?' The careful squeezing of tubes so as not to release too much paint. The scratch of her blade over a line of masking fluid. And her cry of distress—'Ah!'—when she made a mistake, one wash too many, requiring a rush to the sink, where the paper was put under running water. Her palette: French ultramarine, cadmium red, indigo, carmine, cerulean, rose, terracotta. Her style, impressionistic. The mood dreamy. A still life of pears whose blue shadows bleed back onto the skin. A cellist with no features on her face. A woman in a chair, her back to the viewer, her hair in a bun. An ancient statue, blue amongst blocks of sandy stone. A copse of bare trunks, a grey-blue sky, rays of purple and yellow light breaking through, and splashes of pink and red all over (achieved by running her thumb along a toothbrush soaked with colour): my favourite. The walls of the flat are decorated with these paint-ings. Framed in bleached wood. In the bottom right-hand corner of each, her signature painted on a diagonal. The images, which had always been hazy, now faded by time. She will not take up painting again. But nor will she take the easel and the tubes of colour off the dining table. They will stay there as artefacts on display. Objects of historical interest.

In the kitchen, I put my rucksack down on the cream tiled floor and begin to put the shopping away. Vegetables into the dark utility room.

Fruit into the bowls on the counter. Pulses and legumes and rice and couscous into the cupboard beside the cooker. But there is no guarantee these items will stay in those places. When my mother comes home, chances are she will make changes. Like, wash the fruit again and put them in different bowls on the table. Or transfer the vegetables to the icebox in the fridge. Or rearrange the cupboard, swapping the pasta and the muesli around. As far as I can tell, she does not have fixed ideas about where specific objects ought to be. Rather, the moving around of things, the placing and the replacing, evokes in her the pleasurable sensation of establishing a new order. Her order.

'Mum, where's the aubergine I bought? Are you hiding things from me again?'

Perhaps her most unusual habit is that of putting the kitchen utensils, especially the grater and the colander, onto the radiator or the windowsill to dry. Which is to say, after she has dried them with a tea-towel, she puts them out in the sun, or gives a blast of heat, to finish them off. There is a simple point to this, which rationally I am able to fathom: she does not want them going rusty. But there are occasions when I am cooking, with a number of fronts open—something frying and something else steaming and the pasta now ready to be drained—and I am standing in the middle of the kitchen with the pot in my hand and cannot find the fucking colander because it is on the other side of the room, lying upside down on the windowsill, basking in the afternoon sunshine, what may as well be *oceans* away, another continent, and I feel so angry that *my mother is withholding from me what I need* that I am minded to tip the boiling water and the—as of thirty seconds ago—al dente rigatoni over her head.

Standing now in front of the open cupboard, a tin of puy lentils in my hand, the memory of the colander brings with it an angry aftershock, one of such power that I feel a terrible constriction in my chest, over which I lay my free hand in order to massage it in slow circles, so that it does not rise up to my throat and my temples, where it could stay all day and turn into an argument.

If a memoir were ever written about her, my mother would prefer it to be like *Between Them*. In other words, she would prefer to be dead before it is written. I do not blame her. But I think she understands, also, that Ford is writing about his parents as a means to reveal something about himself. He is writing himself through them. And I am doing the same. I cannot see another way. I cannot conceive of a self-portrait that is not painted using my mother's brushes, that is not a reconstruction by me, of me, from the externals of *her* life: this flat, that easel, a tin of puy lentils, and, above all else, her.

Off the main living room, down a short corridor, is the bathroom. The bathroom door opens inwards; at its full extension, it reaches halfway into the room, almost as far as the toilet. If I am not careful and come in too quickly, the inside handle meets the glass of the shower door, making an unpleasant bang. To the left is the sink, which is built into a line of cupboards that takes up most of the room, leaving an area of floor about two metres long and half a metre wide. Two paces and I am at the toilet; when sitting down, my knees are about a handspan from the cupboard doors. Above the sink, a mirror is plastered onto the wall flush with the tiles. These wall tiles are a darker beige than the floor ones. Because there are no windows, when the light is turned on, a fan in the ceiling automatically starts up. The noise of this fan is one of four in the flat which my mother can clearly hear and which bother her (the other three: the washing machine, the fridge, the gas boiler). And, in truth, it bothers me, too. As does the quality of the light. So, when using this room, we both of us tend to keep the door open to let the natural light in and the air out. Since only a limited amount of natural light reaches this part of the flat, we have learned to function in semi-darkness. The open door, meanwhile, serves less to clear away smells than to trouble the boundaries between the public and the private.

What I am trying to say is, my mother talks to me while I am on the toilet. She stands in the open doorway, establishes eye contact with me through the gloom, and speaks to me. I return her gaze and respond. We have a conversation. Usually about something unrelated to the bodily act in which I am currently engaged. But on occasion about that act, too. In general, we do not shy from talking about our shit.

'The system can't cope with our good diet,' she says as she heads towards the toilet with a bucket of water to flush away the latest stoppage.

From my bedroom, I can sometimes hear her shit hitting the water, the deep plop of a stone dropped into a well. I make jokes about this, and she laughs, but actually, for the most part, we take our bowels quite seriously. When they are moving well, we are content. When they are not, we are not. (Though, to tell the truth, my mother expresses few problems in this area. Her transit is, by the sounds of it, robust and free-flowing. The anxiety I am expressing here is mine alone. Freud has some things to say about the sort of person who fixates on his anus, but we will get to them—Freud, my anus—later.)

I am less inclined than my mother to begin dialogues across the bathroom threshold, but I do regularly pass by the open door when she is inside and see her both on the toilet and in various states of undress. She sleeps in just a pair of underpants, no bra, no nightdress, and goes to bed hours before me, so our paths sometimes cross when she gets up to piss. When this happens, I do not fix my gaze or allow it to linger, but nor do I look away. I have seen the naked body of my eighty-year-old mother enough to know it fairly well. And it is beautiful.

I say this without sentimentality. I am not trying to convince myself, or others, that I am one of those (fictional) people enlightened enough to see beauty in absolutely everything. I am acknowledging, merely, that I am glad to possess this picture of my mother's naked body, which she herself has given to me, and which I can now conjure whenever I want, as a memory but also as a certain kind of knowledge (about bodies and sexuality and time and mind and history and women and sons and me).

There were no locks in the house I grew up in. My parents had keys to the front door, but we children did not. We came and went through the back door, which was left unlocked. Neither were there locks on the inside doors of the house. On the bathroom door, not even one of those little bars that slide across. Nada. A lack that was not counterbalanced by a system of rules designed to keep six bodies a modest distance from one another. No, it was a free-for-all. It was not uncommon that I, at age ten or twelve or fifteen or twenty, would be in the shower, soaping my balls behind the thin white curtain, when my mother would walk straight in, no knock, and begin to brush her teeth.

'I won't be a minute.'

A number of habits from my upbringing I have rebelled against or tried to rid myself of, with varying degrees of failure. Communal bath-rooming is not one of them, despite my former protestations against it:

'I can't handle this any more!'

In my relationships, it turns out, I do not respond well to being locked out. *I was fucking you in the arse a minute ago, now I'm not allowed to see you taking a dump?* Or, to put it more constructively, I seek out and thrive in the sort of closeness in which the bathroom door is left open. In which communication continues uninterrupted from the bedroom to the bathroom, and between the sink and the toilet and the shower. I have known profound dialogues to take place while I sit on the edge of a bath and my lover opens his bowels beside me. The end of at least one relation-ship was postponed by a hand passing through my hair while I washed my hole at the bidet. What I am describing is not an imagined ideal state of intimacy, for I know it exists, yet today I find my heart aching as if for something unattainable.

In the final months of her life, my maternal grandmother moved in to our house. On her first morning with us, I (fourteen years old) came out of my bedroom to be greeted with the sight, through the open bathroom door, of her naked figure, or almost naked, on the toilet. My mother was standing beside her, supporting her by keeping hold of her extended arm. The scene, which moves me when I think about it now, embarrassed me then, and I made to slip away. But my mother stopped me:

'Come and say hello to Nana.'

I paused in front of the open door. 'Hi Nana.' And then (that horri-ble Irish tic): 'How are you?'

My grandmother passed her gnarled hand—curled back on itself by arthritis—across her forehead and, speaking over the sound of water falling into water, said: 'I am old.'

Serious question: will my past experience of toilet intimacy with lovers prepare me, train me, make me ready for intimacy with my elderly mother? My wanting to be close to a man when he shits, and my wanting a man to be close to me when I shit: will this desire stand to me if and when I am called upon to wipe *her* arse?

Recently, for the first time, I had a conversation with my siblings about long-term care for her, in the course of which I heard myself say that, when the time came, I would look after her. I would do for my mother what she had done for her own mother. I would sit her on the toilet and hold her arm.

Come and say hello to—

I have lived abroad for most of the past twenty years. During the last couple of these, when speaking to my mother on the phone, I noticed a change in her ability to engage with me and to retain the information I gave her, but I put this down to her hearing loss and to her lifelong dislike of communicating over a wire. Then last summer she got lost while walking home on a route she knew well, which alarmed my siblings because it suggested the onset of a more serious decline. In November of the same year, I came back to Ireland to take up a one-year residency. My mother offered me her spare room for the duration. As soon as I moved in, I noticed a marked change in her behaviour. She was getting confused about time and date and place. She was initiating the same conversation over and over. When I relayed information to her, about where I was going or what I was doing, she retained little of it. She was obsessing about appointments: about where they were and with whom. Was it right what she had written in the calendar?

Since quarantine, the situation has got worse. Or perhaps I just get to observe it for longer periods and from closer range. Whereas before I was spending my days at the library or teaching at the university, seeing her only at mealtimes and as I came and went, now I am in the flat with her for most of the day. Outside of my work, she has become my entire focus. And what I see is a woman whose mind is slipping.

I report this to the others.

'This is only going in one direction,' my eldest brother responds.

So we talk about the future. And I say I will look after her because I am the best placed to do so. It is what I want.

'Are you sure about that?' my sister says.

Yes, I am sure. I do not want her going into a nursing home. I see it as my duty to provide her final care. After all she has done for me, it is the least I could do in return. I will hold her while she goes for a shit. I will reach down behind her and wipe her dirty arse. I will take a wet rag to her breasts, her bottom, her vagina. I will do all of that. Yes, I have thought about it. I have visualised it. I have put myself in her place, standing next to Nana, and I am comfortable there. I am okay with her body.

But no body exists without the mind, and it is that—the mental part—that I am (and my siblings are) more worried about. Will I have the tolerance to answer her questions all day, to repeat myself over and over, and to know that tomorrow will be the same or worse? How long before my own sanity begins to fray? Will I bully her? Will she bully me? Will I be willing to give up work to be available for her around the clock? Will I neglect friendships and turn down relationships because they interfere with my ability to care for her? Will I resent her for that?

'Are you sure?' my sister says.

'Yes,' I say.

But, in the concrete, I am not.

Adjacent to the bathroom is my mother's bedroom. About three by four metres. A single bed. A wardrobe. A chair. A chest of drawers. The walls bare apart from a couple of her watercolours: a Japanese geisha and a female nude reclining on the floor reading a book. My bedroom, a little smaller, is next door. A single bed. A wardrobe. A chair. A bookshelf that I have converted into a standing desk (my laptop on the highest shelf, an external keyboard in the middle, my notebooks and reference texts on the bottom). A spare mattress that sits on its side against the wall in case my sister, who lives outside Dublin, ever wants to stay the night (in which case the giant coffee table in the living room is pushed against the bookshelves, and the mattress put in its place).

The bedrooms, divided as they are by a thin non-supporting wall, form two compartments of a single cell. From my compartment—I am the bug, the rat, the stool pigeon, the snitch—I can hear my mother sleep. At first, in the stage of light sleep, she tends to snore. After that, in deep sleep, she goes completely silent.

(Once, with the aim of getting clean sheets from the drawers under her bed, I entered her room while she was in this silent state. She was lying face-up with her head tilted to the right side of the pillow. In the bar of light coming in from the corridor, her skin looked pale. Her limbs were petrified. Her chest did not appear to be rising or falling; there did not seem to be any air entering or leaving her lungs. I approached her, came right up to her face, and for an instant, before I heard a quiet gurgle in her throat, I beheld a picture of her death. Or perhaps 'death' was merely the name I lazily gave to what would have been, if I had looked more carefully, a picture of undistorted life?)

Later, when she transitions into REM, she sighs and moans and sometimes even calls out. That is when I know she is having her dreams.

'I had a bad dream last night.'

'Yes, I heard you.'

'It was my youngest granddaughter. She needed my help and I couldn't reach her.'

'What was happening to her?'

'She was sick. Or in danger. I can't remember. But I couldn't get there. It was terrible.'

My mother sleeps well. She goes to bed early, around nine o'clock, rarely after ten. Between sleep cycles, she gets up to go the toilet; afterwards, despite the nightmares that often await her, she does not struggle to drop off again. At around seven, she gets up and has a cup of herbal tea and a small bite, then returns to bed to read and snooze until around nine. In all, she can clock up ten or eleven hours. My father was the opposite. He would come home from work at around eight or nine in the evening, have his supper, then fall asleep on the couch. When he woke up, at eleven or so, he would go to bed, where he would toss and turn, plagued by anxiety, until five o'clock—an hour of the morning that has always been loaded with signification for me—when he would get up and go back to work. To his mind, getting out of bed and returning to work was an escape route from the anxieties of the night, yet in reality his work was a principal source of those anxieties. It was a closed loop he was trapped in, going around and around, getting ever more exhausted and maddened, until it eventually finished him off.

Since coming to live with my mother, and especially since quarantine, I have been sleeping longer and more profoundly, while the quality of my dreams has improved. The pictures are richer and more finely detailed than usual. The sequences of images, though they shift and slide as normal, are less interrupted and last longer. I am also remembering my dreams more than I typically do; I am recalling specific aspects, sometimes apparently tiny details, about the characters, the objects, the attire, the environments that I see, all without losing any receptivity to the larger narratives and emotional landscapes that determine the form and the direction of the action.

As a literary experiment—so as to collect these unusually vivid dreams and submit them to interpretation—I have started to keep a journal. As soon as I wake up, be it in the middle of the night or in the morning, I scribble down a few words that I hope will be enough to recall to my conscious mind the full scope of that night's dreams. The entries in the journal are dated, as in a diary. Only a small number are empty (the blank nights, the dreams never to be retrieved). Most of the rest are a few sentences long. A handful run to several pages. My handwriting, bad at the best of times, is barely legible throughout. In the light of day, it takes me some time to decrypt the code, which is usually a case of cracking a key word—*auditorium, orca, slope, boomerang*—and then watching how the dream, the entire moving picture with its attendant constellation of emotions, flows out of it.

Quantitative analysis reveals: men are dominating my nights. Some of these men are imaginary lovers, in which case they tend to be just out of reach. Others are ex-boyfriends who materialise to remind me of what I have lost. The majority, however, are estranged friends. Whom, it irritates me to say, I treat as celebrities. They appear before me as beautiful saviours, and I follow them, run after them, emulate them. They bring me to big events and introduce me to important people, which excites me, though I find I cannot trust what is being said by those gathered there, nor do I understand the emotions being expressed.

When women appear in my dreams, they are, almost without exception, actual celebrities, actors and singers (no writers), some of whom I admire, but many more of whom I do not rate or barely register in my waking life. The A list, the B list, the C list, they are all represented, and no matter where a given celebrity fits into the hierarchy, my relationship with her follows a similar script: I am the only person in whom she can confide because, although my rare qualities have gained me access to the celebrity world, I do not actually belong to that world. The worry running beneath the dreams, which I feel coursing through me as I sleep, is that the celebrity should never be allowed to forget that I am not seeking fame for myself, I am not after her reflected glory or her riches, nor will I desert her when a bigger celebrity comes along; rather, I will always be available to her as a link to the normal life she has given up.

Needless to say, these dream-states embarrass me, their glaring shallowness as much as their obvious deceptions—*not seeking fame for myself? who am I fooling?*—though I am heartened to read that they are not unique.

'Last night I was James Bond': the vivid world of our lockdown dreams.

A group of postgraduate psychoanalytic students at University College London are asking people to fill in an online survey about the dreams they are having during quarantine. In their analyses of the dreams submitted, the students have discerned some familiar patterns. Our material waking lives, they say, have become dull, which is being reflected in a more vivid dreaming life. Our minds are reaching out to try and make something of the few stimuli we are receiving and bringing up things we have forgotten about. We are 'living' more in our dreams. There is a sense of being protagonists in our own films, which might explain why the characters that appear in our dreams are often actors or famous people.

Leaving aside the problem of celebrity culture's infiltration into even our most intimate rooms, our deepest cells, it is uplifting to know that, at a time when there seems to be less life happening and fewer opportunities for memory-making, we are nonetheless finding ways to live and to remember more, and that we are doing so in unison. What is not clear to me, however, is whether our dreams in quarantine have become more significant in themselves, their contents more worthy of interpretation, or whether we are merely having a greater number of insignificant dreams that in ordinary times would be rightfully discarded. According to Carl Jung, while theoretically the whole of a person's previous life experiences might be found in every dream, not every dream is felt by the dreamer to be equally important. What makes one dream significant and another insignificant is the interpretative attitude the dreamer takes to it: the amount of the dream's content that is remembered, the amount of what is remembered that is brought into analysis, and the amount of what is analysed that is understood. (As Freud says, quoting the ancient dream-interpreter Artemidorus, *'the meaning of a dream depends on who the dreamer happens to be.'*) So while all dreams have the potential to be significant, not all dreams end up having equal significance. Which is why Jung makes a distinction between 'little' dreams and 'big' dreams, the former being the nightly fragments of fantasy that come from the subjective and personal sphere, and whose meaning is limited to quotidian affairs; the latter being those that transcend the everyday by seeming to encapsulate an entire personality, and that are remembered for a lifetime.

Looking through my dream journal, I would classify almost all my dreams as 'little'. Had I not written them down, these dreams, I am certain, would have quickly disappeared from my memory, and good riddance. Sometimes, initially, due to the presence of certain characters, or due to the strength of feeling that certain situations evoke, they promise a treasure trove of meaning. Under analysis, though, their weight immediately falls away. With their elements isolated and separated out, they turn out to be flimsy. The meanings they do yield look tired to my eyes: the same self-knowledge with which I have been beating myself for years, each strike a reminder that I am, after all, no more and no less than who I currently believe myself to be.

I once had a dream!

Casting my mind back, I would say I have had, maybe, three 'big' dreams in my entire life. Two of those came in my twenties, in the years after my father's death. They were about my father, contained no characters except him, and remain the only dreams I have ever had featuring him. The third one, however, a whole different beast, happened just a few nights ago, on 28 March, at the height of quarantine. This dream was and is, without a doubt, the biggest of my big three, and the only one from my journal that I have submitted to the UCL study.

My Big Dream: *I am a visitor at the home of my literary agent, R. From where I am standing, I see two walls. Like a stage set, there is darkness where the other two walls should be. I do not know what this darkness is hiding or where it leads. The wall I am facing is painted yellow. To my right, built into the second wall, is a fireplace with an ornate mantlepiece.*

R comes into the room. In her arms, she is holding a small human figure. At first, the figure appears to me to be Lucía Zárate, the smallest woman in the world, whose photograph in The Guinness Book of Records *I used to stare at, mesmerised, as a child. Zárate is very much alive—at one point, she does a little cancan in the air with her tiny legs—but she is got up like a doll. An elaborate nineteenth-century dress. A bodice and petticoats. Layers of ruche and fringe.*

R introduces Zárate to me. 'This is my son,' she says. And indeed when I look again, Zárate has turned into a little boy, although the dress has remained the same. Looking at R's son, I am reminded of those antique photographs of bourgeois boys who have not yet been breeched and who are dressed in an elaborate fashion by their indulgent mothers. R's son's dress is red. On his feet, he has black hobnail boots with a little heel.

'When I wear trousers, I'm a boy,' R's son says, directly addressing me. 'When I wear dresses, I'm a girl.'

'I like your booties,' I say so as not to call attention to the red dress, which is causing me immense embarrassment.

In waking life, I have neither met nor seen a photograph of R's son. I do not know what he looks like. Here, he has sallow skin, brown hair, and brown eyes. Looking at him, I am aware that, even though he looks nothing like me, I am looking at a reflection of myself. Similarly, despite the fact that R's appearance does not change, I understand her to be my own mother. I also realise, as I take in the whole scene, that there is a figure missing, the father. I understand, then, that I am him, and at the same time I am simply myself. I am both things: I am the son looking at his younger self with his mother, and I am the father looking at his family.

Without having to be told, I gather that this room, the sitting room, is where I will be sleeping for the night. I turn away from R and her son in search of somewhere to lie down. With my back now to the yellow wall, facing into the void where the opposite wall should be, I see that the floor extends into the darkness and that there is a mattress lying on the floor, half in the room and half out, the near side lit by the lights, the far side in shadow. It is clear to me that this is my bed for the night.

As soon as I lie down on the mattress, I can tell that it is filled with water. I have only once in my waking life lain on a waterbed, and the sensation in the dream is identical. Every small movement I make creates a wave underneath me that rolls down the entire length of my body.

At a certain point, then, I notice that the water is leaking from the mattress onto the floor. The water is not gushing noisily but rather silently seeping out. The mattress is releasing a much greater volume of liquid than it should be able to hold; there seems to be no limit to the amount it can expel. There is so much of it, in fact, that the room is filling up. The mattress, I notice, is now floating like a raft, and I begin to feel a terrible panic.

It is then, at the onset of panic, that I comprehend the true nature of the situation: I am pissing. The water is in fact my urine.

This knowledge, and the shame that accompanies it, serves to remind me that I am not alone in the room. I become aware once again of the presence of R and her son. Standing in the urine, as if paddling at the seaside, R smiles at me benignly. She is ignoring the fact that her room has become a pool of my urine. In a state of almost unbearable anxiety, I make excuses for my mess.

'Don't worry,' I say, 'nothing will be ruined. The room will absorb everything.'

According to the UCL students, anxiety dreams are having a moment. People are dreaming about empty shelves in the supermarket and about being unable to get their bodies and houses clean. They are worrying about blocked toilets and drains. They are breaking certain rules and being punished by others for it. The explanation the students give for these dreams is that they are supressed irrational thoughts that view the quarantine as punishment for mistakes the dreamers have made or for something bad they have done. Without question, my Big Dream is an anxiety dream of this category. But, to my mind at least, it is also much bigger than that. Mine is a quarantine dream, born of curtailment and restriction, but, paradoxically, within its narrow bounds, it contains the whole of my life.

I tell my mother about it. It is morning and she is telling me about another nightmare she has had about her youngest granddaughter.

'Again?' I say.

'What do you mean? Have I had other nightmares about her?'

'Yes. What happened in this one?'

'She had something on her face. An orange beard that she couldn't get off. And I couldn't help her to remove it.'

'A fake beard?'

'No, it wasn't glued on. The hair was growing from her skin. The poor girl. I couldn't help her.'

In return, I recount as best I can my Big Dream.

'Your poor agent,' she says when I have finished.

'Does it sound childish?'

'You probably just needed to go to the toilet.'

'I feel there's more to it than that.'

'Was it a nightmare?'

'No.'

And, in all sincerity, it was not. Despite the anxiety, the panic, I did not want the dream to end. It was as though I already knew, while I was dreaming about it, that what was happening in that room was important. Looking at the dream material, I can see that it contains elements which, were they to be separated out and reassembled on the page, would make up nothing less than the complete story of me. *The room, the mother, the son, the absent father, the desire for and the turning away from family, the flight, the feeling of shame, the return*: these are the cells that, bonded together, form the canvas on which I am writing the body of this book.

In 1940, the year they moved to Dublin from County Mayo, my grandparents were in their early twenties and unwed. They got married, quickly, in a Dublin city church with my grand-aunt as a witness. In May of the same year, fewer than nine months later, my mother was born. The fact that my grandmother had arrived in the capital already pregnant came to light only much later, around the time of my grandparents' fiftieth wedding anniversary, when the marriage documents were unearthed and somebody did the sums. (While I do not remember any angry displays at the anniversary celebrations, it is hard for me to believe that my mother, who had been raised according to the strict moral strictures of the Catholic Church, had not been furious to discover that her fundamentalist parents had themselves engaged in premarital sex. When I ask her about it today, she is sanguine: 'Imagine it. They'd have had no choice but to pack their bags.')

My grandparents rented a single room—the original cell—on the top floor of a house in the north inner city, which was to be my mother's home until she was fourteen.

'Was it a tenement?' I ask.

'Not quite. It was cramped. But my mother, a proud woman, kept it clean.'

After the third of my mother's four brothers was born in 1953, the family was, as part of the government's social housing programme, cleared out of the room and placed in a house on a new corporation estate seven kilometres to the west. My mother remembers this move well, as it coincided with her removal from school and the start of her working life: 'Although we no longer lived there, I continued to use the city-centre address, because no employer would take on a girl from the estate.'

The house on the estate, in which my grandparents lived until their deaths and to which I made regular Sunday visits with my family, was a small semi-D with pebble-dash walls and two windows to the road. In front, there was a modest garden where my grandfather grew roses (and, as far as I can recall, only roses), and a tiny back yard where he grew (only) rhubarb. My grandmother, never my grandfather, would answer the door to us and, after a kiss on the cheek (our lips on *her* cheek), would lead us into the downstairs room: a table with four chairs in the centre, two small couches pushed against the walls, a cabinet for the crockery, an old radio, a little television, and a single picture (of Pope John Paul) on the wall. Through a door on the Pope's right-hand side (as he looked out) was the kitchen, in style and appointment more akin to a scullery, too cramped to accommodate more than one person, a fact that my grandmother undoubtedly appreciated: it was hard work, fixing meals for all these people, but she did not want anybody's help; there was a system, such a small space required one, but only she could (be allowed to) understand it.

Back in the sitting room, behind a second door under the stairs, was a cavity that served as a pantry, into which my grandmother would, at the crucial moment, bend, her top half disappearing into the shadows, her bony rump persisting on being in the light: this was the sign that we were about to be fed. On our visits to the house, we were given food in two rounds, on arrival and then again later in the day, at a time not fixed by the hands of the clock but decided upon by my grandmother, according to her own intuitions about our general state of digestion—*were we, as a group, beginning to feel peckish again?*—not to mention her own presuppositions about what the role of a mother in a family was: in her eyes, it seemed, a mother was first and foremost a nourisher, *the* nourisher; anything else a mother might do, or turn her hand to, was subordinate to that. Without saying a word, and often in mid-conversation, she—the great mother now—would stand up, and everyone would immediately know what was about to happen. Protests would fly out from the couches, *Sit down, we don't want anything, we're leaving now*, but these would be ignored, stonewalled, a terrifying strength of will emanating from her silence as she delved into the pantry and put on the kettle and laid out the plates once more.

Boiled ham. Stewed turnip. Buttered cabbage. Mashed potatoes. A basket of freshly cut soda bread. A choice of rhubarb or apple tart with cream poured over. A plate and a side plate each. And a thin-lipped china cup and saucer for the sweet tea that accompanied everything we ate. I never once saw a glass of wine or jug of water on the table, though I was often witness to the appearance of a bottle of whiskey after pudding, and to shorts being tipped into crystal tumblers, and to these being passed around—and I did not fail to notice, either, that my parents always refused them.

To me, this refusal had a message: my parents, it said, were different from my uncles and aunts; they had their own mode of living, one that omitted important conventions of Irish social life. My parents' idea of a good time at the weekend was a night at the pictures (French infidelities for my mother, political thrillers for my father) or a long walk on the coast and a bag of chips on the way home—never the pub, for my father did not let a drop of alcohol past his lips, he said he did not like the taste, nor did he much like talking, to anyone, or even being around others who were talking amongst themselves. My mother, meanwhile, associated pubs with waste (of money, of time, of intelligence) and a lack of fresh air. Her talking, which unlike my father's was ready and forthcoming, was done with the strangers she met on buses or on her walks, and with her neighbours when they dropped in unannounced, and above all with her circle of close friends with whom she went for coffee every Friday, and with whom she swapped novels, and with whom she swam in the local pool every morning: sixty lengths, up and down, in their own special lane, pausing every so often to continue the conversation. It is during these extra-familial exchanges, I suppose, that my mother developed a sense of who she was and what she believed, and it turned out she often disagreed with my grandparents and uncles and aunts about the contentious issues (like women priests, or Travellers' halting sites, or divorce, or abortion), and it was clear even to my young mind that, in her pronouncements, as good-humoured as they were, she was going against the grain of majority opinion, that is to say the majority of the entire country, and, as awkward as it made me feel sometimes, I had decided that she was in the right.

(Where exactly my father stood on the issues, what his opinions were, remained something of a mystery, for he refrained from weighing in. He kept everyone in the dark as to which way he voted in the national elections, for instance. When I would beg him to tell me, he would respond with a quip about the secrecy of the ballot. His absolute refusal to give away this information—*refusals and more refusals*—was exceedingly frustrating to me; I interpreted it to mean that, politically, much to my disgust, he was *not* in the right.)

In subtle, mostly unconscious ways, my parents—well, I am really talking about my mother now—had me believe that I, too, was different from my extended family. One way my mother showed me this was by keeping me at a distance from my grandparents. By declining, or simply failing, to leave me alone with them for any length of time. My grandparents did not babysit me, or take me out for the day, as they did my cousins. I was not dropped off at their house, as my cousins were, to spend a weekend with them. I had rarely even been upstairs. For me, the upper floor of the house felt like an out-of-bounds place, a private realm, which I had no business stepping into. (I have retained a mere two memories of doing so: in the first, my cousin is showing me the box room where he is staying while his parents are away; in the second, I am being escorted by my mother up the staircase—which, not unlike that of an Amsterdam house, or the towers of the Sagrada Família, is claustrophobically tight— and into the darkened main bedroom, and towards my grandfather's deathbed.)

The result of this more-or-less manufactured distance—I am not complaining, it suited me fine—was that my grandparents, my grandmother in particular, treated me differently from my cousins. Whereas my grandmother did not hesitate to chastise *them*, or to order *them* around, she did not so much as grimace in my direction; on those extremely uncommon occasions when she dared to complain about something I was doing, my mother was quick to tell her to leave me alone. By which my mother almost certainly meant: 'Leave *me* alone.' The eldest and only girl, my mother had been criticised harshly by my grandmother, and subjected to violence, the hardest blow having been her removal from school at fourteen, which had robbed my mother not only of the chance of a career, but of the permission to perceive herself as an intelligent woman.

My father also put space between me and his parents—but for different reasons. He had grown up in a middle-class neighbourhood just beyond the canal on the south of the city. His father died before I was born, but his mother, his brother, and his sister continued to live in the family home together—I did not think to ask why this might be—and we visited them from time to time, though far less frequently than my maternal grandparents. The house was red brick with three large windows to the front. In the back garden, an apple orchard bore bitter fruit, suitable only for tarts (which here had a thicker crust; I preferred the ones my other grandmother made). In the sitting room, there was an out-of-tune piano, which I enjoyed pounding with my fists. In the kitchen, beside a wood-burning stove, I would sit and drink tea and answer my grandmother's adoring declarations, or my aunt's odd jokes, or my uncle's hyperbolic praise with smiles and blushes. To escape, I would go to the toilet, which was located at the top of the house: up the stairs to the landing, then up another flight to the second floor—*was it lack of curiosity or dread that prevented me from peeping into the various bedrooms?*—and, at last, there it was, in a room of its own, bathed in light from the window; no sink, no bath, no mirror, just the throne itself, whose seat was often broken, and whose chain I liked to pull more than once because it made a funny noise and gave a nice sensation in the arm and was such a novelty.

We seldom stayed long enough to eat, my father being so eager to get away, to pull me out, *we can't stay long*, for he had promised me, *had he not?* that he would take me to the swings around the corner. On the way to the park, we would walk past an ex–prime minister's house that was permanently guarded by a policeman sitting in a little hut at the gate. It excited me to pass by this hut, and to see the guard inside, and to look up at the huge windows of the residence behind, and I was aware, even at that young age, although I could not yet articulate it, that this was a different sort of area from the one my other grandmother lived in; I was aware that this area was wealthy. At the same time, in a similarly inarticulate way, I understood that my own father, despite having grown up on these nice-looking streets, sheltered by these enormous trees, was not in fact wealthy, nor was his mother, nor was anyone in his family. I understood this by the peeling wallpaper in the house. And by the worn carpets. And by the missing bits of glass in the chandeliers. And by the broken keys on the piano. And, most of all, by my grandmother—a daughter of pub owners in Dalkey Village who, as a young trainee sales assistant at Brown Thomas, had met my grandfather, twenty years her senior, and had married him against the express wishes of her family (a kind and generous man but also a gambler who slowly drove the family business, a grocer's on South Great George's Street, into the ground), and who, as hard as she worked to keep everything afloat at home, even resorting to taking in visitors for bed and breakfast, could not overcome the anxiety with which she had tried, for years, to forestall the oncoming catastrophe (which may have been nothing more catastrophic than her own sadness), and who would, without warning, and in response to no obvious external trigger, break down crying, and then apologise for crying, and then cry some more: this was the scene from which my father was forever pulling me away, and which he wanted to avoid seeing himself, if he could manage it.

Which is to say: it was his fear that I might be *like* his family that caused my father to keep me apart from them.

My parents met at a dinner dance in a hotel in the city centre. According to the photos from the time—the year was 1960—they made a good-looking couple. My mother had thick black hair and eyebrows, and high cheekbones, and a slim figure. She worked in a clothes shop in town called Creation Arcade (to which she took a bus from the estate in the morning, another home for lunch, then a bus back in for the afternoon, and a bus home in the evening, for one pound ten shillings a week; she kept the bus fare and gave the rest of her earnings to her mother; on the rare occasions when she asked her mother for some spending money, she was met with what she describes as a 'stony silence'). My father, who had been a Gaelic footballer at school, was strong and handsome, with hair swept back like a screen actor. He had taken his final exams but had not gone to university, and now worked as a salesman for a cereal company (emulating his father, who, after the failure of the grocer's on George's Street, had become a travelling salesman). After their marriage in 1964 (honeymoon: County Kerry), they bought a house, using a mortgage, in a new southside suburb. It took some time for my mother to get pregnant (she talks of lighting candles and going to see specialists), but eventually, in 1969, a son was born, then three years later another. In 1973, after my father got a new job at a fizzy-drinks company, they moved to a larger house even further south. Here, my sister was born. At some point after that, my father left the company to open a shop of his own, a newsagent. My mother worked odd jobs (catering, cleaning schools, demonstrating products at supermarkets) to make ends meet. This was the state of things when in 1978, at the age of thirty-eight, she had me.

The house I grew up in—the 1973 house—was a semi-D in an estate of three hundred, ten kilometres south of the city centre. My parents bought the house new for around ten thousand Irish pounds. I do not know whether or not this price was high for the time, but I do know— and I knew it then—that the estate to which the house belonged was, by Irish standards, middle class. Part of what made it so was its situation, which until at least the late eighties (when the next phase of housebuilding began in the area) was semi-bucolic. On the estate's northern edge, where the city ring road now runs, the Dublin hills began. On the western side was a large park with woodlands, ponds, rivers, a golf course, and an eighteenth-century house. To the east, in fields which today contain flats and houses, there was a cattle farm. These were the boundaries of our little domain. This was the land on which we built our bourgeois dreams.

The houses were of similar design, each with two gardens, front and back, and a driveway, conforming to an American model of life in which people got in to their cars when they wanted to go anywhere, unless they were actively 'going for a walk', in which case they would dress in a manner which suggested they were 'on a walk' and, thus attired, would walk for the sake of walking as opposed to actually getting to a place. One consequence of this was that we, the sons and daughters of the estate, none of whom owned cars, laid claim to its streets. We, not our parents, were the ones clomping up and down to the bus stop; we were the ones roving around on bikes and on skateboards; we were the ones congregating in the evenings in those places which the light from the street lamps did not quite reach, where we would talk about whatever the Americans on television thought we should be talking about, picturing ourselves to be much more impressive than we were.

An outsider entering this world would have found it difficult to distinguish between the different houses, but we, the residents, parents and children both, had an awareness of where the better houses were, and who lived in them. Over time, having started life with the standard four bedrooms, many houses underwent conversions and acquired extensions, transforming in the process into quite substantial buildings: fifth bedrooms built over the garage and sixth bedrooms put into the attic, extra bathrooms under the stairs and out the back and everywhere else, conservatories and sun rooms, bidets in some cases ('handy for washing your feet'), and exterior lights that automatically switched on when you walked past the gate.

We, the children, stayed up to date on the improvements that were being made around the estate. *Keep the front garden or pave over it? BMW versus Mercedes?* These were the questions—rather than, say, the dialectics of revolution—which impinged upon us as we sucked on our Camel Lights. While we were cognizant of the existence of a Dublin working class and of their inhabitation in specific communities, we never deliberately went anywhere that might have put us into contact with them. We knew the areas we were supposed to avoid (White—— Estate, Hill—— Estate; anywhere in the direction of Tallaght or Drimnagh; the whole of the northside, especially the Biblical Hell that was Ballymun), and out of simple fear, which is what snobbery ultimately is, we avoided them. A fine strategy, but one rendered problematic by circumstance, for adjoining our estate to the north, backing on to us—Slough to our Windsor—was a larger, less middle-class, more working-class estate.

The close proximity of this estate—if not quite *neighbours*, undoubtedly *neighbouring*—made it a matter that could not be easily ignored. Psychologically, it performed a dual function for us: it made us a little bit afraid and, at the same time, gave us the nice sensation of knowing ourselves to be the better-offs in life. It allowed us to think that, even though we did not live in one of the city's bona fide enclaves (the residents of which appeared in our nightmares, standing on the thresholds of their period mansions, pointing and laughing at us), still we could consider ourselves members of a higher echelon. Any doubts, we could simply examine the evidence. Over there, on the neighbouring estate, they might have had front and back gardens like we did, but the dimensions were smaller. They had an upstairs all right but with three bedrooms instead of four. The houses were more tightly packed, allowing only modest expansion. There were fewer trees. Less green space. Worse cars. A subtle variation of accent.

Growing up, my friends, all of them, came from my own estate. It was in the houses of my estate that I played as a child and hung out as a teenager. It was to the houses of my estate, not to those of the neighbouring one, that I compared my own house. And I did not fail to notice the differences. At the same speed, it seemed, as my friends' houses modernised and grew, mine deteriorated and tumbled down, and as soon as the significance of this became apparent to me, I suffered a plunge in self-assurance: to my mind, one's house was an expression of one's worth, and it was plain to see that I was not making the cut. Given the state of my house and what this said about the financial health of my parents, technically, *correctly* I ought to have been living in the other estate rather than this one.

As a family, we were not poor, but money was a perennial problem, a source of anxiety, a palpable atmosphere of tension that hung around us. My father's salesman jobs had come with very average salaries, and now the profits from his shop only barely covered the costs. What is more, largely as a consequence of his difficulties in providing, my father struggled with depression and was incapacitated—by which I mean unemployed, unable to provide at all—on a number of occasions. The kind of part-time work my mother could take on, meanwhile, was never more than menial. Occasionally, for example, she did shifts for a catering company, both preparing and serving the food, twelve hours for forty Irish pounds. She seemed to enjoy the work, and I remember catching a glimpse of the cheque and thinking it was a lot of money. But then one day I heard her say that, considering the amount of time she was on her feet, it was *slave labour*. That put a new slant on it.

My parents were not—my ego requires me to emphasise—tight-fisted. Neither of them ever saved a penny. Most of what they earned went to pay the bills, and everything left over was spent on us. Hardly anything went into the house: relative to what was needed for its upkeep (never mind keeping up with the neighbours), a pittance.

It is hard to say whether it was a product of their characters, or whether it was a case of shutting their eyes to what was financially and emotionally beyond reach, but both of my parents, my father even more than my mother, cultivated an active disinterest in home improvements. How the house looked, inside or out, was of only minimal concern to them. Was there a drill on the premises? I do not know. I certainly do not remember my father ever having one in his grip. Things broke and were not fixed. Things fell down and were not put back up. For years, there was no mirror on the bathroom wall, for instance, so we made do with a little hand-held one (the kind that normal families used as an auxiliary mirror to help them pluck hairs or shave) which sat on the windowsill behind the toilet. Eventually, someone's sanity cracked and a new mirror was bought, unframed because the idea was to plaster it to the wall, maybe even use the opportunity to put up a tile or two. As a reminder of the work that needed to be done, this mirror was placed on the sink, in the space behind the tap, and there it remained, and remained, and remained, until its positioning began to appear intentional, the spot it had always been destined for. From then on, if I wanted to check my face or my hair, instead of having to squeeze into the nook beside the toilet to get to the little hand-held as before, I had to plant my feet wide in the middle of the room and bend down, my thigh muscles burning, my arse brushing off the bath edge, a most uncomfortable manoeuvre even when I had the bathroom to myself, but one that quickly began to feel natural, as if this was simply the sensation that attended the act of checking oneself out. My father died before the mirror ever made it onto the wall. At his funeral, one of his (very few) friends delivered a eulogy that included a joke about it. Evidence that the problem was not a figment of my invention; other people saw it, too.

My mother, for her part, was a great gardener who cared deeply for her shrubs and plants. She did not think twice about spending sizeable sums on bags of mature manure (what my father called *the horseshit*) from the garden centre. Towards the house, however, she cultivated an attitude of benign, genial neglect. She kept it clean enough; she was good and rough with the hoover. But mending, extending, knocking through, updating: it was as if caring about any of that were a task too giant, too *ridiculous* merely to contemplate; a vortex that, if approached, would suck her in and strip her of her identity (as an art lover, as a reader, as a socialist, that is as someone who did not care about money because she had never had any to care about).

Despite all of this, on one fateful occasion—I do not know what possessed them—they did secure a credit-union loan to enlarge the kitchen and convert the garage into a 'playroom'. I was still a young child at the time, clearly a snob already and as yet capable of overestimating my parents, because I got immensely excited about this planned change. *Bigger was better, especially when it came to kitchens. At last, we were catching up!* The reality, unfortunately, did not match my fantasy, though it was not until I was older that I got sight of this. The building work had been done on the cheap—*of course! fucking typical!*—creating long-term problems that would not have existed if the place had been left alone. For a start, the new utility room was left unfinished: a concrete floor where tiles ought to have been. Then, the floor of the kitchen extension began to sag and eventually—again after my father's death—had to be replaced. Cracks formed in the kitchen ceiling, and water from the bathroom leaked down. And finally, the lethal blow: after a bad storm, the roof of the new playroom fell right in. My maternal uncles built a temporary ceiling and sealed the roof using blowtorches and strips of felt, but the playroom itself was left as it was, an empty shell, unpainted walls, the rafters exposed, floorboards bare and unvarnished, a receptacle for unwanted things, a store for our failure, the very subconscious of the house—and the source, besides, of a vicious draught in the winter.

(Which was the other thing: the house was cold. There were three reasons for this. One: no insulation. Two: inefficient central heating. Three: my mother's intolerance towards heat. She hated a uniformly hot house; she could not stand to be in a place where she lost sense of what the air outside was like. An attitude which saw her turning on and off the radiators according to her momentary flushes. As soon as the chill left her limbs, she judged it too hot, she was *suffocating*, so the switch would be flicked, and in a matter of minutes the warmth would have rushed out under the doors—or straight out the window, if she opened one of those, which she often did.)

I shared a bedroom with my brother N, who was six years older than me, and towards whom I did not (and still do not) have strong fraternal feelings (whatever they are). I found him a bit mad, to be honest. I was an obedient boy and liked to please my mother and my teachers, whereas he was bold and erratic and had a sense of humour—and a crazy Joker-like laugh—that was all his own. I kept my distance from him. I certainly did not want to share the bedroom with him. Or indeed with anyone else. I wanted the room to myself. Or, more accurately, I wanted *a* room to myself, a room that was not this room, that was not in this house, because this room, this house, I did not like at all.

My room: bare apart from two single beds (no headboards) and a cheap plywood shelf. No posters or pictures. Devoid, in fact, of any expressions of personality. *Is that not strange for a family of artists?* Looking back, I think it pretty shabby that my parents did not give me a say in how my room might have looked or been arranged. That they never asked what I might like to have in it. Not even after my brother moved into a vacated room elsewhere did they encourage me to take possession of what was really now my own room. The biggest step I took in that direction was when, on entering secondary school, I demanded a desk and chair of my own. In fairness to my parents, they complied, but even in the company of this new (second-hand) furniture, I did not feel integrated into that room. It was where I slept, but I did not feel bedded down there. It was where I spent time alone, but, given the choice, it was not a place I would have chosen for that. I did not see it as a retreat. I felt uneasy within its walls.

Part of the reason for this was that I was constantly on guard, expecting invasion. Because there were no locks, there was always a chance that someone would come in on top of me. Worse, whenever a guest came to stay, they were put in my room and I was moved onto a mattress at the end of my parents' bed. A country cousin ousted me for a while. Then my eldest brother, R, and his wife and new baby. Then my dying grandmother. Then my aunt, my father's sister, when she was between psychiatric hospitals; in and out, in and out (she of the asylum, me of the room), until, at last, my siblings moved out and I could permanently take over one of their rooms. At which point, I realised that the problem had never been my room itself, or any single room of the house, but rather all of the rooms together. The problem was that I did not feel at home in my own home.

Out of this sense of unease I developed a neurotic habit of pacing. After closing behind me the door of a room (any room, but especially my room), I would not be able to sit or to lie down, but would be compelled by some inner force to pace, from wall to wall, forward and back, for minutes, even hours, all the while furiously wagging my index finger at the floor (a sort of manic tic). As I did this, my mind would be immersed in fantasies. Some of these fantasies were about the revenge I would one day take on my enemies. Others were about men and romance. But most often they were related to home: the things I would do to this house if I had the money, or the things I would do to my own future house(s). Which is to say, my fantasy life was extremely future-orientated, and contained forms of violence and of sexuality that were bound up with my feelings about settlement and belonging. My revenge fantasies usually involved my enemies learning of my bohemian life in a tasteful home far away and subsequently dying of jealousy. My imaginary relationships, meanwhile, played out in various domestic environments—always stylish, always situated far away, always containing that which my family home lacked—and the men I chose for myself slotted into these environments, melded with them in the same way that the marble countertops and the beanbags did (I had a thing for beanbags).

My pacing habit lasted for years, right into university. In fact, it was a miracle I got a place at all, because the hours I should have been studying I actually spent pacing. Then, at some point during my second year, when I was contemplating dropping out, I realised that the pacing was holding me back. More than that, it was taking me over. Eating up my time and zapping my energy. Taking me further and further away from reality—that is, *from the very place I wanted my fantasies to be realised and played out*. The pacing was, I understood, an unhealthy type of self-absorption, an extreme introversion, and if I continued with it, not only was I going to miss out on the love and the success that I believed were coming to me *out there*, I was also going end up in the madhouse. So, one day, I made the conscious decision to train myself out of it. My method was the same I would later use to get free of cigarettes: every time I felt the urge to pace, I simply said to myself, 'No.' I do not know how many noes I had to issue before the urges themselves stopped. Hundreds. Thousands. Together amounting to a powerful counter-will which, I am convinced, saved my life.

Of all the rooms in my family home, I came closest to liking the kitchen. Why not the sitting room, which had big windows looking onto the gardens and a sofa to lounge on and a long dining table to draw or paint at and hundreds of my mother's books? I cannot explain it, except to say I was not comfortable there. It was where I went to watch television (two channels, RTÉ One and Two, no video player because my mother was against them) or to do my school projects (my books and papers spread out on the dining table) but not to *sit*. Not to *be*. If I wanted to sit or to be, I did so in the kitchen. I think the reason for this was, unlike the other rooms of the house, the kitchen had personality: my mother's. This did not show itself in the cabinets (ordinary) or the appliances ('I would hate a dishwasher'). But rather in the ugly old armchair in the corner where she sat in the evening and rubbed cream into her legs and methylated spirits into her feet. And in the stack of shelves where she kept her reference books for her crosswords, and her collections of short stories, and her poems, and her spiritual texts, stuff for browsing. And, on the other side of the room, in the wonky extension, the side table that was filled with art-related clutter: her easels and her jars of brushes and her boxes of pencils. And, my favourite element, the walls, which were filled with interesting posters that she had bought at museum gift shops or that my siblings brought home from their trips abroad. *Judith Slaying Holofernes* by Artemisia Gentileschi, for one, used to grace the space above the table where we ate our meals. (The painting shows Judith grasping the hair of the supine Holofernes as she slices her long knife through the muscles of his neck, while his blood jets out onto his white pillow in three thin, delicate lines.) In addition, Blu-Tacked onto the fridge door was an ever-changing selection of postcards from galleries around the world. Things like, a still from Matthew Barney's *Cremaster*. A photo of a Giacometti sculpture. A black-and-white portrait of Beckett. And even, for a while—on my honour—a reproduction of Courbet's *L'Origine du monde*.

As I say, I have lived outside Ireland for most of the past twenty years. In leaving, I was disowning the broken-down house I grew up in. Repudiating the material evidence of my parents' straitened circumstances and, at the same time, the bourgeois pretentions of the surrounding estate that made those circumstances so pronounced. For two decades, I moved around Europe, rarely staying in a place longer than a couple of years, always careful to avoid any living arrangement that too closely resembled the suburban lifestyle I had left behind in Dublin. At each of my stops, I lived either in rented rooms or in the homes of my boyfriends. I have never had an entire flat to myself, nor have I ever owned one. Most of the places I lived were ordinary, some were elegant, a couple were spectacular, unforgettable, but even there—especially there—I was never wholly free of the feeling that I was a guest, an invitee, present only at the pleasure of someone else; I was constantly aware of the fact that, if and when I got bored or things went wrong, I would be the one packing my suitcases and getting a plane back to Square One.

Throughout my tour, my attitude to money was, at least on the face of it, matter-of-fact. At the outset, my sole concern was that my earnings should cover the bare cost of life in whatever place I wanted to be. Subsequently, when I began to write, money came to signify the ability to buy time for that. At no point did I put effort into acquiring money for the sake of having it; money was only ever a means to an end. Being able to feed myself I considered a success; reaching the end of the month with a roof still over my head, a triumph. What this meant in practice was a lot of rent payments on the credit card (which the bank had handed to me with a stratospheric upper limit during the Celtic Tiger). These payments I carried out with the terrifying confidence of the bourgeois who believes with all his heart that, when the credit finally ends and the emergency arrives, cosmic justice will intervene and pronounce in his favour: all claims against him annulled. At the same time, rather predictably, I was curating for myself an outward attitude of indifference to the concept of home ownership (and ownership in general). Property was something that other people, the system people, worried about. I was an exception to the rules of the salary-and-mortgage regime. I did not need to worry about any of that because, when the time came, a home—a room, a cell— was simply going to fall out of the heavens onto my lap. That was what I, in my innermost self, believed. (And what, if I stop and look closely enough, I can see I still believe.)

In fashioning this double-faced mask of indifference and entitlement, I had had some training at home. In her discourses, my mother had not disguised her distaste for people whom she considered to be overly concerned with making money, especially those who hoarded their wealth in property. This distaste, however, was at base a kind of fascination, similar to that of the prig for pornography, whereby she would comb through the property section of the newspaper and point out everything that was harmful in it: 'Who on earth needs three reception rooms? It's obscene.'

She could see everything that was wrong with capitalism's fetishisation of property, and she wanted to believe herself above it, yet equally she would rather have died than give up her middle-class house, irrespective of its rotten condition, to return to the working-class estate of her youth.

Today, beneath my veneer of indifference to property ownership lies a wish—suppressed but, when prompted, quick to come to the surface—for exactly that which I am trying to appear indifferent about: a home of my own. On those occasions when the mask slips and I allow myself to express this wish, I notice that I try to be as 'modest' or 'realistic' as I can plausibly be. *All I really want is a small, well-located studio with a door onto a balcony.* But, given that I am in my forties, penniless, in debt, and back living with my mother, and given the real price of a small, well-located studio in the twenty-first-century European city, this apparent modesty, this so-called realism, is really just a grandiose delusion—*a pink princess castle*—in perverted form.

Visually, the room that appears in my Big Dream does not directly correspond to any room in my family home, in either of my grandparents' houses, or indeed in my mother's current flat. In the dream, I am a visitor to the room. I am aware that it belongs not to me but to my agent, R. Having never been to R's home in waking life, I in my dreaming state have constructed a composite of a number of different rooms that I have visited in the past, and have made these the property of R. Both the yellow paint on the first wall and the fireplace on the second wall of the room are features I associate with certain desirable homes I have been to on my travels, and which represent for me warmth, comfort, money, social status, and also a certain type of liberal parenting which encourages children to take up space and voice their preferences and identify themselves in the objects they choose to have around them. In this sense, the room in my dream is a series of overlapping memories which together function as a fantasy, a hallucination of a wished-for object.

As tidy as it sounds, this analysis would probably be rejected outright by Freud. For, as adamant as he is that all dreams fulfil a repressed wish, he is equally convinced that any wish represented in a dream *must be an infantile wish*. This would suggest that the room in my Big Dream cannot be a direct representation of my wish for a material house, as that is an adult wish. Rather, the room must be the expression of a much earlier impulse, one that pre-existed any awareness on my part of the concepts of house or belonging, or indeed of a world beyond my present sensations:

> Cans, boxes, caskets, cupboards, and ovens correspond to the female abdomen, as do caves, ships, and all manner of containers. Rooms in dreams are usually women, with the description of their various entrances and exits leaving us in no doubt as to this particular interpretation. Interest in whether the room is 'open' or 'closed' is easily understandable in this context.

If there is any truth at all to this, then the room in my dream must represent the wish to be enveloped once more in my mother's embrace. To be suckling as a baby at her breast. To be re-enclosed within her womb. To be re-joined to her, to be re-folded into her, so that the meeting of my needs is, one more time, her sole concern and the entirety of my experience.

Returning to Ireland, moving in to her flat, being confined with her in this tiny space for an extended period: for years such a scenario was my nightmare. Yet here I discover that, in actual fact, it is my dream and therefore my wish—that is to say, I do not want it to end, I want it to go on until I am satisfied, until I have had my fill. Tomorrow, as today, I will lose my temper with her and want her to soothe me. Tomorrow, again, instead of answering her questions, I will grunt at her and want her to comprehend me. Though she is old, I will want her to be young, for my benefit, so that I can be helpless again and make her responsible for my feelings. And when she fails to fulfil my wishes, which will be often, I will watch these failures and will make sightings within them of her imminent end, and, within that again, glimpse the moment of being back at the beginning with her.

This feeling of *déjà vu* [Freud again] has a particular significance. There, the place is always the mother's genital region; indeed, of nowhere else can one claim with such certainty to have 'been here before'.

I cannot deny the existence in my psyche of this compulsion to repeat the events of infancy and childhood. There is within me the instinct to restore an earlier state of things, the retrogressive urge to rid myself of consciousness and the responsibilities that attend it, and to be once again, if not exactly inanimate, then certainly helpless and in the protection of a benign force. But I also know this is not the whole picture. Opposing this conservative instinct that impels me towards repetition, there is another force (maybe many others) which drives me towards change and development. A force which, by keeping my mind saturated with images of an imagined future, pushes me forwards, towards their realisation. This second force is what compelled me to leave Ireland in the first place. So forceful was it—so threatened by the opposing drive that would keep me attached to previous states—that it obliged me to hate the land I was leaving and to promise never to return there. Without hatred to motivate me, the force seemed to say, I would stay stuck where I was and never make the necessary move.

What I have since learned is that this hatred of my past is really just an acknowledgement of an element of my psyche that will never be eradicated. Within the instinct to step out, to turn away, to leave behind, there will always remain traces of a contrary instinct: one which will send me searching for the way back. And vice versa, in longing for the past, I am also longing for a route out of it. These two longings are infused one into the other; they cannot survive of and for themselves; their continuance depends on their ongoing, mutual antagonism.

Jung, in his dream analyses, implies that awareness of a room in a dream rarely comes without the further awareness of other rooms, whether or not those rooms are actually seen. For Jung, rooms are not hermetic but permeable; the experience of being in a room is equally the experience of passing through it, while the act of passing through a room is, in turn, the act of searching. In one particularly striking dream that he describes, he finds himself in the upper storey of a house, in a finely furnished salon. As much as this salon pleases him, a curiosity about what lies beneath impels him to leave it. Downstairs, he finds an even older room, the form and contents of which greatly interest him, though not enough to extinguish his drive for further exploration. Descending again, he finds another room, older and darker than the one before, and below that, another, older and darker again.

In my Big Dream, I am prey to a similar feeling of dissatisfaction with the room I find myself in, a similar need to move on. In the dream, the room is home but does not belong to me; it is a desirable façade; it is both closed and open, bright and dark, and this doubleness is maddening; the only thing that keeps me from despair is the intuition that there are other rooms, just out of view, which I can escape to.

In this sense, my dream, like Jung's dream, is a depth-dream. The difference, however, is that Jung's dream moves on a vertical axis, mine on a horizontal one. Because Jung's rooms are stacked one on top of the other, his search is reminiscent of an archaeological excavation, digging ever deeper downwards, as if towards an origin or core. My room, on the other hand, is set on a plane. There is nothing above or below. Instead, through the gap of the missing walls, shrouded by darkness, there is an infinite stretch of ground on which, for all I know, there are built an infinite number of other rooms.

The artist Louise Bourgeois devoted the final two decades of her artistic production to the creation of a monumental cycle of works, collectively called the *Cells*. The *Cells* are architectural spaces constructed using reused and converted materials, such as domestic and industrial doors, wire-mesh screens, fencing, window frames, and mirrors, which, on their own or in various combinations, allow the viewer varying degrees of physical or visual access to the interior. Inside are a variety of personal effects, all of which carry meaning specific to the artist's own life, arranged in such a way as to evoke childhood scenes, or rather childhood traumas. In this respect, the *Cells* are archives (of pain). Repositories (of pain). Boxes (of pain). Rooms (of pain).

The first time I saw a large number of the *Cells* exhibited together—spread out *horizontally* on a single floor—was at a retrospective in Paris in 2008. Normally, I prefer to go to exhibitions alone, at least on a first visit; this time I greatly regretted my solitude. My encounter with the *Cells* so overwhelmed me, left me so *bouleversé*, in such pain—until then, the strongest emotion that visual art had ever evoked in me was a sort of dumbfoundedness—that I felt a desperate need to explain to someone what I had just seen and why it was affecting me in this manner. To that person I would have said that the *Cells* captured, better than any artworks I had seen hitherto, the dual nature of the house. The house as a place of safety, a shield from the public gaze. And the house as a place that silently bears witness to the occurrences within, absorbing the activities of its inhabitants, preserving traces of their personalities, storing up their emotional lives. The contents of the *Cells*, coming as they do from a different country, a different style of life, a different epoch, did not resemble those of my family home; nevertheless, I recognised in their pattern and their ordering, in their blending and their juxtaposition, in their communicating and their clashing, the episodes and the moods of my own childhood. *Was it the same for the other viewers? Were they also seeing into their own infant cages? Did they take in everything? What were they overlooking?*

My second meeting with the *Cells*, which came nearly a decade later, at another major Bourgeois show, this time in Bilbao, was as devastating as the first. At one point, while viewing a *Cell* entitled *Passage dangereux*, I was overcome by a feeling of grief—I stress, a rare occurrence for me—and had to leave the exhibition space. My friend, who thankfully had accompanied me to the museum, found me on a bench by the lift with my face in my hands. We sat in silence for a time before he said, 'What's happening?' (The perfect question; I will always love him for it.)

'I don't know,' I said. 'I think it's the little details. The tiny scraps that Bourgeois has thought to include in the *Cells*, which in themselves appear insignificant, but which are, I think, the emotional nodes of the works. The nerve centres. They touch me so deeply I can hardly bear it.

41

Do you know what I'm talking about? The amulets, and the medals, and the locket? The bits of tapestry, did you see them? The bones jammed into the holes in the wire?'

He touched me on the shoulder, then I had a cry, and after that we sat in silence for a while longer, and I thought about what, if I were ever to construct a 'cell' of my own, I would put into it. Which objects from my family home would I include? *The bathroom mirror*, yes, and *the cracked plaster* and *the exposed rafter* and *the poster of Judith Slaying Holofernes*, definitely, and *L'Origine du monde* and—

Rearing up, then, was the memory of an object so awful, so disgusting, so enraging that I had suppressed it for almost twenty years.

The blue carpet.

'I've just remembered something,' I said to my friend. 'Have I ever told you about the blue carpet?'

It had appeared in the house a couple of weeks after my father's death. Literally, appeared. The doorbell rang. I went downstairs to answer it, but my mother had got there before me. On the step outside: a middle-aged woman, well-dressed. I sat on the stairs to get a better look at her. I had never seen her before, and after that day I never saw her again. She must have been in the house during the wake, though, and seen the state of the carpets, for she had come to replace them. 'I've just put down a new carpet in my own house,' she said, 'but the old one is in grand shape, a waste to throw away. I thought you might like it.' She gestured towards the gate, where a white van was parked, and two workmen were already unloading her unwanted carpet. Panicked, I pulled my mother into the sitting room. 'You're not going to let this happen, are you?' My mother did not answer me except to stare at me with a dazed expression, one which said, *I have seen so much happen recently, and none of it is in my control.* From the hall came the sound of the workmen marching in. 'You have to stop them,' I said. 'You have to say no. For once in your life, say fucking no.' But she did not listen to me and she did not say no, so the hammering began, and the carpet was unfurled and stapled into place, in record time it seemed, in the hall and up the stairs and on the landing: a thick plush of royal blue with an orange paisley-like motif. On seeing it, I was consumed by a rage that was nothing less than a loathing for everyone and everything, above all my mother. I retreated to my (hated) room, perhaps wanting tears but failing to find them in the waves of black anger rolling through me, so big, so loud, that in truth I felt dangerous to myself. Long before, I had realised that, if I was going to survive in this world, I had to get far away from my mother, from this room, from this house, from Ireland, but it was only then, as I ground my teeth and pounded my fists into my mattress and called my mother the most terrible names, that I understood that my going would be for good: once gone, I would never return.

The blue carpet.

Before leaving this 'cell', I lay it down here for people to spit on. To throw their fag ends on. To wipe their shitty shoes on. Anything, provided they do not overlook it.

INTERLUDE: COUNTY MAYO, 1989

Because, growing up, there was money in the house for little more than the bills, we only went on family holidays a handful of times: to the Isle of Man when I was three, my only memory of which is a high diving board I was not allowed to climb up to; to Kerry when I was six, where my sister lost her fishing net while paddling in a river and I was inconsolable; to Clare when I was eight, where nightly my fifteen-year-old brother N would sneak out of our shared bedroom to meet the B & B owners' daughter; and to Mayo when I was eleven, to a cottage rented by my uncle, my mother's brother—he chose Mayo because it was the birthplace of my maternal grandparents, and he, an emigrant living in Los Angeles, nurtured a sort of nostalgia about his West-of-Ireland roots—but at the last minute, he rang to say he could not make the trip after all, possibly on account of one his complicated relationships with American women, so we (my sister, my cousin, my parents, my mother's parents, and I) went to this cottage without him, and before we embarked on the journey from our home in Dublin—where my two brothers had been given permission to stay unsupervised—there was already tension because my mother was annoyed with my uncle for making these plans and not following through on them, this was the kind of thing he used to do, he was unreliable in this way and it made her angry, though she tried not to show it, which was a state I remember my mother being in quite regularly, angry but refusing herself the licence to be so and therefore becoming an object of some fear for me because I would see her face harden and hear her silences lengthen and I could not trust that she was not going to lose her temper over something small; which is to say, in that cottage in Mayo, surrounded by her watchful family and wanting to protect us from herself, my mother put on a front that only served to call attention to her simmering mood underneath, and, every time it seemed like she was about to cool down, she would be brought back to the boil by my grandmother, who, acting with wordless authority, had taken control of the days by deciding for everyone when and what would happen, and where everything would be done and how, and was not allowing anyone into the kitchen lest they interfere with her cooking and baking, activities which she carried out in silence except to pay periodic tribute to my uncle—for his having found this lovely cottage for his family in Ireland, and for his never forgetting to call her every Sunday, despite how complicated life must be over there—which to my mother's ears sounded less like praise for my uncle and more like criticism of her, until, one night, after supper had been cleared and the card games were over and everyone was preparing for bed, it all came to a head: my grandmother accused my cousin of stealing chocolate from the kitchen cabinet, a crime for which she reprimanded him with shocking severity—shocking because I had never been reprimanded by Nana in this way, my mother would not have allowed it, just as now she did not allow it when the truth came out that, in fact, it had been *me*, not my cousin, who had taken the chocolate—but, in any case, by the time the innocent and the guilty parties had been rightly identified, the theft had ceased to be relevant, for the affair had swollen into something larger and more difficult to clarify: for, at last, my mother had unloosed her pent-up feeling and had chosen as her target not me but my grandmother, and what came out of my mother was an anger of such range and depth that at first I could not fathom it, it was like a crack had formed in her chest through which a new force was being released into world, but the longer I listened to it, through the wall of the bathroom where I was hiding—'If you've something to say to me, mother, now is the time to say it'—the closer I came to understanding that this anger, far from being new, was very old: older than my mother, older than my grandmother, older even than the stone walls of this cottage, and that I was infused

46

with it, too, and that one day it would emanate from me in this way and would sound just like this in the air, maybe louder again, more terrible, for it was part, along with all the literature and the art and the laughter, of my inheritance.

CELL II

I am preparing an Asian noodle salad for lunch. I like to have the food ready, or close to it, by the time my mother gets back from her morning walk. I do not involve her in any decisions relating to our meals; rather, I simply cook a dish of my own choosing, put it on the table, and call her to it. Any approach less authoritarian than this, such as the opening of a discussion about what she might like to eat and when, usually results in her refusing to eat altogether. 'Don't worry about me,' she will say. 'Look after yourself. I had a scone on my walk. I'm not hungry.' The doctors think she is underweight. An exaggeration, in my view, but I do think she forgets how old she is, and how much energy she expends on her long walks, and that what she eats when left to her own devices—brown bread and cheese and tomatoes and sliced beetroot and raw peppers, for she has long given up the bother of planning proper meals, preferring to pick at what she can find in the cupboards—is not nearly nourishing enough. So I do not give her the chance to refuse. I tell her the food will be ready presently, and when the plate is actually put in front her, she puts it all away.

She is an adventurous-enough eater and enjoys strong flavours. My noodle salad is one of her favourites. It takes a while to make, but I cannot think of a better way to be spending my time. I look forward each day to eating with my mother. I take pleasure from being at the table with her, my body filling her vision, and hers filling mine, with room left over for little else. It answers a deep need in me, to have her to myself like this, and to know that no one, neither a sibling nor a relative nor a friend, is going to barge in on us. The doorbell, these days, rarely rings, which leaves us free of the tension that arises from the possibility, the expectation, of encroachment; in ordinary times, the outside world feels forever ready to rush in; in these times, we have no choice but to be well and truly with ourselves.

Usually, my mother does the talking while we eat. She tells me about her morning. Goes through her list of fixations. Asks me the same questions she asked me yesterday. I listen mostly in silence. I nod. I shrug. I say, 'Ahuhn.' I answer her queries as succinctly as I can, knowing I will probably have to repeat myself later, and then again tomorrow. In this quietness, I am not holding myself back exactly. My intention is not to protect my mother from my thoughts. There is nothing stopping me from saying what I want to say. She would, undoubtedly, be willing to hear me out. What I am doing, I suppose, is waiting for the moment when the subject arises organically. The moment when, without our even realising, we are already talking about it.

For it must be dealt with.

Delicately, calmly, without a sense of urgency: okay.

But before her mind goes completely, it must.

As I am lifting a spoon of chopped aubergines out of the hot oil, my phone vibrates. I glance over and see that it is a text from my brother N. Sighing, I wipe my fingers on my apron and jab the screen:

—*Ring R* [our elder brother]. *He not answering me.*

Immediately irritated by this interruption, I put down the phone. Return to the stove. Drop another handful of raw aubergine into the oil. Then, my irritation rising, I go back and text R:

—*N is looking for you.*

Then I text N back:

—*He'll call you.*

Five minutes later:

—*Call him again. He not ringing me.*

—*I'm busy, N. I told him to get in touch with you.*

—*Well he's not. Can no one help.*

—*What do you need?*

—*Ask R to ring me. He blocked me the ignoramus.*

—I already called R for you [a lie: I texted him]. *Is there anything else?*
—Ring him again.
—No. If you need anything else, let me know.
—What you mean no? Not a big deal to move your arm.
—Goodbye. I'm busy.
—Why won't you help me?

N's official residence is an eighteenth-century house in the country-side thirty kilometres outside Dublin. Owned by Saint Vincent de Paul, the house is supposed to provide short-term emergency accommodation only; N has been there for a year. Previously, he had been living in supported housing, which had provided him with a room in a shared house in the city and some basic assistance, but he was thrown out for not abiding by the rules. The system would not tolerate his drug use, and he was never going to tolerate such a system. As a consequence, he has ended up where he is, the only place in officialdom that turns a blind eye to his marijuana habit. The price: he must cohabit with ex-convicts and junkies, and be a regular witness to violence and suicide.

Before quarantine, N stayed three nights a week in our sister's house in a small town eighty kilometres from Dublin, three nights being the maximum he can stay away from the facility without losing his place there. When quarantine was announced, he moved in with our sister full time. The question then became: should our sister risk getting infected by allowing N to travel on the bus into Dublin to pick up his drugs? Or should she face an indefinite period of confinement with a man who turns manic when denied his closest attachment?

—Why won't you help me?
—I did help you. R will ring you when he can.
—I don't understand. Did I wrong someone?
—No. I rang R [again, the lie]. *I told him to call you. Do you need anything else?*
—Well ask him again. He hasn't rung back.
—No.
—Why no.
—Once is enough. Do you need anything else, N?

—Don't forget I'm living in homeless shelters so you guys can maintain your lifestyle or lack of. You won't help me with a phone call. Wake up.

This last text is true in its sentiment. (If I am able to stay with my mother and write this book, it is because N has been banished to a place where he can no longer claim such support for himself. And he is right to point out that I did not give him the help he wanted, for in truth I refused to make any phone call for him, stretching myself only as far as a text.) But the details are not quite accurate. N is texting not from the shelter but from my sister's house. He wants R to give him money so that he can get the bus to Dublin—the bus intended for essential workers only—and buy drugs.

I text my sister:

—Are you going to let him go?

—Look, she replies, *the other option is worse. I will disinfect him on the doorstep when he gets back.*

Gripped by a sudden fury, I text N:

—If you go to Dublin to buy drugs, you are to go back to the shelter afterwards. If you go back to our sister's, I will call the police.

I do not get a response.

No police are called.

He will get his drugs.

None of this I report to my mother when she gets back and we share our noodle salad.

Throughout my early childhood, until I was about ten, I shared a bedroom with N. Being six years my senior, he did not play or really associate with me during the day. Night was the only time he spent alone in my company. And it was dark. In the interval before sleep, from his bed on the other side of the room, N took it upon himself to impress upon me certain facts which, according to him, the official education system was going to deprive me of. About the existence of UFOs and alien life on earth. About intergalactic codes hidden in the configurations of prehistoric monuments. About an ancient manuscript found in South

America which accurately described the contours of a lake as seen from outer space.

Sometimes his aim was to amaze me, more often to scare me, and when he managed to do so—when I expressed fright or alarm to him— he would emit a cackle such as that emitted by the maniacal villain in horror films after he has revealed for the first time his true disposition: *AH-ah-ah-ah-ah-AHH-ah-ah-ah-ah-AHHH-ah-ah-ah-ah*—

Sometimes N would bribe me with money (which he did not have) into his bed so that he could kneel on top of me and pull violently on my cheeks: what he called a *cheeky-leeky*.

'I'll give you twenty pee for three *cheeky-leekies*.'

Or so that he could strike the funny bone in my elbow with his knuckles in order to send tingling sensations up my arm: what he called *numb-ers* or *deadners*.

'I'll give you fifty pee for five *deadners*.'

He enjoyed these semi-sadistic rituals immensely. Looming over me, his face was an exhibition of pleasure: eyes focused and bright, mouth opened wide, teeth showing, cheeks flushed. And, in all innocence, I must have liked being dominated by him in this way, for, even though I never got the money promised, I went to his bed whenever he called on me, and, at the same time as I was screaming and telling him to stop, I was allowing him to manhandle me and to push me to the limits of discomfort—I would not call it *pain*—that I could endure.

Afterwards, I would return to my bed exhausted and fall fast asleep. But often I would not make it to the morning. As a younger child especially, between the ages of three and six, I tended to wake up in the middle of the night (perhaps running away from something in my dreams, perhaps running towards something else in my waking life). When this happened, I would abandon the bedroom and N, and go to my parents' room, to my father's side of the bed, and tap on the mattress. Although my aim was to wake my father, I would never touch his body, by prodding it or shaking it, out of a fear that doing so would rouse him too abruptly and cause him distress or anger him (this, despite the fact that I had never, at any time, seen him get angry). Patiently, I would stand barefoot in the dark and tap the mattress, over and over, until eventually he would open his eyes. Then, without complaint, never a word of reproach, he would slide his big hands under my armpits and lift me up and over him—even today I can recall the feeling of being weightless in the night air—and put me into the gap between his body and my mother's. This soft furrow, this nest, remains the warmest, safest place I have known, though my conscious experience of it was brief, for, almost immediately, as soon as my father had pulled the duvet up and fixed it under my chin, I would fall back into a deep, complete sleep, a perfect sleep, the ideal slumber against which all of my subsequent slumbers are measured, always falling short, and to which I long to return at the end of each day (and to which, it would be nice to think, I will return at the end of my life).

In the morning, then, I would wake alone in my parents' vast bed. The curtain would be pulled back, letting in whatever light there was in the day. My father—the big man who had allowed me into his bed and in whose heat I had slept—would have left for work hours before. N and my other siblings would already have gone to school. So I, the only person remaining upstairs, would lie there for a minute, listening to the faint sounds of my mother in the kitchen below, and would be in no doubt as to my specialness. Having had my father for the night, I would now have my mother to myself—the whole of her, unshared, undivided—for the day.

Sometimes, when the weather was bad, we stayed at home and read and listened to classical music and painted and baked fairy cakes and did jigsaws and sewed buttons. Other times, also when the weather was bad, for it did not really matter, we went out together, hand in hand. To feed the ducks in the park. To post letters and do local errands. Or—the happiest days, the days about which I got so excited that I would pace up and down the sitting room while waiting for my mother to get ready—we got the bus to Dundrum or Stillorgan or, the supreme expedition, into town.

First there was usually something boring to do, like a tour of a department store in search of table mats or tea-towels, but the reward afterwards was a trip to a library or a bookshop, where I spent a long time browsing the shelves (not always the children's section, for there was always the chance of a glimpse of something adult and dangerous) and taking in the smell (that specific odour of gum and paper and ink) while my mother chatted to the librarian or the bookseller and to whoever else was nearby, everyone whispering as if in a church, and I was allowed to pick anything I wanted, which normally ended up being something about dinosaurs.

After that, we went to Bewley's. (At that time, there was a Bewley's in Dundrum, in Stillorgan, *and* in town, which led me to believe that there was a Bewley's everywhere; that by national decree every parish had to provide its own Bewley's, and that everyone, naturally, stopped off there on their rounds; no sane person would have dreamt of going home without having paid a visit.) I had merengue while my mother had creamy coffee into which she put lots of sugar, most of which would be left at the bottom of the cup when she had finished. Then we would play a little game whereby I would ask her for the sugar in her cup, and she would tell me that coffee was bad for me, even in small doses, but of course she would end up giving it to me, and I would spoon it out and eat it, and I thought it was divine.

Here I am speaking about Dublin in the early eighties. After two decades of demolition and bad planning, the historic centre had become an eyesore. Unemployment was sky-high. Young people were emigrating in ever-increasing numbers. Heroin use was epidemic. So, although the Bewley's in town was by far the *best* Bewley's, the clientele was far from chic. There was a smattering of Trinity students in long coats and hennaed hair. And on occasion a theatre personality would appear in a loud waistcoat and a pair of coloured socks. But most of the patrons, most of the time, were middle-aged and plainly dressed. A high proportion of them displayed the symptoms of mental illness, or were caring for relatives who displayed such symptoms, although my most vivid memories are of those who sat alone, without family or friends: semi-immersed in the shadows of the booths, further obscured by a film of blue smoke, their belongings divided amongst a number of reused plastic bags on the seat beside them or at their feet, nursing a single pot of tea until it came time—who knows how many hours after their arrival—for them to ship out, at which point they would gather everything up and waddle forth, their negotiation of the narrow paths between the tables made more difficult by the watching eyes and the shifting arses and the noisy pulling-in of chairs, and as they passed by us, invariably—I mean, a statistically implausible amount of times—they would stop to talk to my mother.

For as long as I can remember—back then and still today—my mother has attracted the attention of strangers, above all those who, in her words, *have problems*. Like wasps to honey, they fly to her, land on her; and even then, as a young child, I was fascinated by the change that came over her in their presence. Far from object to their interventions—from standard to high-grade *mad shit*—she went along with them and tried to find their sense. By nodding and beaming and offering the required script—'Isn't that lovely' or 'Isn't that shocking' (depending)—she gave these people permission to be whoever or whatever they were trying to be in that moment. And yet: I also saw that this was not the mother I knew from home. Here in public, faced with these strangers, she was, I understood, putting on a special performance: special because it was played at a notch higher than the other performances I had seen her put on elsewhere, and special also because it had a didactic quality to it; it was, at base, a demonstration to me, and to any other witnesses, of how she believed we ought to treat others who were not as fortunate as ourselves, or who suffered more than we did; it was a lesson to us that in our dealings with different, difficult people we must find it within ourselves to be—that intolerable word—tolerant.

At some point, the tolerated strangers would, without fully turning to look at me, begin to speak about me.

'Isn't he gorgeous? Is he a good little boy? Does he look after his mammy?'

And my mother, then, would half-acknowledge me, by looking at me as if sizing up an unknown child, and—glowing as before, but with a strain in her voice, perceptible only to me perhaps—she would say, 'Yes, this is my prince.'

My prince.

This was how she presented me, so that was who I was.

Her favourite. Her last and best.

I sensed it was not exactly easy for her to express to the strangers what I meant to her, and maybe that was how I knew her feelings for me were true. *What words could describe what we have? Who in the outside world could possibly understand?* Her sentiments were, needless to say, reciprocated. I, too, was head over heels. Completely devoted. She was my beloved and, at that stage, I had no inkling that my place in her affections could ever be usurped. In my surroundings, I did not perceive any rivals. My siblings, though physically larger than me, were, in my estimation of their ability to attract our mother's love, pygmies, gnats, and not even that: outlines that barely registered in space. I presumed my mother saw them the same way, for when they bothered me, obtruded into my little realm, she swatted them away, wafted them out of existence: *Leave him alone, for God's sake.* Not even my father was a match for me. The foolish man went out for the entire day and left her in my hands. When he came home, exhausted, all he could summon for her were a few mumbled words, none of the embraces, the fondles, the kisses that I so readily, so publicly gave her. I saw parts of her—*whole performances*—that he would never see. He did not know her as I knew her. No one did.

That was then. Now, with hindsight, I can guess that what my mother was feeling in Bewley's was pride as she compared me—her bright, blooming boy—to the wilted strangers who approached us; and out of this pride came the attendant shame (for having felt pride in the first place), and from that was born her need to express sympathy for them.

'That poor man,' she would say when he, the stranger, who was more often than not male, had taken his leave. 'He has problems.'

Which was how I learned what *men with problems* looked like. How they behaved. And it precisely matches what my brother N has, four decades later, become. The sort of man who sits in cafés and calls attention to himself, drawing the world's gaze towards his body using the very defences—blackened teeth and long nails and dirty clothes and bad manners—that he has built up to deflect it; and who as a result, in the predetermined way, as night follows day, gets pity poured onto him by nice, normal people, like my mother, like me, who, looking up from our coffee cups and our meringues, do not recognise (or refuse to) the violence, the malignity lurking in our regard.

——

So, the critical question: how and why did I come to be, at forty-two, safe and secure in my mother's bosom, given whatever sustenance I need to make these judgements and write them down, whereas N has wound up over there, on the other side of the café floor, sitting alone behind his pot of tea—or more likely, his plate of chips—motherless, exposed, without a voice, being watched and talked about and, in the worst of cases, explained away in the name of compassion?

What happened?

Which is really to ask: what happened *to him*?

I cannot recount N's childhood. I do not know it, even if I wanted to tell it. But I can say one thing with confidence: my mother did not treat him with the same indulgence that she treated those problem strangers we met. She struggled to allow N, the child, to be whoever or whatever he was trying to be in a particular moment. She fought against him. She wanted to change him. And when finally she did come to pity him, it was out of a sense of despair, a belated recognition that he was beyond her help, outside her control. (Which is maybe what pity is.)

Nor did she spoil him as she spoiled me. I would be surprised if she ever took the young N into town on his own. Or bought him meringue. Or gave him the sugar at the bottom of her coffee cup. Or called him *her prince*. Our mother was the same woman, but N did not get the mother I got.

Seeking confirmation of this, as a formality almost, I ask my mother to describe her relationship with the infant N, and she simply says, 'He did not conform.' When I push her to be more specific, her gaze shifts off me and fixes on the middle distance, as though everything in her vision has become suddenly indistinct, and she says, 'He didn't sit in his pram. He did his own thing.' And then, turning back to me, she sighs: 'I do remember it was a long and difficult birth. A man I once went to talk to, a psychologist, was interested in that.'

Amazed, and not a little shocked, by this response, I give N a rare call to get his version. 'I always got on well with Mam,' he tells me. 'She taught me how to paint.' Really? Does he not remember any tension? Conflicts? 'No. I had a good childhood. My problem was, I listened to my friends too much. I don't have a car or a career because I was stupid enough to listen to them.'

I am appalled. By lying to me in this way, by effectively telling me that my memories are false, are these people trying to drive me mad? I ask my sister to confirm that I am not, in fact, mad. 'I'm afraid I can't really engage with this in any significant way,' she says, 'as this violence is a source—the main source—of my ongoing trauma and so is too painful.'

This violence. Yes, that is what I remember, too. But my recollection of it is fragmented, I struggle to give it form. What scenes took place? What words were used? What gestures?

'I can't remember specific vocabulary,' my sister says. 'And, from my point of view, I would rather it stayed out of the public domain.'

On the face of it, it looks like I have a choice. That I could, if I wanted to, leave N out of this. Out of respect for my sister's wishes, and to protect everyone from further hurt, I could put N's childhood to one side and focus solely on my own. In this run-through, my mother and I could remain centre stage, while N could be placed off the boards, in the surrounding darkness, watching us, seeing what he has been denied—

But, you see, it is not possible.

By separating N off in this way, by removing him from the main action, by drawing a circle around my relationship with my mother and placing N exterior to it, I would be creating a false picture. In point of fact, there is, and was, no such thing as *my* childhood. As a child, I did not exist alone; rather, I was, by virtue of my dependent state, always an essential part of some relationship. When I seek to describe myself as I was back then, I find I must describe *myself and someone else*: primarily myself and my parents (my mother first and foremost), but also myself and my siblings—above all, inescapably, N.

My childhood cannot, without excising it of its emotional centre, be separated from N's. For all of my formative years, from infancy to adolescence, I existed within the same interpersonal microcosmos as him, and, regardless of whether I was always aware of him as a distinct body in space—as a being with weight and mass, an inside and an outside, and a working consciousness like my own—I cannot overlook the impact that he, if only as a story, an idea, a constellation of feelings, had on me. A thorough conception of myself is not possible, I cannot fully exist in my own mind, if I disregard what I know of him, or at least what I think I know—and if I do not admit, besides, that the judgements I make about him on the basis of this presumed knowledge in some way impinge on every other judgement I make, about anything (him, me, my mother, the world).

My memory holds scarcely any visual traces of N as a child. But having a slim cache of images is not the same as knowing nothing *of* his childhood. I remember quite clearly the things that were said *about* him. Sometimes by other children. (According to the gang of boys he hung around with, he was the best artist in the neighbourhood, able to draw or mould or build anything he put his mind to, and popular with the girls as well, though not full of himself, no airs, always up for a laugh.) But more often by adults, usually my mother. I remember, in particular, the tone that she used when talking about him to my father or to her friends: how she dropped into a semi-whisper when it came to describe the precise order of his misdemeanours, how she wove her anger and her disappointment into certain phrases that became résumés, then, of the whole N predicament:

'I hate seeing him moping around with those young fellas.'

'If only he applied himself.'

'I don't know what we're going to do about him.'

I also remember the things she said directly to him: the reasonings, the admonishments, the threats of worse to come if he continued on his road, none of which were ever particularly convincing; our mother had a temper but was not, at heart, a disciplinarian. I remember on one occasion, while she was out of the house, he let all his friends in, and together they ran riot, turning out boxes of toys and scattering Lego pieces everywhere, and on her return she took to screaming: 'You have hurt me!' It was a line she liked to recite. When I replay it to myself now, it rings like a genuine expression of anguish, one which, in its initial airings, might have been effective in eliciting signs of remorse, but which would have lost its power, I imagine, as soon as N was old enough to wonder how *she* could possibly be hurt by actions he had taken against *other people* or even *things*. So he would have developed a habit of answering her back. And terrible arguments would have ensued. And—my mother's hurt breaking out—there would have been violence. I have heard talk of N being beaten with the handle of the vacuum cleaner, though I have no recollection of that. What comes to my mind, rather, are the insults, and the slamming of doors, and then:

'What are we going to do about him?'

Broadly speaking, the narrative of N's development—which over the years I witnessed being constructed, and which I readily absorbed, and to which I contributed in my turn—has three distinct phases. (1) In the beginning, N was 'good'. He was a normal, healthy infant. A big appetite. Energetic. Popular. An artistic streak. (2) But then, through childhood, he began to be 'bad'. To do or say things that caused distress. To choose the wrong company. To play roughly. To be antisocial. To offend against society. That is, to enact the precise scenes—like skiving off school and not returning at bedtime and having to be searched for—which my parents most did not want to see enacted, scenes which they did not want to believe him capable of and which, in their lack of a better explanation, they put down to naughtiness. (3) Until, finally, in adulthood, he went 'mad'. Or more exactly, his behaviour went beyond the tolerable limits of every significant person in his life, so that he could only be regarded as mad.

At base, this narrative—good, then bad, then mad—is about standards. It speaks of N as someone who, for social or biological (or whatever) reasons, was unable to reach, or failed to adjust to, a certain set of norms. N maladapted. He lost contact with the most commonly held definitions of reality. In the last analysis, he did not measure up to the agreed way of being human. The psychiatrist R.D. Laing calls this the *vocabulary of denigration*: a form of disapproving, denunciatory discourse that arises in and around families, and throughout societies, which find themselves harbouring 'difficult children' like N. I do not remember my mother using the word 'mad' while upbraiding N, but she did denigrate him with other words which together in meaning amounted to the same thing—he was 'wild' and 'wilful' and 'unmanageable' and 'rude'—and it is hard to object to all the implications of her doing so. Naturally, she had her standards, many of which conformed to majoritarian views on how people *should* behave, and as a result she was often unable to accept N's habits. Whether he was joining his peers in jeering a teacher until she cried, or whether he was wandering off on his own and sitting for hours atop a nearby hill and watching the cars pass by below, she believed he should desist from *acting like that*. She could not let go of the conviction that there were some worthwhile behavioural and social conventions that he could, with a minimum of effort, abide by.

At the same time, she, an intelligent woman, would have acknowledged that not everyone was capable of complying with the standards she abided by, and that she had a responsibility to try to comprehend and, if possible, come to the aid of those who fell short. 'Much of what he did,' she admits to me now, 'was no different from what a lot of other boys were doing. And *they* grew up to have jobs and lead normal lives. The problem, I think, was that his talent went unacknowledged.'

'What do you mean?' I ask her.

She pauses for a second to collect her thoughts. Then, in a quick bout of lucidity, she tells me the story of being at Mass one Sunday and feeling spellbound by an image of the Virgin Mary on a wall near the altar—only to discover, days later, that N had made it at school.

'He had told me nothing about it,' she says.

'Why do you think that is?' I say.

'I don't know,' she says.

'So what did you do?' I say. 'Did you tell him that you thought his picture was beautiful?'

'Of course I did,' she says. 'I always told him how good his art was. But whenever I did so, whenever I made a special effort to be nice to him, he did not take it in. It was as though he did not believe me. For people like N, only the criticisms cut through.'

—

Jung believed that the behaviours we define as 'mad', such as fits and paranoid ideas and hallucinations, contain germs of signification. That behind psychosis lies a personality, a life history, a pattern of hopes, and that the fault is ours if we do not understand them. It is easier—not free from hardship, necessarily, but certainly more bearable—to define and classify the madness of others, than it is to admit that this same madness functions in an existential context: an individual is not mad in a vacuum but is so in a certain place and time, within a certain culture, amongst a certain group of people, none of whom can claim to have had no part in bringing the madness about.

In other words, N's behaviour would remain incomprehensible to my mother, to me, to us, his family, unless we learned to understand the context in which it arose, and unless we viewed ourselves as integral elements of that context. In trying to understand N's madness, it would be wrong—it would be *mad*—not to consider the (related, relative) madness that pervaded our society, and that pervaded us as a part of that society. N, the mad child, did not exist without us, nor did we—the madly sane, the sanely mad, *the madding crowd*—exist without him. What he was, and what he has become, began with us, in us, and vice versa.

It is even possible—I am reluctant to say *inevitable*, though that is probably what I intend here—that we, the family, are the cause of his madness. That our way of being a family *to him* impeded his capacity to build a sane way of being in relation *to himself*. That our scheme of things did not match what N could live and breathe in, as himself. That when it came to the question of how he was going live in the world, the options we presented him *with* were not options he could live *in*. That the positions, the roles we were preparing him for were just not feasible for him.

So, what did he do? He developed his own vision of how to live. It was either that or go mad, no?

Needless to say, as soon as we noticed what he was doing, we, each in our own time and in our different way, objected. We tried to set him straight. We forced him to see sense, for we, as the sane ones, had to be right, totally right, and he had to be wrong, totally wrong (otherwise where would we all be?). But, after many battles, we realised there was no winning with him, so we reverted to the other method: we helped him along his chosen course by offering him a narrative to explain it: *good, then bad, then mad (after all)*.

Did he truly believe he was going to get round it?

At that: did *I* truly believe *I* was going to?

For, of course, madness is not a rare and isolated aberration. On the contrary, it is the terminal phase of a fairly common line of development extending over years. At no single point on this line can it be said that a critical point has been passed. A precise beginning is well-nigh impossible to locate. The most that can be said is that the ingredients for the outcome have always already been present, albeit in diluted or nascent or dormant form—and this was as true for me as it was for N.

All infants harbour intense needs and feelings. So intense, indeed, that the psychologist Melanie Klein has designated them nothing less than psychotic symptoms. Because the mother (what Klein calls 'the breast') seems to materialise when the infant calls for her, and because the mother makes up the entirety of the world, the infant is under the illusion, according to Klein, that he controls everything that exists. At the same time, the infant fears that the mother, which he believes to be an extension of himself, is actually in control of him. It is these twin fantasies of omnipotence and persecution that are, for Klein, the characteristic anxieties of psychosis. The infant's passing through this psychotic phase is both part of normal development—it enables the young ego to develop necessary defence mechanisms—and the basis for any mental illness that might later arise in him (the same mechanisms that are built to protect the ego can, under certain stresses, cause fissures in the ego's relations with the world). Out of insanity comes the capacity for normality, and inherent in normality is the potential to fall insane once again.

Personally, I find it hard to argue with Klein's reasoning. As a more-or-less adjusted child, I was to a certain extent and at one time or another subject to moods of futility, meaninglessness, and purposelessness. I underwent rents in my relation with the world, and disruptions of my relation with myself. I struggled to be together with others or to feel at home in the world. I despaired at my own aloneness and isolation. I believed myself to be less than complete, or indeed split in various ways. And in all of this, the only thing that set me apart from N was the particular insistence of his moods, the resoluteness of his experiences.

To admit in this way to my own capacity for childhood insanity—or indeed to my own *current, vital, active* flow of insanity—is not to deny N's special suffering. I cannot know what N, as a child, felt from one minute to the next, but I am willing to believe that he experienced agony beyond what I can fathom. I cannot, will not, make light of that distinction. Nevertheless, I do feel the desire to clear some room for my own self in an area of my consciousness—my inner asylum—that N has dominated for a long time.

While I am here, in this cell, I do not ask that N goes elsewhere. (*Why won't you help me?*) I do not need him to vacate. (*Did I wrong someone?*) He can stay where he is and watch me fail to measure up to my own standards. (*Wake up!*) Then together we can be infants, good, again.

In this vein, here is a mad memory of mine. The changing room of the local swimming pool. My mother naked under the harsh artificial light. Her face flushed from the lengths she has just swum; the rest of her skin blotched and goose-pimpled, for it is cold in here. No heating. Zero insulation. Bare brick and breeze-blocks. (In our house, jokes were told about my mother's daily visits to the *Soviet bath house*, about Russia being her *spiritual home*.) She has her foot on the bench and is rubbing cream into her calves: roughly, no relishing, the aim being to finish the task and get her clothes on as fast as she can. From where I am standing, a couple of paces away to one side—wrapped in a towel, a small puddle of water at my feet, putting off the moment when I will have to expose the whole of myself to the Baltic draughts—I have a clear line of vision to the scar on her abdomen; and the full, round underside of her breasts; and her protruding nipple that brushes off her thigh as she bends forward; and, through the crook of her raised leg, a fringe of damp black hair from which a thin ribbon of flesh, her labia minora, is peeping out.

We, my mother and I, are not alone here. Around us, there are other women, I cannot say how many—enough to keep in the air several unrelated conversations—who have assumed poses of their own, in various states of undress. These women are not well known to me, I do not recognise their faces from my mother's coffee mornings at home, but, because they recognise her as a regular at the pool, they behave in a familiar way with her, and address questions and remarks to her. And my mother, between her adjurations to me to *hurry up, dry yourself off, don't let yourself get cold, stop hiding behind the towel, no one is looking at you*, responds to them in a manner that has already become familiar to me: a manner designed to raise other people's spirits and share their burdens and find the funny side of their plights *because sometimes that's all you can do*; a manner that signals a low toleration of nonsense and a deep well of empathy for anyone forced to put up with it; a manner which, simply by virtue of my overhearing it, makes me feel integrated, favoured, stimulated, almost warm.

I delight in being here with my naked mother, amongst these naked women, absorbed in their naked talk. A delight born, perhaps, from my awareness of my penis, or, more precisely, of the strict rules governing the circumstances in which I am permitted to uncover it in women's company, which, excitingly, for a limited period only, do not apply to me. Part of the reason for my dallying must be the knowledge that this exquisite act of trespass will not last for much longer, that in a matter of a minutes, she, I, we will be wrapped up once again and filing out into the grey day, our eyes red, our hair still damp, our skin dried out and smelling of chlorine (despite our having braved the freezing showers), and we will disperse then in the direction of our different housing estates, our different fates, our different men—and I want to keep off that moment for as long as possible, I want to linger here in the women's bath house, I want to stand just as I am, trembling in my towel, until my mother is forced to dry me and to dress me, even though I am old enough to do it myself, for there is always the chance that this will be my last visit before it is decided (by whom? by *me*?) that I am too old and am banished from it forever. And I struggle to imagine what life will be like without this intimate ritual shared with women, and how the alternative—*intimacy with men?*—will function, except that, chances are, it will contain the atmosphere of N, all *Sturm und Drang*, or that of my father, in whose muteness, in whose tenseness, in whose insularity my delight will shrivel up and turn to dust.

As much as I am enjoying inspecting my mother's body like this, the presence of the other women in the room makes it unlikely that I am openly staring at it. More probably I am stealing glances. Collecting what I can before looking away in apparent disinterest. Which is clever of me, really, because, on top of concealing the true object of my fascination, which I know to be proscribed, it gives me the opportunity to compare my mother to the other examples of women. And how pleased I am by what I find. What satisfaction this juxtaposition yields. No one seeing what I see could deny it:

My mother is indeed a goddess.

The evidence is overwhelming. Whereas these women are squat and have large reserves of fat on their stomachs and on their bottoms and on the back of their arms, whereas their flesh gathers in rolls and collapses over their waists and ankles and wrists, my mother is tall and slim, her limbs lean, tapering elegantly to the joints. While these women's cheeks and chins and necks and breasts droop and sag, my mother's remain upright and firm. The rashes and the broken veins that blight these women's faces are, on my mother's, converted into rosy discs that sit high on her cheekbones, given an added lift by her near-constant smile. And when she speaks—her voice being merely an outgrowth of her physical grace—she does not have a coarse accent like theirs, but one that leaves each word distinct, shaped and crisp, uttered with no contortion of the face, demonstrating an ability, in spite of a lack of formal education, to make language perform for her, as it does at gatherings of family and friends, when she recites Paul Durcan or William Butler Yeats.

Later, from my adolescence onwards, my mother—everything about her, including her body—will be the object of my most searing criticisms. But, for now, she represents for me the quintessence of beauty, incomparable, occupying the celluloid chamber in my mind that would in subsequent years be taken over by the likes of Anna Magnani and Sophia Loren and Isabelle Huppert and Julianne Moore. The strange part is, unlike those famous women, my mother appears to be above reproach precisely because of her proximity. But the opposite is also true: the enjoyment I find in my mother's body, the reassurance given me by her caresses, the lessons I learn from her affectionate play, the utter certainty I have that she alone can satisfy my needs—somehow all of this coexists with my view of her as magically other, exactly like those famous women, always just shy of my capacity for understanding, never completely under my ownership. When we are alone together, we act like conspirators, mapping out secret routes through the days, yet even then she seems to be following orders from an authority that is independent of me. Disturbingly, she appears in charge of her own life, as well as mine. She is, on the face of it, just as fulfilled when she is acting for herself in the world as when she is doing so on my behalf. As happy, it seems, to waste her time reprimanding N as to fill it praising me!

Which perhaps explains the anxiety and the disappointment that attend my love for her. True, it is with her body that I associate love; my feelings for her are like those between men and women who love. Yet, no matter what I do to make her see it, she does not seem to fathom, or does not seem to take seriously, the depth of my love for her. Often, when it would be easy—when it would be *right*—for her to acknowledge our special bond, by simply returning to me feelings of comparable magnitude, instead she chooses to scold me, to belittle me, to manipulate me, to ignore me, to feed me words (and things: let us not forget the chocolate and the ice cream and the toys) that even I, at my age, can see are false gifts, designed merely to mollify. My love, I fear, is not wholly requited. I am haunted by the idea of being dependent on her for an incomplete love, for the rest of my life.

It is nothing less than misery to see love offered to me, but to know that I should not get too close to it, for fear that it is smaller, lesser, weaker, paler than I have anticipated. It is hell to want the love that is provided but to be torn by guilt for believing that it is not enough; to get the love, but also to be constantly preparing myself to reject it as insufficient. For this reason, while never ceasing to love my mother, I find it easier, sometimes, to hate her. For when I hate her, I do not get hurt so much as when I love her, and I still get to be alive and to feel things. My hate, moreover, is not an eliminator: in the throes of it, my mother continues to mean something to me.

So, when it can no longer be kept in, like dark ink injected into a pure pool, I release my hate into the space between us. I explode with righteous anger. I stamp and slap and kick and bite. *If my love feels so dangerous to you, then what do you think about this?* And, honestly, I feel it would be wonderful to be hit by her, as N is, for it would show that she really cared about me. In beating me, she would merely be trying to return me to a state in which I am untouched, unharmed, at peace once more.

But, in this, too, she disappoints. She does not, as a matter of course, spank me or thrash me or put me over her knee. Occasionally, yes, she tightens her grip on my arm until it hurts. And once, just the once, she slapped me across the face. But I know she is capable of more. Deep reservoirs of anger exist within her. Formidable, unacceptable rage. Murderous resentment. At certain times, in certain lights, especially when N is around, I can see her quiver from the effort of holding it all in, of absorbing it into herself. Until she can absorb no more and must take it out on something.

Like: the coal fire in the sitting room. Which we light when we arrive home cold from the swimming pool, and which we gather round in our pyjamas for my night-time story. But which must be cleaned the following morning and the ash taken to the bunker in the back garden. I watch her doing this chore—from the breakfast table, I peer down at her—and it is obvious to me, from the way she is banging and clattering the dustpan and brush, and from the quiet remarks she is making to herself as she carries the bucket out, that she is furious. (*Is it with me?*) She wants to be doing anything else than this profitless work for this ungrateful family, for this greedy boy, yet she will not put it down for a second to have it out with me, or to take it out on me. (*Why not? Am I not worthy of it?*)

Then, when all other routes are exhausted, she gives it to N (the *N*ot me, the *N*ot good). Through the doors and the walls, I hear her at it. And I am jealous of N, almost, that he gets to see what her hate looks like when it comes out. That he is trusted enough to witness its turning explicit. And, perhaps most of all, that he is able to receive it so excitedly, so joyfully:

AH-ah-ah-ah-ah-AHH-ah-ah-ah-ah-AHHH-ah-ah-ah-ah—

Why him? What is wrong with *me*? Would she treat me differently, I wonder, would she give me what she gives N, if she knew that there are days when I believe, just as N does, that the stuff I am made of, far from being gold, is rotten to the core and ought to be burned, incinerated, thrown on the ash heap?

The primary school my mother enrolled me in was not the one nearest our house. (That one, St P——'s, where N and my other siblings went, had been split by some perverted adult minds into separate boys' and girls' schools, making it a no-go area for an effeminate boy like me: this, I would like to think, was my mother's reasoning, though her choices for my later education make me doubt it.) Mine, St A——'s, was a newer, mixed school about half an hour away on foot: its distance, its mixed-ness, its newness, its difference, all sources of great pride for me.

My mother and I set out for it at around twenty past eight each morning. Initially hand in hand. Then, when I got old enough to feel embarrassed about that, side by side or even a few paces apart. The journey took us down the long curving road of our estate, through the stretch of wasteland known locally as the Shortcut, past the petrol station and the church, then onto a thoroughfare that cut through the cluster of estates from which St A——'s took most of its pupils.

Few children from my estate went to St A——'s. In my class, I was the only one. Which meant that my mother and I were mostly alone on our walk. Only as we neared the school did we come into contact with other people—my classmates and their mothers—whose entrance onto the scene I resented as an encroachment. Seeing my classmates outside the school boundaries, that is outside the system of rules governing our treatment of one another, was disorientating to me: their behaviour here was different from that in the classroom, and I wondered whether it was ever right to call attention to this difference, or whether I was, in fact, bound by an unspoken pact to keep silent about it. *Should I pretend not to know what people are really like?* Similarly, with their mothers I felt a duty to be someone other—*better? nicer?*—than who I was used to being with my own mother, which caused me a fair amount of anxiety. Much more content, much more at ease I was when it was just my mother and me, being ourselves with ourselves, and when our destination—the problem of others—was still far away.

The school itself was a complex of single-storey buildings built in dark-brown brick, with a large yard, some playing fields, and, at the back, the flat blocks of a working-class estate. My mother would drop me off at the gate, and would be there again, with an ice cream or a chocolate bar in hand—she always came with something—when the final bell went in the afternoon. Then we would walk home together, and I would eat the treat she had brought, and we would chat, or we would let our minds wander in silence, just as we had done in the morning. This routine was utterly constant, my mother absolutely reliable. I was never met by a neighbour or a relative or a paid babysitter; it was always her. Whenever she forgot to pack my lunchbox, she would cycle back down to the school with it—the box in the basket on the front of her bike—and come in to the classroom to hand it to me personally, grinning from ear to ear, and my classmates would raise a hullabaloo—*Ooooohhhhh-oooohhhh-ooohhh*—and I would go puce, on cue, but really I was grateful to her, and pleased to be her son. How many of the other mothers did this sort of thing? How many were as recognisably good as she? Always there, always smiling, always congenial; everyone knew her for exactly this: how happy she appeared, and how friendly she was, and I loved her for it. (How on earth I grew up to be so *unhappy*, so *unfriendly* is a mystery to her. It mortifies her. So much so that she has mastered the art of subtly apologising for me to strangers. Compensating for my rudeness, as she sees it, by laying on her version of the opposite. Which, to me, of course, is a red rag to a bull: *Are you with me, Mum, or shall I leave you alone with these lovely people?*)

Only once, when I failed to notify her of an unscheduled half-day, did she fail to appear at the school gate to accompany me home, and have to be rung. On that day, I sat alone on a bench in the sports hall, listening to the cleaning ladies gossip over the noise of their vacuum cleaners— doing a job which, in later years, my mother would do—and, although I put on a brave face for the janitor when he came to fuss over me, I was, in fact, teetering on the brink of panic. To be the last child left in the building, perceived as someone who had been forgotten, was a kind of horror, and I never, ever wanted it to happen again.

Later, when I was allowed to walk to school on my own, my mother would accompany me as far as the hall door and smear a layer of Vaseline onto my lips and cheeks; then she would stand in the open doorway and wave: a long-armed, wide-arced gesture that lasted until I had cleared the gate and disappeared behind the neighbour's hedge. As soon as I knew my mother's gaze was no longer on me, and I was properly alone, my left hand, acting without my will, would come out of my pocket, and the index finger would begin to wag, and my thinking time would begin.

I walked with my neck bent forward, looking at the tops of my feet. The movement of my shoes in and out of my vision worked to wipe away awareness of my body and the surrounding world. The singing of the birds, the wind in the leaves, the rain hitting my hood, the engines of the passing cars: these sounds faded to nothing. The discrete objects of the world flattened and blurred as they were pushed to the edges of my consciousness. And I entered, then, a state of hallucination and delusion; lost my connection to the outside under an assault of fantasies.

I would not go so far as to call the visions I conjured *my own worlds*, for they were not complete, or coherent, or even especially original and creative. Rather, they were a composite of secondary images taken from the television, from fantasy books and comics, from newspapers and magazines, interspliced with memories and immature sexual preoccupations, which my mind arranged into series, and played in loops, over and over, inexhaustible, sometimes sticking to a fixed order, other times changing the sequence according to an unfathomable rationale. These imaginings were extremely important to me. Freud says that daydreams, like nocturnal dreams, are wish-fulfilments, and I think he is right in this sense: it was not simply that I *wished* the content of my daydreams to come true in my life; rather, my daydreams were, in and of themselves, *already* true in my life; they *were* my truths; they *were* my life. Nothing that happened to me at home or at school or at play was as exciting, or as real, as what happened to me in my mind as I walked. No friendship I had offered me the intimacy that my imaginary companions did. No lesson was as meaningful as those passed on to me by my private voices. No measly religion or moral code was going to survive for long in this fire. I set my subjective psychological processes above the objects of the world. I gave myself—the sum of the visions in my mind—a higher value than the things and the beings I saw around me. I declined to give outward happenings any advantage over me.

And in this, I imagine, I was just like N.

This attitude shifted dramatically, however, as soon as I crossed the threshold of the classroom. Once enclosed within those four walls, merged with my peers, placed under surveillance, put to work, I subordinated myself to others; or more precisely, I gave others' opinion of me a higher value than my own. What I thought of myself, and what I thought of them, was less important than how I came to think of myself *through* them. What mattered, suddenly, was how others took me: what they said and did in response to me, or for me, or against me, or with me. I no longer lived for myself, for my daydreams; now I was trying out for parts in other people's dreams.

Unlike N, who seemed so effortlessly to win the affection of his friends, I perceived a lack of approval from my classmates and worked hard to gain it. N was simply popular; I wanted to be universally so. This meant I had to put a lot of time into chasing and barging with the boys, as well as doing what I really enjoyed, which was skipping with the girls. At playtime, the yard was divided into two: a larger section where all pupils could congregate, and a smaller corner reserved for the girls, where they could skip without being disturbed by boys running through their ropes. It was not that I objected on moral grounds to this gender apartheid—I did not mount a principled challenge to it—rather, I simply acted on the presumption that the rule did not apply to me. Instead of asking for permission to enter the girls' yard, I just went in whenever I wanted to. The girls always let me join their games; they never rejected me or made fun of me. And the teachers on yard duty never threw me out. There was, you could say, a sort of unspoken understanding that I had a special pass.

'Remember, boys,' said the school principal one morning at assembly, 'under no circumstances are you allowed into the girls' yard. That goes for all of you. Except for one notable exception.'

Everyone turned to look at me, and I felt the requisite shame. But at the same time, I was thinking: *That's right, watch this spot. I wouldn't swap it with any of you, not in a million years.*

(I mean, imagine living in a world in which, just because you are a boy, you are discouraged, forcibly so, from experiencing the vertiginous joy of waiting in the skipping line, of watching the bodies ahead of you snake round and jump through, of the nerves intensifying as your turn gets closer, of the arrival of your big moment, and the exhilaration of rushing in and leaping over the moving cord and escaping before it whips you in the back. Or, if it is your lucky day, of being the one who happens to come into the centre when the last word of the rhyme is being sung, which obliges you to jump the rope as many times as you can, at an ever increasing speed, until eventually—nothing can go on forever—it catches your ankle; and, although this is presented as a terrible punishment, the worst thing that can befall you, it is all that you long for, a chance to show the world that you can get past your current record of three rapid skips, and maybe make it to five, or—why not dream?—ten!)

That being said, in girls' society, I was never *quite* allowed to belong. I was let in, but the underlying message was: do not get too comfortable. There were boundaries I would not be able to cross. I was an ally, maybe one day I would be counted as a real friend, but I should not think I would ever be a *sister*. Likewise, there were activities in which I was never going to match up. My fancy paper, for starters, was not as desirable as theirs (I used to cut squares out of my comics and spray them with perfume, in a vain effort to pass it off as the genuine article), so I was often left out of their bartering. I did not have long hair, so I could not braid or be braided, as much as I desperately wanted this. I had no rings, no bangles, no hairbands, no nail varnish (and so forth), so I was on the outside of many (to me, scintillating) conversations. When push came to shove, regardless of how different I was from the other boys, I was still a boy, and therefore had to be made to accept at least some of the conventions that regulated boys' behaviour. For this reason—in the name of preserving civilisation—I could not be allowed to get too close. I had to be kept at a certain distance.

So it was with my teachers, the first three of whom were women. Miss D, Miss B, and Miss J: I had a strong attachment to them all. I idolised them, in fact. Was devoted to them. And feared, furthermore, that the other children would win their love away from me. This, in spite of the clear lines that they drew on the ground for me: our relationship could go this far, but no further. I accepted these confines, as I knew I must, but that is not to say it was easy for me to do. To my mind, these women were, quite concretely, my mothers. Or rather, as much as my own mother, they represented Mother. When my own mother disappeared at the school gate, these women took over from her as nourishers, providers, comforters, guides. Like my own mother, they were reliably there and kind. Like my mother, too, they harboured a deep perceptiveness, and had no truck with foolishness and silly behaviour. I watched their eyes move around the room, with knowledge shining out of them—a knowledge which, for me, was identical to love—and I saw my appearance reflected in that light. When their gaze happened to fall upon me—purposely so, I believed, and more often than upon the other pupils—I recognised within it a positive image of myself. And I recognised, also, a certain expectation: to live up to the love I was being shown. My identification with this expectation was, I would say, complete. The formation and development of my identity was entirely bound up with my ambition to impress these women and draw from them expressions of pleasure in me. Learning their lessons was easy, in short, because I was in love with them and wanted to satisfy them. I was, in their realm, under their guidance, the antithesis of N, who, while not always disliked by his teachers, acted as though earning their disapprobation was just as worthwhile as winning their praise, as though the one (the dark) gratified him as much as the other (the light).

Gavin is an excellent student, and very popular, especially with the girls.

At the end of each year, I brought home to my (first) mother a glowing report card. *Outstanding. A+. Go han-mhaith.* I was able to draw, so my pictures were pinned up. I could act and sing, so I was picked for the plays. I could run and jump, so I won gold medals on sports day (beating all the little heterosexual boys). My greatest triumphs, however, were with language. I was regularly awarded full marks for my essays and my stories, and called upon to read them out loud to the class. And when I was doing so, I felt I was nothing other than what I had written. And what I had written was, I was told, good, which made me, not only tremendously happy but, at least for those few moments of praise, in possession of a self: a knowledge of who and what I was.

Once, as an award for writing the best story, I was allowed to choose a book from the class library to take home that weekend. I chose an illustrated book about butterflies, which, over the course of that Saturday and Sunday, I did not read so much as carry around like a trophy, propping it up in conspicuous places and standing in front of it to bask. On Sunday night, instead of putting it into my bag with the rest of my things, I propped it up on my bedside table, its cover facing out, so that it would continue to transmit its glory onto me while I slept—with the result that, the next morning, halfway to school, I was woken from my usual reveries by the realisation that I had left it there, in my bedroom, even though my teacher had warned me expressly *not to forget to bring it back in*. In a state of extreme agitation, I dashed back to get it, then ran all the way to school. Arriving twenty minutes late, unheard of for me, I entered the classroom winded and already weeping. I was manic. Unhinged. On the verge of wetting myself. For I had ruined everything. Given proof that, really, under the *excellent student* mask, I was N. That is to say, I was vile. Despicable. Totally undeserving of the amorous embrace, the soothing caresses which, in contravention of her own policy, my teacher was now giving me.

And this was not the only breach. My inner N revealed itself—the return of the repressed—on many other occasions. It sometimes happened, indeed, that for whole periods of a day I would be heedless and giddy, a state which, when fuelled by whispered jokes from O (the cleverest and the funniest girl in the class, and still a close friend today), could spill over into hysteria, in which case my teacher would put me standing in the corner, facing the wall, until I had cooled off.

Or, without warning I would drift off into a daydream, from which I would emerge long minutes later, ignorant of the instructions for a task, or sometimes having missed a whole lesson. Once, roused from a reverie by the final bell, I realised I had not taken down the homework from the board. This was a disaster for me, both because I liked to be the first to finish taking things down and because I liked to get on the road promptly, I did not like to dawdle. I picked up my pen with the aim of quickly scribbling the homework down, but, with the other pupils packing their bags and making their way for the door, I was gripped by anxiety and found I could not do it. My hand was paralysed. I was unable to write. Panic rose up through me, and I began to shake, then gasp for breath, then sob, until, again, my teacher had to come and, with her touch and her gentle words, settle me down.

I was cruel, too, off and on. There was, to give an instance, a boy in the class whom I adored. I used to sit beside him and hold his hand and kiss him on the cheek and help him with his work. But, on one occasion, I jeered him for a mistake he had made in his copybook, which was overheard by my teacher and which sent her into an uncharacteristic rage. I was shocked by this sudden change in her demeanour, and it took me a few moments to understand that her ire was directed at me. When I finally grasped that indeed I was its object, I became perplexed. My only recourse was to interpret her anger as illegitimate, since her job, surely, was unceasingly to provide the leniency that I required in order to do my best for her. I protested, or tried to explain, which only served to inflame her bad feelings towards me. With a shouted command, and a pointed finger, she put me standing in the corridor outside. Familiar to N, perhaps, humdrum even, but for me the ultimate position of shame. Exposing me as a wrongdoer to any teacher who passed by.

The ignominy!

But, also, the injustice!

For the truth was, I loved the boy whom I had jeered. It was out of love for him that I had disparaged him: was that not how it worked? Could my teacher, whom I loved with the same love, not comprehend that? In the middle of that same school year, the boy moved away. From then on, I would only ever see him in my dreams. Even today, some forty years later, he drops in to me at night, and I help him, and I kiss him on the cheek, and I think he is beautiful, even though I no longer have a face for him.

So there was home, and there was school, which stood in for home, both of which were under female jurisdiction, and neither of which my father belonged in. Unlike my childhood memories of N and my other siblings, those of my father are numerous and vivid; yet, oddly, he is a figure whom I remember as being absent in those spaces where, for me, life was populated and bright.

For a start, he was someone who entered the home when the sky had already darkened. His exhausted presence was in tune with the atmosphere of ending, of preparations being made for rest; what interventions he made were too few, too weak to reverse the sense that that day's chances—of feeling, of understanding—had already drained away. On those occasions when I saw my father in the hours of daylight—on the weekends, or on one of his unusual days off, or on late-summer evenings, when he had more energy, certainly, and often took me on outings—still then, my experience of him was less physical, less doting, more remote, quieter, more for-himself, than my mother. In the long periods I spent with *her*, I learned how to gauge her emotional state. By keeping a fairly constant eye on her face, I got in tune with her and could judge for myself when she was open to engagement and when she wanted to be left alone. My father, on the other hand, was a mystery to me. Physically, he was robust, a sportsman, yet his moods, or rather his one overriding mood—tiredness and depression—appeared to drain his body of the spirit required for human connection. He spent long periods in silence, allowing my mother's voice to dominate—'*You'll have to talk to N'*—until, out of the blue, he would, in a muted tone, utter something droll (*spitting out the side of his mouth,* my mother called it) which would send her into hysterical laughter. *Strong or sad? Dull or quick-witted?* I found him impossible to read.

(Or maybe the opposite is truer: that my readings of him were correct, that he simply *was* the contradictions that I saw, and that, in actual fact, what I did not want to face was the terrible question of why, in that case, my mother should have chosen this contradictory man as her husband. Why she had not gone, instead, for a man who was always strong, consistently quick-witted, incapable of depression? A question which, if I had ever posed it, would have transformed my mother into the mystery, unsolvable, and that would have been intolerable.)

Unless she was caught up with N, in which case I would have to wait until she had calmed down, my mother gave her attention to me without my having to fight too hard for it. I did not see N as competition because I understood that she preferred me to him. N was merely something that had to be dealt with and put away in order that normal relations between us could resume. With my father, it was a different story. As soon as he walked in the door, he became a distraction for her, and a link in the circuit connecting us would be fatally interrupted. Her world no longer revolved around me; now it was all about him. Clearly, my father was highest in the pecking order, higher even than me, commanding a special kind of respect, but she did not appear particularly willing to provide this. She did not offer him any words of affection. Nor share with him any stories. There was no *How was your day?* Rather, because my father usually came home after the rest of us had had dinner, my mother would stop what she was doing and return to the kitchen, where she would bang around, pulling together an impromptu meal for him—'Have you eaten?'—as if she had not expected his return; as if, far from being her overworked husband, he was a guest who had just floated in to ruin her evening. This, I can only interpret today as a failure of organisation on her part, born of her resentment at having to do something—devise a large meal, cook it, allow for the possibility of two sittings—which did not come to her naturally, and which she did not enjoy. She struggled, as far as I can remember, to take pleasure in her role as nourisher. Rather than finding a set of recipes she herself liked to prepare and to eat, she fixated on the unwelcome work that the act of cooking created—the shopping that had to be done, the vegetables that had to be chopped, the surfaces that had to be wiped, the plates that had to be washed—which made mealtimes stressful, and turned food into a fraught subject, one emptied of its potential for delight.

Yet she did it. She did what she so clearly disliked—for *him*. Which told me that he held something that she wanted. What it was, I did not know. But I wanted it from him, too, nonetheless. To this end, regardless of how exhausted he appeared, I demanded his regard, usually by bringing a book to him and holding it out in his direction, as a sign that I wanted him to read to me. This was something he clearly did not want to do, yet I insisted, and my mother goaded him until he agreed. Then, I would sit on a chair beside him, or simply stand by his side, and place the book on the table by his plate, and he—dutifully, far from thrilled with the task—would read to me between mouthfuls. As he spoke, I would look not so much at the book as at his mouth, for I was fascinated by the pauses he would make to chew and to swallow, and by the way the muscles of his face moved and the bones of his jaw came through the flesh and then disappeared again, and by how he could so easily break, without any qualms or repercussions, the momentous social norm of not speaking while one's mouth was full.

What is this thing called 'man'? What is going on in there?

My father did not have a space in the house that belonged exclusively to him. He did not have an office or a television room or workshed (no tools) or even the corner of a room that he could retreat into and be unseen. After his meal, he would just go to the armchair in the sitting room and turn on the sports highlights or read the newspaper, and that would become his lair, though in fact it was not remotely private. Once installed, he would last only a couple of minutes before tiredness took him over. At which point, he would stretch out his legs, push his two hands down the front of his trousers to cup his penis and testicles, let his head fall back onto the rest, and fall asleep. Watching him in this pose—which

I could do without fear of being caught, for his snoring acted as a kind of warning system—I was interested, most of all, in what he held in his hands, and in the question of why he was holding it in this way, and my conclusion, I imagine, was that this was the area of his body where his secret power lay, that his penis was what my mother wanted—nothing else represented a satisfactory explanation for her attention—which was why it needed to be protected while he slept.

(Protected *from* her, though? Or preserved *for* her?)

There existed, I knew, stringent rules about access to my father's penis, which I had to be clever to get around. Whenever I was on his lap, I would make sure to stand on it, or to rub my legs or my arse against it. When he got changed, I paid close attention to its unveiling, and then to its re-cloaking, and I memorised how it looked, and recalled the image later when I was alone. If I happened to come upon him while he was pissing, I would go and stand by the toilet cistern and observe the entire operation, taking careful note of his handling of it, and its response to this handling.

(One tragedy of child abuse by fathers, I think, is that the victim is robbed of this chance to be in close proximity, and to remember being in such proximity, to the father's penis, and, in all innocence, to admire it, to fathom both its power and its defencelessness, and to want this, all of it, for oneself. *'Memories often come to mind much later,'* writes Louise Bourgeois, *'[like] my father walking around in his night shirt while holding his penis.'* How productive such a memory can be for a person, like Bourgeois, like me, who has never been molested; what a nightmare it must be, on the other hand, for a person who has.)

After an hour or two in the armchair, my father would wake up, or my mother would wake him up, and he would go to bed, where he would lie and worry for a few hours, before getting up at five and leaving the house again. Or, as sometimes happened, he would get a call from the police, telling him that his shop had been burgled, in which case I would come out onto the landing to see what was going on, and I would catch sight of my father getting dressed, and my mother would lead me back to bed and stroke my head and tell me it was nothing, even though

I knew—by the nerves I could sense in the atmosphere, I knew—that it was something.

From time to time, after much nagging, my father would agree to take me with him to the shop, which was in the F—— housing estate in West Tallaght, one of the most deprived in Dublin (a community centre, a church, a school, and that was it, for a population of six thousand; no health centre, no doctors, no pharmacies, no dentists, no bus route; my father's shop was one of only two). I adored riding in the car to F——, buckled into the back seat and peering out at what were then mainly country roads, the bends of which required my father to turn the wheel a great deal and perform lots of gear shifts. Through the gap in the middle of the front seats, I would witness his big hands carry out these manipulations, and the muscles of his left thigh clenching and unclenching, and, if I craned my neck a bit, the bunched-up part of his trousers underneath which his penis would be, in that very moment, vibrating.

The shop, rather than being part of a strip, or integrated into a block of houses or flats, stood forlorn on a patch of green, in the middle of which there were sometimes burnt-out cars. The windows were barred and grilled. My father's full name was printed on a sign above the door, alongside the word *Newsagent*. Which meant, in essence, that he was the area's prime purveyor of fags, sweets, tabloids, and boiled ham. When a customer came in, I would beg my father for permission to press the buttons on the cash register. 'Next time,' my father would say until he could not, in good conscience, put it off any longer. At which point, he would sigh, 'All right, come on,' but would first check with the customer that she was not in a rush, for I was bound to slow her transaction down. Then, even with her permission, my father would make a point of apologising to the customer, 'I'm sorry about this,' while he was lifting me up and holding me over the register, and he would continue to apologise in between speaking out the numbers I needed to press, in the order I needed to press them.

Soon, by force of circumstance, the shop went bust, and my father had a nervous breakdown (not his first, not his last). He was admitted to St P——'s Hospital in Islandbridge, where, to my memory, my mother brought me only once. We, my mother and I, got the bus in. Being only four or five, I was not told why my father was in hospital, or even that he *was* in hospital. Nothing was explained to me. All I knew, on that journey, was that the vague atmosphere of anxiety that normally surrounded my father had been diffused and was now palpable even in the places where he was not: it had been in the house before we left, it was on the bus now, and it would be in the city streets, too, hovering over the Liffey as we walked down the quays.

On arrival, we took a roundabout route to my father's ward, down unused corridors and closed-off wards. We did this, I have since learned, in order to avoid bumping into my father's mother and my father's sister, both of whom, unbelievably, were patients in the hospital at that exact time, recovering from their own individual breakdowns. By avoiding them in this way, we were helping my father to keep his committal a secret from his similarly committed family.

And we/he succeeded.

I refused to enter my father's room. Or my mother kept me from entering it. Or the hospital rules said no children were allowed. Or my father did not want me coming near him. Whichever it was, my memory is of being out in the corridor, holding my mother's hand, and looking into the room, through the open door. My father is standing at the end of his bed, with his back turned. Although it is broad daylight, he is wearing a dressing gown. He does not look sick. At the moment just before my memory ends, he turns to glance out the door, and our eyes meet—and, I swear, even then, at that young age, I recognised in them genuine, unadulterated shame. And I recognised, too, that what I was feeling was also shame, though it would take much longer to understand that the shame I saw in my father's eyes *was* my own shame: it was the shame I felt for him, and, at the same time, it was the shame I felt for wanting (to be) him.

This is the desirable object that draws my mother away from me?

This is the man I must become if I want to attract someone as good as her?

—

As at home, so, too, at school. A regime of motherly diversion interrupted, in the final hours, by the mysterious laws of man. After six blissful years under the guardianship of three goddesses, in came the god.

The entrance of the Pater.

But Mr S, my teacher for my final two years at primary school, was not the same kind of man as my father. That is to say, he was, to my eyes, everything my father was not. He was alive, and in my life, implacably *there*. I had no choice but to get to know him, to perform for him, to expose myself to him, and, eventually, to have him find me out, just as I would find him out. In the mornings, he would charge into the room with his cup of coffee in one hand, his acoustic guitar in the other, the smell of last night's beer and his morning cigarettes wafting from him, and, as he trundled towards his desk, I would search his face for his mood: that was my first and most important task. If his mood looked good, then the day itself might be good. He might, for example, get out his plectrum, and we might pass the hours learning Bob Dylan songs. Or he might tell us to pull back the tables, so that we could have a debate or do some drama improvs. If his mood looked bad, however, he would stay behind the desk and sulk. Today I understand why he might have done this; his *was* thankless work. But, back then, I was not so understanding: quickly losing patience, I would put up my hand and tell him, in a more or less polite manner, *to do his fucking job*. In response to which, he would bark some orders at us, or write mundane tasks onto the blackboard in his swirly writing, and we would open our books and do what were told—or not. When we did not, he would lose his temper with us, and tell us what he really thought of us as a collective, which was usually pretty mean. Or, more commonly, he would choose one of us to bully. Not me, so much. I was not his primary target. Sure, I got dumped on from time to time, but not to the same extent as a couple of the other children. This was because I, unlike the others, had made the effort to learn how to fight with him.

And, oh mother, we fought like dogs. We fought in a way that I was unable to with my father, who, at the merest whiff of confrontation, would simply walk out of the room. Mr S and I, by contrast, were eager armies in a hot war. Whether I wanted his opinion or not, he gave it to me, and vice versa. He shouted at me, I shouted back. He pointed in my face, I pointed in his. He stood up and threatened me, I followed suit. He sent me out to the corridor, I gladly left and slammed the door. At one point, our relationship deteriorated to the point where he would no longer speak to me, until one morning I was informed—by whom, I cannot remember, but it was not him—that I would no longer be a pupil of his, that I was being moved to another class. Two interminable weeks I ended up spending in the room next door, sitting amongst a crowd of total strangers, seething, choking on my rage—I mean, absolutely *panting* for revenge against the man who had humiliated me in this way.

Without realising it, I was beginning to understand why N fought against authority as he did; to identify the circumstances in which such struggles are justified. Interestingly, though, by the time I was finally let back into my own class, I had become subdued. Outwardly I had gone quiet, just as inwardly I was no longer in torment. For I had settled on a single position. I had reached the point where I could, without any fuss, plainly, straightforwardly, hate him.

Because, until then, of course, I had also loved him. He was not espe-cially handsome—not a patch on my own father, I can see that now—but he possessed certain traits, like dark eyes and a hairy chest, which, to my immature mind, were markers of a kind of unattainable, and therefore superior, masculinity. And what is more, this unattainable man, this god actually *saw* me. He did not look past me, overlook me, ignore me, get bored by me, walk out on me, as my father did. On the contrary, he noticed me. Picked me out. Laughed at my jokes. Asked me to join in. Brought me to the centre. Encouraged me to speak, to act. There were times I felt he reached the deep insides of me, but this was probably just an effect of my propensity to show him everything of myself. In different modes, overt and covert, I confessed to him my violence, my aggression, my cruelty. I revealed to him my dreams as well as my terrors; in particu-lar, my fear of abandonment. By trying to be everything for him, I wanted him to be jealous of me, which implicated me in a constant rivalry with him—*and* with my classmates, all of whom I considered competitors. For I was ambitious. I wanted to be chosen. To be number one. And this was exhausting. That is to say, loving Mr S was exhausting, for I was constantly vacillating between wanting and not wanting him to see it, which produced in me a profound insecurity, a dizzying lack of self-esteem: he was a god, and I believed myself to be a littler god, whom he, in his turn, had to adore, and it was terrible—*terrible*—when he did not.

I loved him because he accepted me as his enemy—in a way my mother reserved only for N—which made me feel special.

And I hated him, too, because he asked me to accept that I was less than perfect, limited, unable to control or satisfy the world, that my own desires were not paramount.

The end-of-year play in fifth year was *Joseph and the Amazing Technicolor Dreamcoat*, and I was Joseph. I was chosen, as I had been chosen for so many other productions and events before, because I had a singing voice, but also, let me put it baldly, because I was prone to certain episodes in which, driven by my profound insecurities and my concomitant need for approval, I passionately refused to accept that my will did not reign supreme, which led to an irrational belief in my own abilities. ('*I have found that persons who are aware of being preferred or singled out by their mothers show, in life, that special self-assurance and that unshakeable optimism that not infrequently appear heroic and compel true success.*' So said Freud of Julius Caesar. And we all know how things turned out for *him*.)

As soon as Mr S announced that we would be putting on *Joseph*, I, in my mind, without knowing anything about the play, was already Joseph. I was not even remotely surprised, or even that excited, when I got the part, for it was merely the world catching up with reality (which, obviously, was synonymous with my destiny). I learned the songbook in a matter of days, and took the rehearsals extremely seriously, and I could tell that Mr S, who was directing, was pleased with me, that he could depend on me, that he believed my strength would make up for the weaknesses of others. And on the night, I did not fail to hit the notes:

Close every door to me,
Hide all the world from me
Bar all the windows
And shut out the light.
Do what you want with me,
Hate me and laugh at me
Darken my daytime
And torture my night.

The following year, our last, it was decided that the play would be *Rumpelstiltskin*. This, in an instant, put me out of the running for the lead role. As one of the taller boys, I was never going to be cast as the imp. My ambition, meanwhile, ruled out the part of the king, for he carried no weight in the story; really, he was just a souped-up walk-on. The only other character of any interest was the miller's daughter.

'Who would like to try out for *her*?' said Mr S.

A girl called L auditioned first, and she was good. She chose to portray the scene in which the miller's daughter, locked in the tower room, has to spin a bundle of straw into gold by morning or else the king will cut off her head. L's approach was to highlight the scene's tragic aspect. By the end of her two minutes, she was crying real tears. Mr S was impressed.

'Anyone else?'

I sat down in the chair that L had just vacated and looked around at my classmates' faces. I had spent the past eight years with these people. They did not frighten me, nor did I them. There was nothing I could do, by now, that would shock them.

So I crossed the leg over.

And I did the wrist.

And I did the hair.

And I did the lashes.

And I did the nail file.

And I put on the Yank accent.

And, when I stood up and walked around the chair, I did the stiletto heels.

None of which made me a girl. By all appearances, I was still a boy. But that was what made it funny, right?

When I was finished—well over my two minutes—Mr S laughed and said, 'Are we really going to do it that way?'

And my classmates, bless them, roared: 'Yes!'

Here, I want to return, for a second, to my Big Dream:

> *My agent, R, comes into the room. In her arms, she is holding a small human figure, her son, who is got up like a doll. An elaborate nineteenth-century dress. A bodice and petticoats. Layers of ruche and fringe.*
>
> *'When I wear trousers, I'm a boy,' R's son says, directly addressing me. 'When I wear dresses, I'm a girl.'*
>
> *'I like your booties,' I say so as not to call attention to the red dress, which is causing me immense embarrassment.*

Even as I dreamt my Dream—*any dream will do?*—I was aware that, when looking at R's son, I was looking at a reflection of myself. That the little boy in the red dress—*my dreamcoat?*—was a representation of myself as a child. Now, in the role of interpreter, I can be even more precise: R was the personification of the feminine nature of my unconscious; she was my enduring image of woman, of the beloved Mother; while her son represented my own desire to please that Mother by acting like her, by wanting to become her. In the dream, I was both proud to be the son of Mother, and ashamed that I was behaving in this outrageous way to impress her. What would Father think?

A serious question: what would he think?

Because ultimately it was for *him*, was it not, that I put on the dress?

The school hall on the night of *Rumpelstiltskin* was packed. My father was in the audience, of course, along with my mother, and my uncle who was home from Los Angeles for Christmas, and all of the other parents and teachers, and plenty of local hangers-on besides. As I waited in the wings for my cue, I was aware of the singularity of what I, at eleven years old, was about to do, and that it would be threatening to those who witnessed it, though I could not yet know what it would mean, in the long term, for me.

We teach children that only certain possibilities within them are liveable, writes Adrienne Rich. *We teach them to hear only certain voices inside themselves, to feel only what we believe they ought to feel, to recognise only certain others as human. We teach the boy to hate and scorn the places in himself where he identifies with women.*

Is going on a stage in a blonde wig and a tutu, with red paint on your lips, identifying with women? I wonder. But I will say this: while I was on those boards, under those lights, while I was revelling in the audience's gaze and soaking up their laughter, while I was twinkling my fingers and cocking my hip and twirling around—not imitating any woman in particular but rather replaying fantasies of the fantasy of women, that is, repeating those gesticulations, those affectations, those stylisations, which were supposed to sum up the experience of womanhood—while I was doing all of this, I did not know if my appearance was masculine or feminine, nor did I know if my essence was either of those things; in fact, part of the pleasure was not really knowing what or where I, essentially, was.

Is this Gavin?

Is this?

Is *this*?

And the source of my joy was that it did not really matter. There was nothing natural or necessary about any of my gestures. None of them were original. All of them, derived. Technically, any of them could be, or could become, if I practised them often enough, me.

After the performance, I joined my family in the front row. I had taken off my costume and wig, but I still had the make-up on my face. Lipstick. Rouge. Eye shadow. Because there were no free seats, and despite being far too old, I sat on my father's lap. In this position, father under son, we watched the other performances, none of which came close to surpassing mine. I was the star of the night: no one in their right mind could deny it. But then the thrill of my triumph began to wane, and, beginning with an uncomfortable prickling on my neck, I turned to feeling cold and exposed. Twisting my neck round, I chanced a look at the people in the hall. Together, as one, they looked back at me. And I saw, then, that all the faces, which just moments before had been full of admiration for me, were now sneering at me. Scorning me. The respect I had won from them was not, could not be, a permanent contract between us; it was, I now realised, the fleeting effect of an exceptional circumstance. The house lights had come up. The true state of affairs could no longer be disregarded. They—*what could I possibly have against them?*—were the sane majority, and I was the mad one. To reach their standard, and to stay there, I would have to keep trying, keep practising, keep rehearsing. And, make no mistake, they would punish me when and where I failed to get the performance right.

INTERLUDE: ÎLE D'OLÉRON, 1993

With summer came the foreign exchange students, and with *them* the question, inwardly and anxiously posed by us, the teenagers of the estate, of who they would fancy, and who, regardless of who they fancied, they would end up with, and, even though I, as the gay one, was out of the running for the going prizes—a badly spelled love letter, a walk into the bushes, a hand-job—I did not fail to be stirred by the prospect of their arrival, then captivated by the reality of their presence in the group: the Spanish, the French, the Germans, they appeared to me higher-level beings, products of a better diet, beneficiaries of a giving sun, exemplars of both orthodox manners and an alternative sort of modernity, carriers of culture, utterly covetable, and for these reasons completely out of my reach; so the only thing for it was to get a foreign student of my own, which my parents agreed to do, even though they could not really afford the costs, 'Thank you!' I said, hugging them, 'thank you!' but then when the application form arrived in the post, my father refused to let me fill it in, or even see it, instead he took it away to complete on his own, which sent me into an indignant rage, 'Mum!' I screamed, 'You must stop him! I'll have to live with the boy who comes!' but she did not intervene, or even try to find a compromise, and when my father came back and showed me what he had written on the form, how he had described me and the sort of boy he believed I should be paired with—both pitiful little versions of *himself*—I felt no pleasure in seeing that I had been right, that he had done exactly what I had expected him to do; and sure enough, as soon as I laid eyes on the boy, E, whom my father had ordered for me—

clean-cut, sporty, clearly unread, *plainly* the progeny of reactionaries—I could tell he was not for me, we were not going to get along, and, lo and behold, we did not, could not, for I was who I was, and he was, to say the least, a stupid, arrogant son of a bitch; nevertheless, by introducing him to the liberty of the suburban wastelands, by getting him drunk as often as possible, by constantly censuring my judgements of his comportment, by ignoring the ramifications of absolutely everything he said, I managed to get through our three weeks in Ireland without clashing openly with him: a triumph, a miracle, which he then proceeded to undo by not granting *me* the same tolerance when we got to France, so it was there, on his home turf, that the real shit went down, beginning, as a matter of fact, on the first evening, in the sitting room of his house, when, during a conversation with his father, I, without thinking, used the informal *tu*, and E, without hesitation, exploded, '*Vous! Vous!* Use *vous* when addressing my father!' in response to which his father, though he evidently agreed with his son, sheepishly said, 'It's all right, don't worry,' but, for E, what was at stake was nothing less than his father's honour—*was that not him in the white navy uniform in the photos on the wall? did such a man not deserve the world's reverence?*—so he berated me some more, until his father finally snapped at him, and, from that moment on, we, E and I, were at war, which I waged using the best, the only weapon in my armoury: whenever E lost his temper with me, which occurred with increasing frequency as the days passed, I would respond by not responding at all, by acting as if I had not heard a thing, by giving him my silence, which was its own kind of violence, perhaps even worse than his, though, trapped as I was, I did not think I had an alternative—until one day it dawned on me that the reason E spent his days on his own, throwing a basketball at a hoop in the garden, was that he had no friends, and from that moment on, out of pity, I began to punctuate my silence with the odd smile, pitched witheringly in his direction, which I actually think he appreciated, for it told him that our feelings of hatred were mutual, so at least he was not alone in this hell; and this, I think, would have been as brutal as the hostilities got, had his parents not decided to take a trip around the country in a camping car, that is, had they not decided to confine us to a tiny cell, four metres by two, for ten days and nights—what was, for me, the slow process of dying from being deprived of a room of one's own—and at several junctures the thought occurred to me that I was not going to last out, that my personality was on the verge of dissolving into psychosis, that, as an urgent matter of survival, I had to get away; and then, on Île d'Oléron, *la lumineuse*, I saw my chance: in the morning, after breakfast, while the family was busy contemplating a map of the island, I stepped out and, feigning a trip to the communal toilets, started to walk, and continued to walk, and did not stop walking, up and down the paths, and across the dunes, and along the shores, stopping every now and then to buy bread and chocolate and sweets, and to smoke one of my secret duty-free Lucky Strikes, until it began to get dark and a search party made up of ordinary people from the campsite found me and escorted me back to the camping car, where E was boiling with predictable rage, 'Are you stupid? Are you mad?' and where his father gave me a stern lecture about the dangers of wandering off alone, to which I listened silently, offering no apology, for I had every intention of repeating my walk of freedom the next morning, only this time I would make for the public phone box I had located near the beach, and, using the calling card I had purchased, would ring my mother, and she would get me out of here: though, in the event, my opportunity to flee did not come until the afternoon, when E and his parents were in the sea together, which meant that I had to walk unprotected under a harsh sun, and the interior of the phone booth, when I entered, was swelteringly hot, my clothes instantly stuck to my body, and my breathing became laboured, and, as I waited for her to answer, water welled up in my eyes, and I knew as soon as I heard her voice that I would break down—*just as I had broken down the summer before, when I had rung her from the Connemara Gaeltacht and begged her to let me come home, for I was miserable, the other students were horrible, the food was inedible, and, to top it off, someone had just stolen my spending money that I had hidden in the drawer, a crime which I could not report to the host family because my Irish was not good enough, and anyway I could not be certain that they were not the culprits*—only this time, this year, on Île d'Oléron, I was not going to take no for an answer, my mother was

93

going to come through for me, she was going to book me safe passage from this unhappiness: 'What do you expect me to do, Gavin? Call the agency? I can't do that. I'm not booking you a new flight, I'm sorry. You'll have to stick it out,' and there was nothing I could do to bring her round, I ransacked inside her for a feeling and came out with none, and, I wonder, in all truth, had I anticipated a different response? or had this fresh abandonment been precisely what I had bargained for? and was I surprised, honestly, when she picked me up from the airport a fortnight later, and took me to Bewley's in town on the way home, and I had meringue and she had creamy coffee, and I told her all about it—was I surprised that, instead of taking my side, or even just making an effort to see my point of view (*these people were Gaullists, for fuck's sake!*) she folded her arms and hardened her look and said in the tone of a woman who, at my age, had long since built her own shields against the forces that surround us, 'You're immature, that's what's wrong with you. You went and wasted the experience'?

CELL III

Normally, my mother does the dishes after lunch. She prefers to be in control of that. But today, because I have noticed that she is particularly tired, I insist on taking over. She yields, but only if she can dry. Tea-towel in hand, she assumes a close position on my left side.

'God, Gavin, you don't have to wash them so hard.'

'What do you mean?'

'You sponge everything three times and rinse them for ages. They just need a quick swish.'

I laugh, thinking of her method: the strict order that must be followed, and the weird little habits like the scalding of the cutlery with boiling water from the kettle. Then I feel a bit false, thinking of how we must look through the window, a picture of happiness, like one of those ads that begin with the mother pondering how she might increase the son's intake of good bacteria, for she is much concerned about his overall intestinal health, and end with her wiping something, a foodstuff, from his nose, then beaming into the camera, as though she has just solved his life.

'Are you going to work today?'

'I work every day, Mum.'

'I know you do. You're too hard on yourself.'

'It's what it takes.'

'You're driven. It's frightening. You're like a plough carving into the earth. Nothing will stand in your way.'

She is right. It is frightening. And it is tiring. Sometimes I would like to sit back. Take a break. But I am a servant to the delusion that I will

write one sentence, one chapter, one book that will be enough to satisfy me and enable me to stop.

'That'll never happen.'

'I know.'

'You won't be filled up by any one thing you do. Better to find fulfilment from the simple fact that you have a career, with all its highs and lows. That's more than a lot of people can say.'

'You know, Mum, you're driven, too. In your own way.'

'Me? I'm like water. I flow.'

I let out a single laugh, which she is expecting. Then I turn serious again.

'I don't know what it is,' I say. 'I guess I have something to prove.'

'To whom? Not to me, I hope.'

'Maybe to you, a little.'

She twists the tea-towel into a tube to get it inside a cup and puts all her attention into the action of turning it around to collect all the moisture hiding down there.

'To the people at my old school as well,' I say, unexpectedly broaching the subject.

Sensing that she is being blamed for something, she turns away to put the cup into the cupboard.

'Probably to the people from my school most of all,' I say. 'Success would be my way of taking revenge on those motherfuckers.'

I say this, but my mother is right: it is anger towards her that I am feeling. And, paradoxically, it is this same anger that stops me from saying any more. As though the anger itself knows that it is not the right conduit for the message I have come to give her.

At some point in my final year of primary school, a change took place, one for which I had been given no preparation. There was, quite suddenly, an increase in the frequency with which my classmates—groups of them, sometimes more girls, sometimes more boys—failed to show up to school. When I enquired, I would be told that they had gone to an 'open day' or were undertaking an 'entrance exam'. These expressions were new to me; it took hearing them many times, over several weeks, for me to absorb their significance. In the meantime, I went around in a state of not quite grasping what was going on, an experience akin to that of returning to awareness after a period of daydreaming, and of realising I had missed an entire lesson, and of having to pretend, then, that I had understood everything, in the hope that, by watching what everyone else was doing, I would belatedly catch on. The day after their absence, the missing pupils would return bearing parental notes, which they would queue up to give to our teacher, and then, amongst themselves in the yard, they would exchange anecdotes about what they had seen and done on their private excursions, and, at some point, out of the blue, the question that everyone was asking was 'What secondary school are you going to?'

'What do you mean?' I said the first time I was asked this question, for naively I had thought we would all be going to the same place, that our passage together through the system would continue, uninterrupted, to the local community school, located just a couple of hundred metres away. That was where my siblings went, and it was, I presumed, where I would be going also, along with everyone else. Did the others now have a different idea?

'I got a place in St M——'s,' said my friend, referring to a private all-boys school, which I had never heard of before, but which I rightly took to mean that he and I were about to embark on different paths, and that, once separated, we would never see each other again.

I was devastated.

A witness to the advent, in a single instant, of two imminent losses: the first, that of my friendships; the second, more terrible, that of my love affair with my mother.

All at once, I felt very bitter against her. It was she, not my father, who had jurisdiction over my advancement, my cultivation—at least, that is what it looked like to me—yet, in this role, she had never spoken about secondary school as something that was chosen. Something weighed up and considered. Something I might have a say in accepting or rejecting. Rather, in her communications on the subject, which were not many, and which were mean in detail, and which certainly did not take the form of dialogues, secondary school *was* the community school, and that was that. I had never thought to question this, to question *her*, until now—too late—I found myself vigorously doing so. Had it occurred to her to explore a number of possibilities, as the other mothers had done? Had she put my name down for entrance exams elsewhere? Had she applied for scholarships in my name? Had she ever, once, looked at me and thought that, perhaps, given the type of the boy I was—the type that skipped rope with girls and wore pink tutus on stage—some research ought to be done to find a place that would suit me?

It came as a shock to understand that such questions had not entered her mind. A shock that was not lessened by the consideration that, perhaps, given the financial circumstances, she had not allowed them in. In my eyes, it came down to this: she had made me *her prince* under false pretences, for, when push came to shove, not only was I going to be denied special treatment, but I was also going to be treated *worse* than my decidedly less princely peers.

One day, after staying late for some reason or another, my teacher, Mr S, gave me a lift home in his little car.

'I shouldn't be doing this,' he said as we sped up the main road towards my estate.

'Why not?' I said.

He shook his head, knowing that I knew well why not.

To change the subject to something lighter, he asked, 'What secondary school are you going to?'

'The community school,' I replied, quite naturally, seeing nothing controversial in these words.

'Oh,' he said.

'Oh?' I said, noticing his tone.

He sighed and, after a weighty pause, said, 'You shouldn't go to that school.'

I went red. A flush of anger: 'Why not?'

'Uhm,' he said, fumbling for the right phrasing, 'all I can say is, it's not the right place for you.'

I had turned to look at him while he spoke. Now that he had finished, I switched my attention to the road ahead, and to the trees whizzing by, and, in the ensuing moments of silence, there arose in me resentment of a magnitude that outdid anything I had felt for him before, and that, by its great force, impelled me to make a pact with myself, right then and there, never to get in to his car, or to be alone with him anywhere, ever again. I had reached the pinnacle of my aversion to him. Hatred could not get higher than this. Yet, as I peered out from this new vantage point, I could not deny, either, that my feelings for him were part of a much larger landscape, one in which my mother, in actuality, was the dominant feature. What did Mr S know about the community school that *she* did not? Or did she know what he knew, and choose not to tell me? Or, out of disinterest, was she simply neglecting to pass the pertinent information on?

And then, appearing on the horizon, hovering at the edges of my perception, this alarming proposition: the man I despised as an enemy was trying to protect me, while the woman who was my everything was proving incapable, or unwilling, to do the same.

And layered over that, infusing the air like a noxious gas, this certitude: I would not share Mr S's words with my mother, I would bury them in an out-of-reach place, I would protect her, both of us, from them.

It's not the right place for you.

What voice could I give to this phrase, what meaning could I attribute to it, that would not lead to the irrevocable break-up of my most cherished relationship? That would not, in fact, like the finest of blades, divide my very self, as though it were glass, into two?

A recent novel by Édouard Louis gives an account of homophobic bullying in secondary school. In the opening chapter, as an entry point to the subject, the narrator, a gay boy, recounts a scene from his old school corridor, in which he is spat at and pushed and kicked. People looking at such a scene from the outside, he says, tend to focus on the emotional torment—the fear or the humiliation—but what he, the protagonist, remembers most clearly are the blows to his stomach and the crash of his head hitting the wall; what has stayed with him is the physical pain.

I was—I take pleasure in reporting today, from my ivory tower—the star of many such scenes. Preparation for my role, by a large margin the most consequential of my life, had begun some years before, in primary school, with a campaign of jeering and taunting of gradually increasing intensity (what in gym-speak they call *pyramid training*: start light and build up to a top weight). But induction into physical violence—the climax, the ejaculation, what the hard-working people have paid their money to witness—I was denied until, like a bull in a ring, gone demented from provocation, I was nigh on begging for it, pleading for the sensation of body striking body, praying that after the next insult a fist would finally follow, for it promised to bring to a conclusion a humourless spectacle that had dragged on far too long.

Here I am. This is my body. Which is for you.

Like the narrator in Louis's novel, I was on many occasions spat at and pushed. I was elbowed and kneed and kicked. I belong to that hallowed minority which has heard, reverberating through a dimly lit corridor, the sound of their own skull knocking against a wall.

'He was asking for it.'

Once, on the way home from school, a matter of metres from my house, I was surrounded by a marauding gang, who, having scoured the area in search of me—'There he is! McGay! You faggot! We're going to burst you'—pulled me to the ground and pounded me with their feet and fists.

On a separate occasion, during the summer holidays—for there was, you see, no official break from the hostilities—I was in a field near my housing estate, sitting in a circle with a few of my girlfriends, smoking and chatting, when I heard my name being called: not my proper name, mind, but its bastardisation, which, by that stage, I had become habituated to. Cupping my cigarette to conceal it, I stood up and looked around. Marching in my direction was a group of five boys, strangers to me. None of them was from my school, but in terms of the probability of my being singled out and called upon in this way, that no longer mattered, for the use of the moniker I had been given at school was no longer confined to it: *Gayvin McGay* had spread—with no social media to conduct it, remember, so sort of miraculously, from one believer to the next—throughout the entire neighbourhood.

'There he is.' (There was a lot of that: the pleasure of identification, recognition, discovery.) 'Come here, McGay, we've something to tell you.'

I stepped out of the long grass into the nearby clearing. (There was a lot of that, too: the offering of myself to my executioners.) I dropped my precious cigarette onto the ground and stood on it. Put my hand in my pocket, where I had a packet of ten Marlboro Lights, which, I supposed, these boys were going to want. Was it better to give them the packet up front, as an oblation to their god, or to wait until I was commanded?

The group stopped a couple of paces away from me. Four of the boys formed a loose arc around the fifth.

'Do it,' they said to this fifth boy. 'Go on.'

It is significant, I think, that, even after all the violence I had suffered up to this point in my adolescence, I did not immediately grasp what the four boys were ordering the fifth to do. While I waited to find out—it was a matter of seconds, yet it felt like the world, that is to say people everywhere, not just those in this miserable field, on this miserable island, were on pause and standing by for the cue to proceed—I examined the fifth boy's appearance. He had his hair styled in a bob, tucked behind his ears, with a bit of an undercut, as was the fashion for middle-class suburban boys at that time. He was thin, like me, but a bit shorter. In the face, good-looking enough. Converse runners, jeans, a green shirt kept open to reveal a grey T-shirt underneath. In brief, he was himself *and* he was me *and* he was a thousand other southside boys, never quite free of the suspicion that we enjoyed conditioning our hair a little too much, that we wore our runners a little too clean, that we defended the girls' honour with a little too much gusto.

'Fucking do it,' they said.

And without further ado, he stepped into the empty space and did it. A hard, closed-fisted punch to my jaw.

Strangely, although I can only have experienced this from the inside, what occurred in my mind—a creative elaboration of what I glimpsed out of the side of my eye as my head swung to the right—was an image of myself as seen from the *outside*: my own long hair fanning out in the air, blond against a cloudless blue sky.

And that—banality of banalities—was that. I put my left hand over the place where I had been struck. Checked for blood. (None.) Then went back to my friends (none of whom had defended me, and none of whom was remotely put out by the treatment I had received). The boys—*were they satiated? had they admitted and accepted their violence?*—went away.

The next time I saw the boy who punched me, the fifth boy, was in a gay bar in the city centre about a decade later. *There he is*, I thought when I caught sight of him standing by the wall with a friend. *I've been waiting for this*. And I felt the pleasure, then, of identification, recognition, discovery. *Fucking do it*, I thought. *Look at me*. And, as if willed to, he did. Straight in the eye.

One dreams of revenge, and then it simply drops into your lap.

I had, at that stage in my life, not yet mastered many things inside myself. But, for that second, I came close to the superiority which I so badly wanted. This was the fifth boy's belated gift to me.

Unlike Louis's narrator, however, when I look back at the long decade—ages ten to twenty-two—in which I suffered relentless, daily homophobic abuse, it is not the physical pain that returns. I am unable to recall what, precisely, it felt like to be punched or kicked or spat at: it seems those sensations left my body as soon as they came in. In fact, the pain that comes to me when I remember that time, the pain that I constantly relive and give new life to, is of a completely different order and of a vastly greater magnitude than that which attended the physical violence. It is a pain which takes its nourishment from an entire field of experience, of which corporal brutality constitutes only a few scattered hotspots. A pain whose terrain is, for the most part—I should say, wholly—taken up with language. The action of naming and renaming. Of attaching words to things. Each time I recollect the words that my abusers once used to define me, each time I look at myself through the lens of those words, each time I interpret myself using their (multiple, contradictory, impossible) meanings, I become, again, an inhabitant of that terrain of pain, and, more often than not, I get lost in it.

Would it be possible, now, to draw a map of this terrain, one that shows a safe route through its most dangerous features to a frontier, an exit, beyond which—who knows—there might be a home waiting for me, and a mother who takes me in her arms, and brings comfort to me, and gives me peace?

My secondary school was situated next to my primary, so my walk there was similar to that which I had taken as a younger child. The only difference was that, instead of skirting around the neighbouring housing estate, I had to cut through it. At the entrance to this estate sat a petrol station, beside which there was a small piece of wasteland (the uncompleted, or badly completed, driveway leading into the local youth club). This was the meeting place of a large gang. I did not know, beyond a handful of the names and faces, the precise make-up of this gang; I did not know its factional alignment, its hierarchical structure, the nature of the relationships amongst its members, whether their affiliation was based on where they lived or what school they went to or something else entirely; in other words, I did not know what someone had to be or do to *join*. But I do know this. Whoever they were, wherever they came from, when they congregated on that scrap of dirt beside the station, they held sway over the world. Even on a relatively quiet day, with only five or six of them gathered, sitting in a line along the low wall or skulking in a pack, they made a menacing impression, one that dominated the environment, forming a cynosure which, as I approached, demanded my complete attention, but at which I knew better than to look too hard. This doubled experience—*be aware but do not be seen to see*—was magnified a hundredfold when the whole gang happened to be there. (Far from being planned, these mass convocations seemed to come about randomly, the momentary coalescence of normally chaotic forces.) On such occasions, as many as thirty bodies would be crammed together in a space that could comfortably fit only half that number, and the noise they made, their screams—*under which, surely, was the longing to call out softly with love?*—would travel a long distance in every direction, and I would know, from far off I would already have been warned, that I was in for it.

Each day, I had to walk past the petrol station at least four times: on the way to school in the morning, on the way home for lunch, on the way back to school in the afternoon, and on the way home after the last bell. It was inescapable, maddeningly so. Like a toll booth on a motorway, there was no going round it; the only way was through it. Which is why it constitutes the first landmark on my map. Picture a large red dot marking its position. Now see, emanating from this dot, semicircular lines in the same red colour—sound waves—and the figure of a boy approaching on the path, being struck by these waves at an increasing frequency. Observe this and ask: do the waves break? Do they wash over him, around him, past him? Or do they enter him? Penetrate his cells? Colonise the places in his mind where, in silence, better thoughts might well have developed?

Gay. Gay. Gay. Gay. Gay. Gay.
Gay. Gay. Gay. Gay. Gay. Gay.
Gay. Gay. Gay. Gay. Gay. Gay.
Gay. Gay. Gay. Gay. Gay. Gay.
Gay. Gay. Gay. Gay. Gay. Gay.
Gay.Gay.Gay.Gay.Gay.Gay.
Gaygaygaygaygaygay
Gagagagagaga
Gggggg

It took about ten minutes to walk from my house to the petrol station. Normally, I started to hear the voices—calling for me, at me, against me—from about minute seven or eight, as I left my estate and turned the corner into the gang's view. When the sound hit, however, the sensation was that of déjà vu; as the voices entered my consciousness, they met, already active, memories of those same voices. This was because, before leaving the house, knowing that to reach my destination I would have to pass the station, and that the probabilities of crossing the gang were therefore high, I automatically, without noticing what I was doing, rehearsed what I expected to hear from them. Silently, to myself, as I got ready to leave, I called myself the name that they had assigned to me. Ventriloquising their voices, speaking to myself as though from above and afar, I named myself as they had named me. On my way down the road of my estate, I even imagined myself in my neighbours' houses, at their windows, shouting this name at me, or simply peeping through the curtains and *thinking* it in my direction.

It was a kind of paranoia.

A personal pattern of defence that I had, over time, unconsciously developed (and that I would, over more time, develop further, and expand, and generalise, so that it would no longer apply only to a single gang located at a specific place but to anyone, more or less, who showed even a passing interest in me). A psychological mechanism, it was, whose aim was the deflation of an oncoming verbal attack by the replication of that same attack. A stab at emotional desensitisation. At mental inoculation. And it worked, in its own perverse mode. For when the attack then came, in the precise form that I had predicted, there was, mixed up with the anger and shame, a distinct feeling of relief: I had *not* imagined it, I was *not* deluded, what I had foreseen *had* come true, this *was* happening to me, and it *was* going to happen to me again tomorrow—and that, sadly, gave me some compensation.

From the petrol station, it took another ten minutes to get through the neighbouring estate. On this portion of my journey, especially in the narrow laneways that connected the different roads, I had to contend with other smaller gangs, or fragments of the larger one, each of which presented me with the same word: *gay*. Sometimes, they lobbed it as a single grenade, to get it out of their system. Other times, they machine-gunned it, magazine after magazine. Or maybe the better metaphor is that of a chant, one which my appearance instantaneously roused up in them, though as an incantation it lacked any meditative consistency; rather, it came at a frantic pace, in a range of tones and inflections, at different volumes, sometimes solo, other times in duets, or in harmony, or in chorus; and it went on, this inglorious prayer, until, several minutes later—a fucking eternity—I had disappeared from their view:

Gaaaaa a a a a a a a a a a a a a a a a a a a a y

I powered on, my head down, my face neutral, and did not say a word. The stoic. That was the part I was playing. *A role for which my grandparents had trained my mother, and for which my mother had trained me in turn,* and it was far from a noble one. I just did not know any other that would have fitted me. That would have got me through.

Leaving the estate by its northern exit—the underarms of my school shirt wet with nervous sweat—I came into a wide clearing: a conglomeration of green fields, mostly grass, very few trees, cut through by roads, and bordered in the far distance by the façades of terraced and semi-detached houses. At the centre of this expanse, inside a wooden fence (later substituted for high metal railings) were two single-storey buildings, sitting side by side, east and west. The walls of these buildings were orange brick and featureless. The windows were set high, just underneath the roof (the kind that required a pole to open and close), preventing anyone from seeing out or in. Add a chimney and some white smoke, and they could have been a chemical factory. Switch out the uniforms of the people converging on them: a barracks. Put a watchtower in, and some barbed wire: a prison. Or, leaving them exactly as they were: a low-security detention centre for juvenile delinquents.

My homeroom was in the west building, access to which was by one of three double doors. Each of these doors gave onto a corridor that ran straight through the building, to identical doors on the other side. Vertical slits of reinforced glass in these doors provided the only natural light in the corridors. For this reason, fluorescent bulbs in the ceiling were kept on at all times. When a bulb broke, or there was an electrical fault, the corridors were plunged into a depressing gloom. Some industrious past pupils had painted murals onto the grey bricks of the corridor walls. One of these murals was Picasso's *Guernica*. In which, as far as I can see, the most important figures are the ceiling lamp and the hand-held candle, without whose light the horrors taking place below would remain black, invisible.

For a free, state-run institution with an open-door policy (anyone, regardless of their record at other schools, got a place), and a commitment to lowering the dropout rate (getting expelled was virtually unheard-of), and an emphasis on technical and vocational training (metal work, mechanical drawing, home economics), and a genuinely admirable scheme of disability inclusion (most classes had at least one wheelchair user), my school was fond of its strata, all the same. We, the pupils, were divided into forms according to our age, and then, within each form, into streams according to academic performance. Our academic performance—our *potential*—was judged based on the results of a single entrance test, which we had taken before entering, at the age of eleven or twelve. Getting a place in the top stream, as I did, was far from a guarantee of a good education, though it *was* an escape from an absolutely terrible one, which was no small matter. (*If, for some reason, I had flunked the entrance test and had been placed in a lower stream, would my mother have accepted this, or would she have stepped in and demanded that I be elevated?*) Nor was being in the top stream a sign, necessarily, of advanced academic or intellectual or artistic or athletic capacity. At the school, the hierarchy peaked at 'mediocrity', and, in line with this, my classmates and I were, by every measure, mediocre—though, as chance would have it, there was one bona fide genius amongst us. (This was O, my friend from primary school, who would be my saviour in this place, and who, later, at the age of nineteen, having suffered as much as I did here, but at the hands of different people and for different reasons, would enter the same psychiatric hospital that was treating my father, and eventually share a ward with him, so that when I visited him, I was able to nip down to her, too, and, as in the arrangement of mutilated bodies in *Guernica*, there was an awful randomness to this, but at the same time a sense of order, of inevitability, as though this was the only possible shape of things, given everything that had gone before.)

The way the system worked, we went to the teachers; they did not come to us. After the morning roll in our homeroom, we spent the day mooching from classroom to classroom, teacher to teacher. With nine periods a day, five before lunch and four after, this meant a whole lot of standing up and sitting down, putting on and taking off our jackets, unpacking and repacking our bags (there were no lockers). It also meant a lot of time spent in the corridors. While waiting for a teacher to arrive at a particular room, we would loiter outside, leaning against the wall, watching and being watched by students from the other forms, the other streams, who might as well have been from a different country, for all the contact we had with them. As average as we at the top were, we were surrounded by people who were under the illusion—one created not by anything *we* said or did, for we did not say or do anything that would call extra attention to ourselves, but by the structure of the streaming system itself—that we were poshos. Snoots. Brains. Swots. (Depressingly, having money and having brains were, in the contemporary parlance, indivisible. And, ironically, part of the reason my mother sent me to this school was to fight against this very prejudice.) The job of the other streams, as they saw it, was to knock us off our pedestals. Cut us down to size. Put a pin in our inflated heads. This reverse snobbery—a vicious form of intimidation that not only went unpunished but, it seemed to me, was actively encouraged by the authorities—blended easily with the all-pervasive culture of homophobia, which was not so much fostered as considered an already intrinsic part of the atmosphere, as natural, as rightfully *there*, as the air we breathed. What could one do about something that was everywhere?

'*You fucking posh queer.*'

'*State of you, bleeding gay swot.*'

(Intersectionality *avant la lettre*.)

One day, the dean glided into our homeroom, her fingers clicking. (This woman, who was also our Irish-language teacher, did a lot of gliding and a lot of finger-clicking; if anyone could have been accused of having airs in that school, it was her.)

'I have received some serious complaints about you,' she said, addressing the whole class. 'The other streams have informed me that you have been behaving in an arrogant and condescending manner. That you have been looking down your noses at them.'

As a rule, I have never needed to reach for anger. It is there, and it has always been there. But what I felt as I listened to these words went far beyond what was customarily available to me. This, here, was the anger of the trapped animal. It was the anger of the tortured man who is blamed for his own torture (*'Only you can stop this'*). It was the anger of the prisoner who is made to answer for the manipulations that the prison system itself carries out on his spirit. It was the anger I felt when my brother N slapped me on one cheek and then, when I turned away to protect myself, slapped me on the other. And it was an anger so black, so bitter that it felt dangerous and made me want to walk out of the room.

Speak bitterness or eat bitterness? My mother, who had put me here: what would she have me do?

Before raising my hand, I looked around at my classmates. They sat with their arms crossed, peering up through their eyebrows. Weary. Incredulous. And angry, too, as I was, though they perhaps had a calmer way of being so.

'What you are saying isn't true,' I said, my voice shaking. 'If you had bothered to ask us, instead of just launching these ridiculous accusations at us, you would know that we are treated like dirt in this place. Subject to daily abuse by the students from the other streams. And we don't answer back. Never. We keep our mouths shut and walk on. Why? Because we're frightened.'

I was happy I said this, and about the impact it had. (We did not hear any more from the powers on the subject.) But in truth, my words were only a fraction of what I could—*should*—have said. Today I am struck more by the cloud of unvoiced thoughts surrounding my utterance than by the utterance itself. I can feel as a sensation in my body—in my gut and my chest and my throat—the immense pressure of all that I left unsaid: years and years of declarations and protestations generated in my mind and kept in silence there; an accumulation, an amassing which I can only describe as pain. In that classroom, in audience with the dean, I was given an opportunity, the only one I ever got, to acknowledge this pain, even to avail of it as a kind of strength; an opportunity to stand up and testify about *my* treatment at the school; an opportunity to move out of this blubbery 'we' and into the indisputable 'I', and to say: *I am frightened. I am hurt. What is happening to me here, in these corridors, has to stop.* And I failed to take it.

So, I am taking it now.
Here, mother, is my school report.

On my map of hurt, I am marking my secondary school as a discrete landmark, separate from the petrol station and the surrounding housing estates, because the abuse I endured within its walls, while on the face of it familiar, part of a by now standard routine, was in fact of a special order and quality, arising in a singular environment, resulting from a specific set of power relations, providing me with a distinct and distinctive knowledge of pain (or, if you like, knowledge of a distinct and distinctive pain).

Whereas to the gang at the petrol station I was an outsider—an external repository for their own unwanted feelings, relevant to them, not as a person, but as a distant figure, a marker, from which they could get their bearings and locate themselves, as men, in the world—in school I was very much *in*. Could not be anywhere other than in. Because, in that place, there was no outside to be in. No tribes to be on the outside of. We, all of us, pupils and teachers, were members of the one uniform, and uniformed, cell. The environment was rough and wild, but it was not *in* the wild. Ours was an artificial, closed-off, internal domain in which adults ruled over children. In which adults, as the established authorities, carried out suppressions and repressions on those children. But it was also a domain in which these same adults did not really understand exactly how their authority functioned or what its consequences were, and would not have been able to do what they did without the willing or unwilling, innocent or not-so-innocent, contribution of the governed, the repressed: us, the children.

The principal, who cultivated a Walter Mitty persona—an ill-fitting suit, a tie permanently flung over his shoulder, his hair wispy and ruffled— would be seen dashing down the corridor to his office, his gaze set high, apparently oblivious to what was going on around him, when in truth he was oblivious to nothing. (Later, after I had left the school, he would be fined €88,000 by the Irish courts for bullying another teacher, first by personally stalking her and then by employing a private investigator to do so, behaviour that the judge described as 'truly terrifying' and 'most serious harassment'.) When it came to harassing the pupils, however, he, perhaps believing himself above it (he held a doctorate after all), handed responsibility to his bulldog, Mr T.

This Mr T, broad of body and dense of face—*bully about the muzzle*, as Leopold Bloom might say—his mouth frozen into a grimace, his eyes blazing like an animal on the hunt, stalked the corridors in search of boys (it was always boys) to berate, to demean, to physically assault. His mission, which was no secret, given that he sprayed it into the faces of the ones he cornered (and which was not actually *his* mission but *the* mission of which he was merely an obedient functionary), was to instil discipline into those parts (of the body, of the mind) that had been denied it at home. He hated the boys for whom he was responsible: hated them for being loud, for being rude, for being rough, that is for being everything that he himself was. Many of the boys were undisciplined, no question. But, to my mind at least, the discipline Mr T tried to impose on them was nothing other than the boys' own resistances coming back at them, in a form only barely disguised: born in the same furnace, iron and steel crashing heads.

One day, on ducking out of a class to go to the toilet, I witnessed Mr T taking grip of a student, P, and flinging him against the wall. P, who was in the lowest stream of my form and one of the most feared boys in the school, a real hard case with a penchant for outrageous flour- ishes—rumour had it he had once flashed his penis in religion class—did not resist. He allowed himself to be thrown back, and then kept himself obligingly still to give Mr T the thrill of taking him by the collar and barking into his face. (This, even though, technically, P could have, and in any other context probably would have, floored Mr T with a simple knee-elbow-fist, one-two-three.) Crossing the otherwise empty corridor, I caught P's eye over Mr T's shoulder. And something—a message— passed between us. It took a second for this message to cross the space that divided us, and another second to read and understand, so our gaze was locked for what was, in comparison to how long one would normally want to be holding P's regard, an extended period of time. A shimmer of recognition. A glint of solidarity, tough man to *gay*, masculine to feminine, positive charge to negative. *We cannot be friends,* it said, *for in this place we are, by force, pitted against each other. But I see you, what happens to you here, and I know what that is like. I will remember you.* And then it was over. And I was in the toilet. Locking the cubicle. Lighting my cigarette. And wondering, *Did that just happen?*

Girls in the school were allowed to wear make-up—and many did, too much of it—but, because masculinity was the preferred mode of behaviour, the pole to which both sexes were urged in our attitudes and our preferences to tend, the style was utilitarian. Layers of panstick to cover acne and blemishes. A glob of mascara to harden the eye. And a strong brown line drawn around the lips so that people would not miss who was talking. Perms were in, sprayed into hard helmets, not for touching. Popular were signet rings and claddaghs, worn on all fingers like knuckle dusters, and gold chains hung outside the jumper. The rules governing the uniform were strict, though girls were given the choice between a skirt or trousers, and most chose the latter. When the rule against high heels was broken, the offending shoe would be a clunky platform, full to the ankle, with a heavy buckle on front.

Boys were given no such leeway. The regulations governing their masculine appearance were rigorously enforced. This was done in the name of tidiness, neatness, in preparation for what was called *working life*, though the larger purpose, it seemed to me, was to limit our expression, to eliminate ambiguity from our gestures, to stop short any outward shift on our part in the wrong direction. (Androgyny? Forget about it. Trans? We were living in the stone age.) Boys' hair was kept short and hardened with gel. Those who grew their locks moussed them back, smoothed them close to the scalp, and tied them into little ponytails, mafioso style. Any boy who dared to grow his hair, shampoo it, condition it, and wear it loose in the wind: this boy was a pervert, and was told to tie up his shame, hide it, have a barber to it. No boys wore make-up or nail varnish; if they had, they would have been beaten up, and, failing that, would have been ridiculed by the teachers and sent home. What incited this feminine panic more than anything else, however, what turned the meter of masculine hysteria up to ninety, was the sight in the male ear of the humble earring. As it happened, the pupils were largely immune to this hysteria because, according to the complicated rules of the street, it was in fact a feat of hardness for a man to pull off a hoop without metamorphosing into a pussy. The adults, though, were uncommonly susceptible. Above all, Ms V.

That Ms V was heavily invested in her own femininity—statement jewellery, garish skirts, loud stockings, and something shocking, always shocking, on the lips—did not mean she *liked* femininity wherever it manifested itself. The opposite, she could not tolerate its eruption in boys (for, without polarity, right? without the separation of electrical charge, how would molecules form, on what would the universe be built?). On entering the classroom, after her little act of disrobing, first this colour, then that colour, then—look!—another colour, she would sit behind her desk and stare in silence at each bejewelled boy, and would continue to stare in silence until, red-faced, he would remove the offending article. She would not start the lesson, that is *she could not possibly have taught us about ionic and covalent bonds*, until all the boys, and only the boys, had taken off their adornments.

In a not unrelated matter, Ms V also despised intelligence in girls. She felt radically threatened by O, whom she could see was bored and unstimulated and way ahead of the rest of the class—and of her. O was destined for an A1, and Ms V knew it, and it made her crazy. One day, when Ms V got into a fluster because she was failing to explain a basic concept, O said to her, quite simply, quite plainly, without any pretension or derision in her voice: 'You have to reverse the polarity.' And this— simply, plainly—was the end for her. 'We appreciate intelligence,' Ms V replied furiously, 'but there is no need for cockiness,' and from that day forth, she made it her daily task to avenge herself on O, by isolating her from the rest of the class, by making her sit alone at a separate desk, by taking every opportunity to make petty comments about her, by directing snide remarks directly to her, until O simply stopped attending. Daily sick notes written by her mother.

Would my mother have written such notes for me, if I had asked her?

In the school, there did not exist a specific locale, a central hub similar to the petrol station, in which homophobic feelings could be marshalled and from which they could be dispatched. Rather, these feelings, the power to express them, was funnelled through anyone who happened to witness male femininity—which, in the absence of any openly homosexual men, stood in for homosexuality—and felt ready to identify it. The abuse, in other words, came from everywhere and anywhere. In any room, in any corridor, in any building, at any time. On occasion, from teachers. (My English teacher, for instance, scratching his long, tobacco-stained fingernails across the entire width of my desk, and, apropos of nothing, saying, 'Every day is a *gay* day, Gavin.') But most often from other pupils. From top streamers and middle streamers and bottom steamers; from all the forms, first to sixth. Hundreds of points in space. Hundreds of faces. Of which I do not remember a single one. What I have retained, rather, are the voices, which flew at me, now from here, now from there, here there here there here there, many frequencies, equal intensities, so that by the end of any given day, they came to fill, like static on a detuned analogue television, the entire panel of my consciousness: a blank of quivering cells.

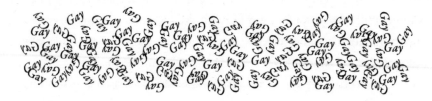

Each of these utterances was, by itself, a tiny local event with its own history, its own trajectory, its own connotations for the speaker, the target, and the witnesses, its own special place in our outlook on life in that sliver of time. But, added together, over the course of a month, a year, five years, these little remarks amounted to a force much greater than the sum of its parts. Extending upwards and outwards in all directions—from school, to church, to playing field, to office, to pub, to home, and back to school—they attached to and harmonised with ever more general forms of social domination, until they were indistinguishable, in my mind, from (1) laws that criminalised homosexual sex (still in place while I was at secondary school); (2) institutionalised discrimination against gay people as customers, employees, and employers; (3) religious stigmatisation of the expression of gay voices and choices; (4) cultural censorship of gay opinion, art, and literature; and (5) *mothers who failed to protect their gay children*. These utterances—these throwaway comments—functioned as extrajudicial sanctions enforced at a granular level on behalf of, or in concert with, the more respectably institutionalised prohibitions against gay beings. In reality, the people in high positions in church and state who claimed to wield power for the purposes of clamping down on homosexuality remained distant from the actual workings of power itself; the boys in my school, and countless others just like them, did the necessary labour, without consciously knowing or asking why.

The impact on me of this amalgamated force—high and low, global and local, authorised and unauthorised, institutional and familial and individual—was drastic. It penetrated my body in depth. Absorbed into my skin and muscle. Flowed through my veins to the furthest extremities. Working ostensibly for the good of my health, to man me up, it produced in me new gestures and actions and habits, and ultimately reconstituted my very material, gave me a new kind of physicality altogether. While as a younger child I had walked with my head down as a means of erasing the phenomenal world and entering a pensive state, now, as an adolescent, I was hunched in pre-emptive defence against attack: my shoulders lifted high and pulled forwards, my shoulder blades protruding out of my back like fins, my entire skeleton crowding in around my breastplate to protect my heart; all the time trying to fold myself into invisibility. My hands in my pockets were clenched, as was my jaw. My facial features were scrunched and, although I often laughed—O's jokes were my lifeline—I rarely smiled.

And it was not only my body that changed. The united force of homophobic repression, on passing into my body, came through my mind and always ended up back there, the inevitable terminus, where it yielded new ways of thinking and speaking. My conception of myself, as a man, as sane, as a human was now moulded by, against, in relation to this repression. Even as I mentally argued against it, or ignored it, or tried to drown it out, I could not escape responding, resisting, obeying, enduring, hopelessly forbidding it. What I was caught in was a sphere of mind control in which I was being taught to conform to non-homosexual, that is masculine, categories of thought and behaviour. The aura of happiness that had surrounded me in primary school, the shine that came off my talents and my accomplishments, disappeared. I stopped caring about winning, or achieving, or being liked, or being good, or even having manners. I now hated the part of myself that had once yearned for these things, and I worked to strip it out. In the void left behind, I fabricated a surrogate out of the basest of fantasies. Revenge. Violence. Sex. Money. Fame. Whatever it took *to show them*.

These were the walls of my new transparent cell. Inside, sealed off, without oxygen, I stopped growing. Concerned only with protecting myself, I became a danger to myself. I was on pause and had no guarantee that there was such a thing in life as being *unpaused*. Unreachable, unfeeling, yet also trying to make myself felt, I made the shapes which I thought proved the existence of an imposing personality, but in actual fact I was merely exposing myself as a mimic, a braggart, a poseur, a humbug. A fake.

In my daydreams, which I would nourish and prolong when I should have been studying, I rode on a motorcycle and lived the rebel's life. In reality, I was unattractive, unmotivated, depressed, resigned, subjected, broken-down, docile—and totally celibate. I started to act up. To answer teachers back. To disrupt lessons. To get thrown out of classrooms. In my final year, with nothing left to lose, I produced a leaflet entitled *Underground News* and left stacks of them all around the school. On one side of this leaflet, underneath the clenched fist of socialist revolution, there was a notice urging all pupils to stage a walk-out in protest against the ban on boys wearing earrings. On the other side was a satirical sketch, written in the voice of a gay fashion designer, excoriating the dress sense of some of the teachers. I can still remember a line from it:

Let us pray that God may grant Sr L a new blouse.

The teachers were understandably furious. A couple of them threatened to take legal action. Against whom though? I had hardly signed the thing. When they accused me of being the culprit, I denied it with a smile. Where was their proof? I dared them to say: *Only a pupil from the top stream could have written this*. Or: *A gay fashion designer? This could only have been you.*

Mr T let me know that he knew I was the guilty party—that *everyone* knew—by taking me by the collar one day and, just as I had seen him do to P, pushing me against the corridor wall. In his tirade, he did not accuse me of making the leaflet, for he did not want to give me the satisfaction of denying it once again. Instead, he took the time to tell me, in vivid detail, what he thought of me, and what he believed my prospects were. He did not say the word *gay*, but it was there on his lips, in the gobs of spit in the corners of his mouth. After a while of this—in a bit of gorgeous synchronicity, of the sort that can happen only a handful of times in a life—P appeared in the corridor. I clocked him out of the corner of my eye, and was glad, no, more than that, I was excited, to see him. Taking his time, P swaggered down, then sauntered by. When I glanced at him, he received my look and smiled.

(As Joyce says: *If we were all suddenly somebody else.*)

I smiled back. And he winked. And so it was that P and I became, if only for an instant, comrades. And I knew, then, that my *Underground News* had been a success. Totally worth it.

A few days later, I entered the toilet nearest my homeroom with the intention of smoking a cigarette, and found P there with four other, much younger, pupils. They were standing in a semicircle by the sinks, passing around a single fag. I hesitated. My instinct was to leave immediately, but I resisted. Suddenly conscious of my body, not knowing what else to do with it—I knew better than to produce my own packet, as it was liable to be taken from me—I took a step forward, then another. P acknowledged me by tilting back his head once. I raised my eyebrows in return. Then he did one of the most generous things anyone has ever done for me. He said to the boy who was currently sucking from the fag, 'When you're finished on that, give it to him.' P chucked his chin in my direction, and the smoking boy turned to blink at me. I nodded. And the boy nodded back. Then he gave the fag to me. And I took a drag, making sure to withdraw a good load of smoke and to inhale it well, and then handed it on. And, as I did so, I thought, *So this is what it's like.* And I cannot say that it did not feel good.

Meanwhile, my grades plummeted. I took to saying nasty, stupid things to my classmates, and became unliked even amongst the more sympathetic of them. As an exercise in masochism, I put myself forward, at the height of my unpopularity, for class representative and got a total of one vote (from O). Incorrigible, I continued, afterwards, to lie and speak badly of people and say outrageous things just to get laughs. Without even noticing—for it felt like just more of the same air, in and out, give and take—I myself had turned into a bully.

M's crime was that of being absolutely himself: sensitive, a bit nerdy, handsome in a left-field sort of way. Whenever I witnessed the other boys in the class giving him a hard time, I felt sorry for him. But then, when-ever he deigned to annoy me, even faintly, I lashed out at him. Poked fun at him. Made remarks about his tall forehead and his other unusual but actually rather interesting features. *On the grand scale of Normal*, was the message I was passing on to him, *I need you to be further down a notch.* And like this, I completed my meshing with the system. No longer could I claim to be merely an inert or consenting target of power; I had attached myself to the very forces that were suppressing me, and had come to rely on them, and was now a carrier for them. Not the opponent of power, I was one of its effects. A vehicle of power's articulation.

Thus, I had reached my nadir. My basest state.

Never had I known such misery.

Fear is pain, writes Louise Bourgeois. Often it is not perceived as pain, because it is always disguising itself.

At school I was afraid, of course I was. Yet I was not able, at that point in my life, to identify my pain as such. In my comprehension, I was not even in pain: I was just indignant. Privacy, what people like me have always been equated with and defined by—*either, 'We need to know what you do in private because we want to make laws about it,' or, 'We don't care what you do in private, as long as you keep it there and don't put it in our faces'*—was the very thing I was now being denied. I, a private citizen, was not being allowed to walk in a public place with my privacy intact. My right to a personal life was being taken from me *in order that* I should never, of my own accord, publicise matters which (by public order) ought to be kept to myself. I was being called *out* as a means of pushing me back *in*.

We see what you are. We know about you, and we care deeply about what we know. For your own sake, you ought to learn to hide it better.

What exactly I was doing that was causing my sexuality to be revealed to others in this way, I could not say. Far from undertaking a declarative act, I was, I believed, simply walking, talking, being. If, in doing so, I was broadcasting intimate information about myself, it was an unconscious transmission. I was baffled, and not a little unnerved, that the invisible contents of my mind could apparently, without my noticing, leak out onto the surface of my body, insinuate themselves into my gestures, where they could be perceived by others and, moreover, provoke in them extreme hostility. How, simply by reading my body, could my abusers gain access to my thoughts? What, just by looking, could they understand about my internal experience? What did they know *that I did not*?

While it was true that, from a young age, I had been having romantic thoughts about male companionship and, more recently, since puberty, sexual fantasies centred on the male body, at that point—as I walked through the school corridors—these thoughts and fantasies were still unstructured, unarticulated. I had not yet integrated them into a larger sense of self. As yet, I was in a state of ignorance about the meaning of these mental products, about what influence they might exert over my actions, or how they might determine the configurations of my actual relationships with other people; which is to say, I was still a stranger to my own sexuality, and to sexuality in general. I was smart enough to understand *that* I was having same-sex desires—an understanding that never, ever, ever caused me a moment's torment—but I was innocent about *what* these desires signified for me as a person in the world. The most I could say about these desires was that they did not seem to be fully mine; by some mysterious process of expropriation, they were constantly being taken away from me and put on public display; they were an open secret.

There was, it seemed, no way for others to look at me without finding such desires everywhere, all over me.

Today I can marvel at the eloquence of my body language, its ability to express what I did not yet have words for, but back then it was all very confusing to me. It would take me many more years to see—and I regret not having seen this sooner, for it would have saved me a lot of agony—that the type of desire that my abusers imagined to be *on* my body, bore no relation to the desire that occurred *in* my body. The only common factor was the object-choice: men. In every other aspect, the two desires existed in entirely different planes of consciousness. Whatever phantasmagoria my abusers conjured up about male-male desire—judging from their reactions to it, it must have been terrifying—could not possibly have encapsulated the variety of genital acts, and the diversity of sexual roles and scenarios, and the richness of mental and emotional involvement, and the contexts resonant with meaning, and the connectedness, and the stories (God, just so many stories spontaneously shared!) that arose naturally in my desires. If, by some divine intercession, they had been given a glimpse of this, they would not have been able to undermine it without also undermining their own corresponding—I would hazard, identical—notions of ideal friendship and romantic love.

Needless to say, there was no intercession. No one to spit on their eyes and put hands on them. So, in their blindness, all they could see was: *gay*.

Now and then, they opted for a synonym or two, as an excitement. In the main, though, this word—*gay*—was their preferred choice. They liked *gay* best. And, clearly, they wanted the best for me.

So what did *gay* mean for them? Why was it such an important term in their shared vocabulary?

The setting, remember, was a distant suburb in one of Europe's smallest capitals. The backwater of a backwater. The intense hatred my abusers were articulating did not come from contact with living, breathing homosexuals. For them, *gay* had little to do with perceiving and experiencing their own or others' actual feelings and activities. They were—this is my strong impression today—incapable of conceiving of *gay* as a fact. A sexuality in its own right. *Gay*, rather, was a collection of rarefied, the-ologised visions that they had gleaned from the tatty imaginaria of pop culture and religion. *Gay* in their mouths was an accusation, a curse, a damnation directed at this kaleidoscope of images, or, more accurately, at the people, like me, onto whom they projected those images. By calling me *gay*, their enterprise—if indeed their actions deserved such a title, given that they conveyed no ideas, no scheme, no constructive impulse, no originality—was simply what Eve Kosofsky Sedgwick calls *detecting and excoriating male effeminacy*. Rather than a means of identifying a member of a distinct sexuality, it was a means of passing judgement on a breakdown, a malfunction in the One True Sexuality, in which, by force of nature, men were essentially masculine and women were essentially feminine. Their difficulty with me was not that I might be having sexual relations with other boys (they were as aware as I was that there was little chance of that in these parts, and that on the special occasions it happened, it usually involved a circle of heterosexual boys, showing off to each other). Rather, I was failing to live up to certain unwritten, unde-finable, but all the same indispensable standards of how a boy ought to appear, dress, move, and talk. Basically, I was not being accused of being a homosexual (a permanent state of affairs, extremely rare, semi-mythical) but of acting like a girl (a temporary performance, therefore alterable, not hopeless). Implied by girlishness was *gay*, and implied by *gay* was the possibility of redemption. *Gay* was nothing that a bit of tough love could not put right. After the proper punishment, fairly meted out, *gay* would go away.

The excitement that my abusers felt at the sight of me, the fits of hysteria that my presence brought on in them, their urge to gain pleasure from inflicting harm on me were clearly residues of infantile behaviour. As well as childishness, however, theirs was also a display of recently manifested manhood. The stimulation and glamourisation of the energies of adult-like masculinity. Which at base was a burgeoning form of male-male desire.

Not direct sexual desire, man for man.

Nothing as straightforward as that.

Rather an unconscious or semi-conscious inclination to emulate, verbally and nonverbally, other desirable men, so as to be desirable in turn, not only to women, but also to other men (for a woman, the belief seemed to be, could only know that a man was manly, and therefore desirable, when she could see that he was desired as a model of manhood, by other men).

My abusers' desire for each other—that is, the permission they shared out amongst themselves to desire each other's manliness, in the form of masculinity—was the preservative of their bond. It was their masculinity that permitted them to be in close proximity with one other, touch each other, perhaps even be naked together, regardless of whether they did these things in actuality. Femininity was a toxin to which no one was immune—*everyone had mothers, did they not?*—which was why my abusers needed always to be on guard, and to shame out of existence any signs of intoxication shown by anyone in their vicinity. By making me the representative of the feminine in men, and by publicly measuring themselves against me, they could make their own level of femininity seem negligible. Indeed, if I appeared often enough, and regularly enough, and if I was feminine enough on each appearance, they would be able to give the impression (to whoever happened to be interested, which was only themselves) of being immune to femininity altogether, of having expunged the feminine from themselves entirely, of having banished femininity on a permanent basis from their souls.

By declaring *gay* to be a specific sort of outward feminine deportment (as opposed to an intricate arrangement, or disorderly assortment, of impulses, desires, and acts) and by making *gay* sound so disgusting, so deviant that no one in their right mind ever would want to appear that way (just by the way they pronounced the word, they achieved this), they tried to make *gay* hurt. And in this they succeeded. In my innocence, heedless, I allowed myself to be drawn in to their project of hurt.

This hurt, I stress, was not caused by my desires, which have never been anything other than a source of pleasure and comfort for me. It was caused, rather, by my exposure to, in Sedgwick's words, *a high ambient hatred* for something called *gay*, which I then mistook for my own experience. The term *gay*, in itself, I had no objection to, as long as it touched upon, even lightly, the complex, multifarious, ever-changing nature of my desires, as they occurred in me, unwilled. The problem was that, in the service of my abusers, *gay* bore no meaningful relation to any of that. Obviously I was not *gay*, as my abusers imagined *gay* to be, for the gay that I was, my gay, provoked none of the panic and the dread that their *gay* provoked in them.

This distinction is clear to me now, looking back, but was difficult to make out at the time. This was because the word *gay* belonged to people who, in a sick way, adored it. People who loved to feel the shape of it in their mouths, to hear the sound of it in their ears. People who were phenomenally eager—I would say, gagging—to put it to use.

Gay you *gay* you *gay* you *gay* you *gay* you *gay* you...

As I waded, over and again, through this sonic ocean, *my* gay was by degrees reduced to a mere blip, a narrow beam from a distant galaxy. Caught in the deep, and drowning, I found it difficult, eventually impossible, to hear my gay for what it actually was—gentle and quiet and harmless and exciting and fabulous and beautiful and really nothing to be surprised by—and to prevent its transmutation into the *gay* that was pressing in from all sides: vociferous, ugly, shocking, shameful.

What this amounted to was the seizure of my right to define my own feelings by those who claimed, not only to have no personal experience of such feelings, but to have an active aversion to them. I was being condemned to a lifetime of explaining my feelings in the negative, in opposition to opinions and hearsay. ('That is *not* what I like. That is *not* how I feel.') I was being punished for things I did not do, on the one hand, and being asked to defend things that did not need defending, on the other. I was, in short, being forced to fight for permission to have my own interior life (to inhabit myself, to experience myself for what I was, to develop the independent voice that I warranted, to turn my energies to my own account). And this, ultimately, was my pain.

———

Most days after school, I arrived home with a headache. My mother would ask me how my day had been, and I would say, 'Fine.' I would open the fridge and look into it: other than a few yoghurt pots, a litre of milk, a packet of rashers, and a couple of blocks of cheese, it would be empty. My mother hated an overstocked fridge, the sight of old mustard pots and half-squeezed tubes of tomato paste. Everything had to be used quickly, washed out, thrown out. 'Fucking nothing to eat,' I would say as I slammed the fridge door shut. Then I would bang upstairs to my room. Flop onto the bed. Look at the bare walls. And fume.

Or, because, on several occasions during my adolescence, I had to vacate my room, give it to someone else, and sleep instead on a spare bed in my parents' room, I would pace around the small area of free carpet there, and fume.

I despised my school. To me, it represented debasement. Humanity's rot. The decay of civilisation. The sight of it, the mere thought of it was enough to bring on despair. When I daydreamed of getting out of this suburb, out of Ireland altogether, my most burning wish was to put space between me and my school; such was its size in my mind, its weight on my moods, that I believed I would never be happy until there was at least one sea, preferably more, separating us.

And when I was not fuming, when my internal weathervane swung in the other direction, I was consumed with shame.

Shame for how I acted at school.

Shame for how my body looked, how my voice sounded.

Shame for ever having wanted to be visible to others.

Shame for having a house like this, a family like this.

Shame for not loving my mother any more, for being able to see, now, what she was doing wrong, what she had always done wrong, and having to blame her for it.

Once, she came into my room (no knock) while I was lying face down on the bed. On the chair that doubled as my bedside table was a packet of cigarettes that I had bought with money I had stolen from her purse and that I usually kept hidden in a drawer. She hovered at my side, long enough to take in the cigarettes, and said, 'Why aren't you studying?'

'I've told you already,' I said, not lifting my head from the pillow, 'I don't care if I fail. I will repeat my exams somewhere else. All I want is to get out of that school.'

'A grind school? Is that what you're saying?' she said, already leaving, for this was a conversation she was not going to stay around for. 'How will we pay for that?'

Another time, when we were eating alone in the kitchen, I said, 'I'm not going back to that school. I'll finish this year, but I'm not going back next year.'

And she said, 'Don't be ridiculous. Where do you want to go? To a private school, like your friends?'

Then, soon after that, this secret little back-and-forth of ours went public. At Easter, with the entire family seated around the table, she said, out of nowhere, 'Gavin wants to move school.'

Faces turned to me, incredulous, condemnatory, as if I had just been outed as sex criminal or something.

All my siblings had gone to the same school. My brothers had not had an especially edifying experience there, they had fought against the system, but in the end they had got on with it, or had left early. They had no patience for this talk of changing. *What*, their faces now told me, *was Gavin's problem now?*

'Get over it, Gavin,' my eldest brother, R, said, though I was not sure what exactly he was telling me to get over. Did he want me to get over the fact that he had never shown the remotest interest in me, nor furnished me with a single piece of fraternal guidance or advice?

My sister, visibly conflicted, did not say anything. She was the only one who had got on well at the school. Obedient. Good grades. Student of the year. Our time there had crossed over for two years, we sometimes passed each other in the corridors, so it is hard for me to believe that she did not witness something, hear something. In any case, she did not step in, either.

My mother, I remember, was moving around behind the chairs, spooning roast potatoes out of a tin onto the plates.

'He wants to go to a private school,' she said.

At which moment I understood what I had long suspected: that she had turned away from me inwardly. That I was no longer *her prince*. The words *I want to go to private school* had not, in her company, nor in anyone's company, ever passed my lips. That she would distort my confidences to her in this way meant that she did not care about me as she once did. Where and when it mattered, she did not care about me at all. More, it seemed as if she felt the need to harm me, to make herself hated by me. And, in this, she succeeded.

You are my vessel, you are my cell. You have my hatred. This, now, is my identity.

My sister-in-law, a teacher in a working-class school in Tallaght, took pleasure in twisting the knife:

'Why, Gavin, what are the people in your school *like*?'

I ate that day, and I drank. I stayed at the table for pudding and coffee. I listened to the conversations, receptive to every layer of subtext, the entire tonal range. I was surrounded by my flesh and blood, I was being nourished in my body, yet my rage was my only satisfaction; expanding and retracting, advancing and retiring, pulling the world in, then pushing it back out, lending everything its colour, its taste. Immersed in it, I would willingly have watched my mother and my family, all of them, choke and die.

Yet I did not say a word.

In my Big Dream I appear in two places, in the centre and on the peripheries of the room, and in three guises: I am a young boy in a red dress being held by his mother; I am an older version of myself, looking at my younger self and my mother; and I am also my father, looking at us. As the outside perceiver, I feel embarrassed about the young boy's appearance and behaviour. This embarrassment is nothing less than the shame that I myself feel about my femininity and my sexuality, which I then disguise as my father's feelings about me.

Is this not how my shame functions, from day to day? As a mental trick in which I apparently gain an objective stance in relation to myself, and, from there, judge myself according to beliefs I attribute to others but which are in fact my own?

In the dream, my mind is using the figure of the father, in the first place, to give my shame the authority it needs for me to believe it, and, after that, to hide the shame from myself, to make it look like it belongs to others, and therefore keep it out of my reach, beyond help, beyond resolution.

My father hates the red dress that I am wearing. It makes him shudder. 'Why is my son making such a show of himself? He looks like a freak.'

The anger I feel at being shamed in this way—anger which I cannot direct at my father because of my deep-seated belief that he, as a masculine man, has a natural right to be ashamed by me—I direct at my mother. And these are the questions which accompany it: *Why is she pretending not to see the red dress? Why is she acting like I am dressed ordinarily, when clearly I am not? Why isn't she recognising me for who I am, and standing up for that? Why isn't she defending me against my father's shaming?*

These questions take on a special significance when I bear in mind that in the dream my mother, too, can only be me in disguise. (Me, disguised as my mother, disguised as my literary agent.) My intention in taking on this double costume is to ensure that I do not see myself, and thereby maintain the illusion that my mother is the person I am truly angry with. *If I get sufficiently angry with her, a sufficient number of times, I will be relieved of my anger, for then it will belong to her.* Yet, in this, I am setting myself up for disappointment. For all the costumes succeed in doing is call attention to their own artificiality, to the places where the seams do not join and the masks slip down. And once I have become aware of these faults, I can no longer accept that the external aspect of what I am looking at matches what I really mean to see; from then on, I cannot stop seeing myself: *Why aren't I defending myself against other people's shaming? Why do I insist on shaming myself in their name, long after they have stopped shaming me?*

The anger I feel towards this part of myself that I call my mother, together with the preceding shame which I attribute to my father (but which I cannot bring myself to blame him *for*), make up the pain that I associate with the third and final point on my map: home. And it is this pain, emphatically *this*, which I feel most acutely today, and which I find hardest to talk away. (Because *it* is so often doing the talking.)

The regime in my house functioned like this: when I failed to help my mother in some way, say, by overlooking some dishes on the draining board that needed to be dried and put away, she would get upset and rouse my father out of his silence: 'You need to help your mother.'

To which I would say, 'She can ask me to do anything, and I will do it.'

In response to which would come the statement, the mantra: '*She shouldn't have to ask.*'

As far as I could see, *asking* was, for my mother, the same as voicing a need, which was an affront to the teachings of her upbringing. So, because she *should* not ask, then she should not *have to* ask, and she therefore did *not* ask, choosing instead to get angry when her unspoken demands were not met.

'Don't worry. I'll do it myself.'

Mine was the sort of family that sneered at the sort of family that used a roster, but honestly I would have preferred that—a big board on the fridge door, in place of *L'Origine du monde*, on which our tasks for each day would be highlighted in different colours—than being expected to know, telepathically, what my mother wanted from me at a particular juncture, and then having to swallow her bitterness, when, out of laziness or neglect, I failed.

Yet, equally, I expected my mother to know, without my having to say anything, what was going on inside me, what was happening to me.

Why doesn't she notice how unhappy I am?

Well, you've never actually said anything, have you? You've told her you want to move school, but you've never told her why.

I shouldn't have to!

This refusal on my part to speak to my mother about my pain was, undeniably, the mendacity of homophobic denial. I did not want to have to tell her about the part of me that people seemed to hate so much. In general, I felt fundamentally uncertain about who was in control of information about my sexual identity, and I feared people's reactions to, and uses of, that information. I saw that what felt light and free in me—almost nothing—became, in the minds of others, substantial, heavy: something. I could not trust that it would not be the same for her, and that, like all the others, she would not want to get rid of that weight, by throwing it back on me. It was easier to believe that mine was an unkeepable secret. A secret I did not have to tell because it had already been told, by others, thousands of times. Safer to bed down in the lie of *I know you know*.

Or rather, the imperative: you *must* know.

Yet it was also the case—my silence spoke for itself—that I did not want her to know. By not speaking out, I made sure that she could not know, not definitively. *You must not know.* I wanted my mother to be ignorant of what was happening to me on the streets and in school. Which was the same as wanting her to be ignorant of my sexuality (for what was happening on the street and at school was, at the point, the sum of my sexuality). Ideally, she would act as though she knew, while I would make sure she could not possibly know for sure. In this way, she would be, at one and the same time, omnipotent and in the dark. Holding sway over everything, including my happiness, but understanding nothing.

(What I wanted, that is, was a mother like that played by Sophia Loren in *Una giornata particolare*. The mother who knows that her husband is a fascist but does not really know what fascism means. Who knows her son possesses a pornographic magazine, but does not know enough about pornography to be able to discipline him for it. Who is exhausted by the demands of her role as a housewife but does not know any other. Who is always beautiful without ever quite knowing it. Who, without knowing, foils her neighbour Marcello Mastroianni's plan to kill himself. Who kisses Mastroianni without knowing that he is a homosexual and an anti-fascist. Who, when told of this by Mastroianni himself, slaps him and pretends not to know what he means. Who, even as Mastroianni chases her down the stairs screaming, *'I'm a faggot! A faggot! And you are an ignorant woman!'* does not know what to do, except to continue to long for him. Who, in taking Mastroianni's hand

and putting it on her breast, and in kissing him on the eyelids like a little boy, does not know that he has become her son, and she the all-powerful, unknowing mother. Who, in the end, reveals to Mastroianni everything she knows of her husband's affairs and of her ignorance that facilitates them: *'An ignorant woman can't do anything because she'll never be respected.'* But who, even with this final knowledge, will do nothing to change her circumstances, and will instead content herself with being a changed woman within them.)

At the same time as I was nourishing my mother's ignorance through silence, as if wanting to stretch that ignorance to breaking point, I started to dress gayly. I dyed my hair and wore eyeliner. I bought cheap T-shirts in second-hand shops and cut them into belly tops. I wore silver-coloured runners and flared trousers and sparkly shirts open to the navel. And, building up my courage in increments, I eventually took the leap and got myself a faux fur coat. I would hide these clothes in my school bag and, after the last bell, catch the bus into town, changing out of my uniform in the back seat on the top deck. Like a creature emerging from its chrysalis, I would get off at Hawkins Street and, finding my gait, with a little more swing of the hip than I would normally risk, would open myself up to the wonder and pleasure of the passers-by.

This was my spectacle of the closet. The private cell exploded outwards. Shame masquerading as brazenness.

Through College Green I would strut, then down Dame Street, around Temple Bar, up George's Street, through the covered market a few times, before finding somewhere conspicuous to stand (in silence) and smoke a cigarette (in silence) and soak up the laughs and the whistles and the comments (in silence).

Even in my outrageousness, I was silent. My silence itself was, in its ever-growing proportions and ever-diminishing meaningfulness, outrageous. As was the silence of my mother. Who, when at the weekend she saw me dressed up and on my way out the door, would say nothing more than, 'Don't drink too much,' or, 'Remember this is your Leaving Cert year,' and I think she saw in my attire a criticism of her as a parent, and was glad, actually, to see that I was going away from her in this way, liberating myself from her authority. Perhaps she understood that, if I had taken measures any less drastic, I would have failed to get away at all.

It took my father, the taciturn one, to put an end to the quiet. At around three o'clock on a Sunday morning, midway through my final year in school, I came in the back door (no lock, no key) to find him sitting at the kitchen table. I had spent the night dancing at a gay club in town, and was conscious that I smelled of smoke, which I wanted to conceal from him, so I tried to keep my distance as I made my way to the other door. I got as far as the fridge, about halfway, before he spoke, and it was only then that I remembered what I was wearing: a green belly top with a print of Andy Warhol's *Banana*, a ring in my belly-button, a pair of brown cord flares, my favourite silver shoes, and a pair of pink Jackie O's perched on top of my spikey, bleached-out hair.

'You look—'

And it was only when I registered what he said that I realised that the era of speechlessness was now over, and that a new time was beginning, one in which I would no longer simply suffer power but would exercise it, at the top of my lungs.

'—like a freak.'

Later that morning, my throat raw from shouting, I packed my bags and went to stay in a friend's house around the corner. I was determined not to return home, which had lost, once and for all, its meaning for me as a home. *A mother who had sent me to play with the wolves? A father who, under the sheep's clothing, turned out to be a wolf himself?* I was not safe there, with them, and I was a fool ever to have believed I might be.

A couple of days later, my mother phoned asking me to come back and talk. At this meeting, which took place in the kitchen, overlooked by Judith and Holofernes, not a lot of talking took place.

'I'm not saying anything until *he* apologises,' I said, gesturing at my father.

'I didn't do anything,' said my father.

'You called me a freak,' I said.

'No, I didn't,' he said.

And, in that instant, any residual respect I had for him burned away. He sank lower in my estimation than even my abusers at school, who, as cowardly as they were, would not have denied what they had against me, and what they had done as a consequence.

'Are you gay?' my mother asked then, abruptly.

Surprised, my face still flushed with anger for my father, I turned to her. Her expression was hard because this was hard for her. She wanted me to come out, to pull the plaster off the wound, to get it over with. But I was only going to do so for a good mother, and I had lost my conviction that I was under the influence of one.

'You're not ready for the answer,' I said.

By which I meant: *you're not worthy of it.*

INTERLUDE: ROME, 2004

For four years in my late twenties I was in Rome, sharing a flat with two other single gay men in San Giovanni, an area of the city I particularly liked because it was off the tourist trail but central enough not to require a car or a scooter: if I gave myself enough time, I could walk to most places I needed to go, while taking the opportunity, as I went, to observe the city at a speed conducive to the appreciation of its different historical strata; so, for instance, to get from my flat to the main train station, instead of taking the busy thoroughfare to the Basilica of San Giovanni (324 AD) and then climbing the hill with all the traffic towards Piazza Vittorio (1880), I often went the back way, along an ancient defensive wall (270 AD), down a bit of the Appian Way (312 BC), through Porta San Sebastiano (275 AD), past the crumbling Terme di Caracalla (212 AD), up the slope to Villa Celimontana (1580), before descending and joining the crowds again at the Colosseum (72 AD), and from there making my way through the streets of Monti to Termini (1947); and, along the way, with each glimpse of the exposed understructures of human civilisation, with each encounter with the historical magnitude contained in each moment, my own past grew a little smaller, moved a little further away, became a little more remote, as was essential for my growing sense of confidence as a self-contained man in the world: alas, achieving this distance from my past did nothing to diminish the anger I felt *about* my past—an anger that more often than not centred on my mother's failure to protect me from this anger-filled future—nor did it eliminate any of the loneliness I felt in Rome, the gap I perceived between myself and other men, for, although while walking I fantasised about a chance meeting with a man—olive skin, important nose, greying hair, a walker like myself, who would accompany me on my wanderings, speaking only when absolutely necessary, and next to whom I would lie on cold white sheets in the middle of the day, and whose embrace would obviate any need for friends or family or a world outside—at the same time, I was conscious of the unlikelihood of such a fantasy becoming a reality, for, as much as I pined for men, I also avoided them, choosing streets I knew would be devoid of them, and times when most of them would be busy earning a living; and it was this masochistic hiding-and-pining, more than any monument, that my mother observed when she came to visit me and we took this route together: simply from the way I was walking and pointing things out—stone carved by men to look like men—she could see I was lonely and angry (that my loneliness and my anger were giving birth to one other), and she was terribly kind about it and did not mention the apparent absence of friends in my life, or the clear incompatibility between my banker flatmates and me, or the fact that I did not talk about boyfriends: the closest she came to remarking on the subject was after our walk, on the bus to the Vatican Museums—the number 64, *l'autobus dei ladri*—where a middle-aged priest in full collar, not unhandsome, flirted openly with me, saying suggestive things to me in Italian knowing my mother would not understand, but she, smarter than any priest, easily figured out his game: 'I think he liked you,' she said when we get off, to which I said, 'I think he was desperate,' and in that moment I felt deeply proud of her—this woman, my mother, raised by fundamentalists at the height of a theocratic regime—and in the queue for the Museums I joked with her some more, about Pope Ratzinger and his red Prada shoes and the things I imagined his beautiful personal secretary, Georg Gänswein, was expected to do to them, and when my mother laughed I felt a lot of warmth coming from her, which I soaked up like a dry sponge; but as soon as we gained entry to the Museums, in the courtyard outside the main door, she turned serious again and said, 'Now what'll we do if we get separated?' and I said, 'It's simple, Mum, we won't get separated,' and as I turned to inspect a sculpture in a nearby alcove, I thought to myself, 'So typical. Why is *separation* even on her mind?' then when I turned back, she was gone, *vanished*, and immediately a panic gripped me, an uncanny feeling that my mother's anxiety about getting separated had actually been a premonition, that these were the first instants of a bad event, one which I had brought about by not heeding the warnings, so I searched the courtyard, going round and round the central fountain, pushing through the bodies and calling out, 'Mum! Mum!' and once I was certain she was no longer there, I went inside and ran along the banks of the human river flowing down the long corridors in a futile attempt to identify her head amongst the other hundreds—*remembering this now, I am also reminded of a holiday in Kerry as a child, chasing a fishing net that was being carried away by the stream's current, and in fact my feelings on the two occasions were identical: helplessness, loss of control, an ache in my groin that was both a need to piss and a desire to punch myself there*—the difference in Rome being, I was an adult and therefore supposed to be able to fix problems without breaking down, so I waded into the flood of people and let myself be taken along as it penetrated deeper into the Museums, and after a time we reached Raphael's Rooms and still my mother was nowhere to be seen, and I was beginning to feel hysterical, so I approached one of the museum guards, whose job it was to prevent the torrent of pink flesh from engulfing the precious marble, and I hurriedly told him my predicament, and he asked me to describe my mother and then relayed my description into his walkie-talkie so that the guards further down the line could look out for her, and I experienced his patience and his sympathy as a gripping ache in my chest, and I managed to say, 'You are a gentleman, thank you', to which he showed his bad teeth and put a hand on my shoulder and told me, 'Calm down, son, this happens all the time, chances are your mother will be waiting for you in the Sistine Chapel or outside on St Peter's Square, or, failing that, she will already be at home writing her postcards', and I said, 'I hope you're right', though I did not see how he could be, for my mother did not have my address written down, nor did she carry a mobile phone, nor did she have a spare key— we were simply not *organised* in that way—and, sure enough, she was neither in the Chapel nor on the Square, and the only thing left for me to do was get the bus home and hope that a miracle had got her there: and when, an hour later, I arrived at my street and saw her sitting on the step outside my door with bloody feet where her sandals had cut into her skin, instantly all suffering left my body and I felt that I had entered a biblical scene, that time was slowing down and action in space coming to a stop, such that when we—my mother and I—would reach out towards each other, at that infinitely precise moment before contact would be made, our bodies would freeze and *that* would be the picture of us that posterity would preserve, leaving our actual coming together, our reunion—our final pose—forever unseen: an omission in the record.

CELL IV

Once she has washed and put away the dishes, my mother goes to her chair, and my expectation, then, is that she should be quiet, resting, for the remainder of the day. The act of feeding her, of making sure she is satisfied makes me feel competent and useful; my further motive, however, is to ensure that, afterwards, she is subdued and serene, fit for little more than a few paragraphs of her book, and a crossword clue or two, before she puts her head back and dozes off, at which point all motion in the flat will cease, stillness will descend, and I will be able to work in peace.

She, for her part, wants to be good. She respects my work and is eager to see me do well. She would hate to be seen as belonging to the category of person who bears down too hard, who irritates, encroaches, disturbs, demands. So when I tell her, as I do every day, that I am going into my room, and ask her—remind her—not to interrupt me, she does not recognise herself in my request. *You must have the wrong woman. When have I ever bothered anyone?* But then, often just moments later:

'My phone doesn't work.'

She is in, without knocking. Standing right beside me, her face close enough that I can smell her breath. Jabbing her shitty flip-top into the sacred space between me and my computer screen.

'I'll have to bring it back to the shop.'

'Shouldn't you be relaxing?'

'I want to make a call and it isn't working.'

'The phone is fine, Mum.'

'It needs to be fixed.'

'You just don't know how to use it, that's all.'

In the shop where she went, unsupervised, to buy this phone, *good morning, my requirements are big buttons and a loud ring,* the young sales assistant spent half an hour drawing a detailed, life-sized, colour-coded diagram of the device, all arrows and smiley faces, with instructions about what each button did and how to reach each function.

'I hate it.'

'I know, Mum. But that doesn't mean it's broken.'

'Well, I must say, you're a great help.'

She leaves and comes back an hour later.

'There's something wrong with this.'

This being: *this, this, this, under my nose.*

'Mum, listen, if you need me to send a text for you, write it down on a piece of paper and I'll do it later. Or just post a card in response like you sometimes do.'

'I don't need you to write any messages.'

'All right, good.'

'However, do you see that little light there?'

'Yes.'

'Make it stop flashing.'

Then an hour after that:

'Look at th—'

'No, stop. I can't talk about your phone again.'

'Don't be so narky.'

'We've already talked about it several times today. I'm not doing it again.'

'Well, I forgot.'

'I know you did, and I'm sorry about that, but I've got my limits.'

'All right. I'll go for another walk.'

'Good. I hope you get lost.'

'You'll eat those words.'

While she is gone, I search through the drawers in the kitchen and find—*I cannot quite believe it, I have to test it several times before I am convinced it is real, and then I actually cry out with joy*—a key to my bedroom door. Supremely pleased with myself, I lock myself in and get back to work.

When she returns, she tries to come into my room. I hear the door-handle creak and the door-frame rattle. Then again. Then again. Then silence.

Later, at supper, she says:

'I feel insulted that you've locked the door.'

I knew she would be hurt. I would feel the same.

'I feel more comfortable having it locked while I work.'

'I won't be barging in.'

'In that case, you won't know if it's locked or not, will you?'

'Don't be so smart.'

'For me, it's an insurance policy. I can relax knowing I won't be disturbed.'

'One day, you'll lose the key and get locked in, and I'll laugh. I'll cackle with laughter, you'll see.'

The next day, I do not lock the door. The act of keeping my mother out, of blocking her access to me, is, I notice, causing me discomfort. The belief that my writing *about* my mother is more important than the flesh-and-blood woman who is my mother seems suddenly—well, it seems cruel. But then:

'Do you see this—?'

She is in on top of me again, with her phone, and I am shouting:

'For fuck's sake! Is this important?'

'I was just wondering, can you—'

'Christ almighty!'

I can feel my blood beat in my neck and cheeks as I stare—harder, harder—at my screen. Her figure recedes. The door behind me closes.

A while later, she comes in and drops a stack of folded clothes onto my bed, then leaves in silence.

When I emerge later that night, she has already gone to bed. There is a note on the kitchen counter. Written on a postcard. The image on the front is a watercolour of a robin perched on a branch: a leftover from Christmas. Her message is written in large letters in blue ink:

Gavin
Just to remind you I am NOT A SERVANT
Mum

(Signed. As if I would not know who the message is from. As if I might mistake *this* servant for one of my many others. As if I, *her prince*, could ever truly see her as something other than a servant to my needs.)

I get up late the next morning. She has left for her walk. After breakfast, I leave for my own, and our paths cross by the river. I hug her. She accepts my embrace.

'I got your note.'

'Note?'

She is pretending not to remember. By now, I can tell the difference.

'I lost my temper with you. I'm sorry. Are you all right?'

'I've walked it out.'

'I shouldn't have spoken to you like that.'

'It's all right.'

'But I must insist, Mum, that you don't interrupt me when I'm working.'

'I don't interrupt you that much.'

'It may seem that way to you, but to me it feels quite often. I'm not used to it. I find it disruptive.'

'So I am in the wrong.'

'It's not about right or wrong. These are conversations that any two people who live together have to have. I'm just asking you, please, to respect my space. Especially when I am working.'

'All right.'

'And you don't have to fold my clothes. If you feel you must, you can leave them out on the couch, and I will deal with them when I can.'

We hug again.

She goes off on her way.

'I'll see you at lunchtime,' I call after her. 'I'm making those spicy lentils you like.'

Servant indeed.

——

Around the same time of year, twenty-odd years ago, I was sitting at the kitchen table in the family house. Spread out on the table were the Sunday supplements. Playing on the stereo, a CD I had chosen. I had slept late, my hair was unwashed. A towelling dressing gown of green-and-blue stripes, *ungirdled* like Buck Mulligan's, hung loosely about my frame; its ends cascaded over each side of my chair. I was in my final year of university. My exams were approaching. I would have to study later in the day, but for now I was enjoying having the place to myself. No interruptions.

None of my siblings lived here any more. My brother R and his wife were in a place of their own near the city centre. My sister was doing a postgraduate degree in another city. N had emigrated to New York a decade ago. The day, therefore, was bright. Judging from the movement of the branches in my mother's garden, there was a light breeze. The birds were whistling. My parents had not left a note to tell me where they were, but I imagined they were on one of their seaside walks. Which gave me a couple of hours. A rare window in which I would not have to wonder, 'Are they finished with the bathroom yet? Is the kitchen free? Is he going to barge in here? Does she really think that now is the apt moment for *La traviata*?' A chance, that is, to be at home and—at the same time, on top of that—to have privacy. To be and to think in peace.

Not that there was much of a war going on these days. My relationship with my mother had, after the tumultuous years, stabilised. Or rather, the shock of our rift had abated, the hurt had been counted up and invested (for future returns), and we were now settled into a semi-bearable bond of mutual annoyance. She got on my nerves, I got on hers: this, we had come to believe, was how one experienced the other.

Gradually, though not without resistance, I was learning to accept that she had come to the end of her ability to sacrifice everything for me. It was dawning on me, unpleasantly, that the changes she underwent during my adolescence, the shift in her priorities that saw her turning away from me towards other concerns—babysitting her grandchildren, working as a nurse's aide, going to her painting classes and meeting her friends for coffee, sitting in her chair in the corner of the kitchen reading her novels, chopping raw fruit and vegetables and laying them out as a spread, in lieu of a cooked meal, with a note saying, *Love, Mam*—was not going to reverse. She was now asserting herself, for herself. She had more pressing demands to meet. She was invested, now, in pleasing others more than in pleasing me. She was not willing to overlook their needs in her determination to fulfil mine. I just had to get on with it, without her.

My frustration about this, my high irritation, I moulded into criticisms of her, which I parcelled out in little jibes. And she, in return, or sometimes as an opening salvo—it can be hard to pinpoint the starting point of these behavioural systems—was loose with her own tongue-lashings, that is to say the reproaches that as an infant I had craved, and that even now, as a grown man, with more knowledge of the suffering behind them, I was glad to receive; they were better than nothing. A love/hate routine, I guess you might call it, which took shape in both the private and the public spheres but assumed especial vividness in the latter. From time to time, for instance, we would go together, like lovers, to the art-house cinema in town to watch the genre of film we both liked. Bleak and uncompromising family sagas set in rural Russia. Or complicated romances involving plain-looking French people who managed also to be handsome, who were unfaithful and cruel while never ceasing to be civilised. The more inconclusive the ending, the better. For this allowed us, afterwards, to wonder what might have happened next. *'Do you think she took the flight?'* Or: *'I don't believe he left her for good, do you?'* The sort of question which used to drive my father demented, but which I enjoyed as evidence of the existence, both in my mother and in me, of a rich inner life, an imaginative (foreign) other world that made this (Irish) world liveable. But then, at some point, the spell would break. I mean that *she* would break it. Like, once, on the bus home from the cinema, responding to her obvious need for validation from strangers—*'Excuse me,'* even though she was not disturbing anyone; *'Would you like this seat?'* even though there were plenty of free places around her—a man began to offload his opinions onto her about a delay in the construction of a motorway caused by a group of environmentalists living in trees. 'Progress halted once again by the lunatic fringe,' he said. And, instead of telling him what she really thought, which would have meant contradicting him, falling out of his favour, she nodded along and gave a vague, semi-approving smile. Which, to me, was an inexcusable capitulation. *Was this the same woman who had demonstrated against the construction of office blocks on the Viking settlement of Woodquay?* 'Lunatic fringe?' I hissed at her when we got off the bus. 'You *are* the lunatic fringe.'

The only way out of this suffocating bind (mother as expressive paramour, mother as silent betrayer) was, I believed, to get far away from it. After everything that had happened—my mother's dumbness in the face of abuse, which had become inextricable from my experience of Ireland, of being Irish, of being an Irish mother's son—I knew that I would have to go abroad, and that this departure would probably be permanent. I had also concluded that the kind of life I wanted elsewhere would be impossible without a good university degree, maybe even two, so, for the first time since primary school, I was taking my studies seriously. Staying late in the library every night. Going hard at my essays. Making up for all that time in which, intellectually and spiritually, I had been errant.

My father was delighted by my renewed studiousness. I showed him the A-pluses that I was once again getting for my compositions, and he was genuinely amazed. On that night, years ago, when he had called me a freak, he had been fearful, I think, that my look and my manner, my insistence on flaunting my femininity, would cut me off from society, deprive me of success, and he wanted to shock me out of it. Now, seeing that I was, in spite of these apparently self-imposed handicaps, beginning to thrive again, he wanted to help. When I rang him, as I often did, late in the evenings from the public phone box outside the library, he did not hesitate to get back into the car, after a day spent in it, and collect me.

Since his recovery from the breakdown that had resulted from the failure of his shop, he had worked as a salesman in a large national food company. Every day he drove around the country peddling rashers and sausages to shops and supermarkets. A job that required him to meet and make small talk with the managers of the various shops he visited as well

143

as the members of his sales team: a large number of men. For someone as antisocial as my father—a man who did not go to pubs because he did not drink, who did not go to restaurants or play golf because he could not afford to, who did not have friends because he had never learned how to make phone calls or write letters, who did not really know anyone because he was at a loss as to how to talk to them—this was a kind of hell. Back-slapping. Dirty jokes. *'Where are you going on your holidays?'* This was the meat of the job, and he hated it. So much so that it—the meat, the hate—was slowly killing him. Exhausting him by day, and by night generating in him bouts of anxiety so severe that he barely slept and was unable to recuperate.

Our drives home from the university were mostly spent in silence; perhaps because of this, they were the most intimate occasions we would ever share. I was able to be in the seat beside him, simply be and not feel the need to enter battle with him, because I did not resent him, as I did my mother, for not having protected me. In truth, I did not see him capable of such protection. My mother, I believed, had that capacity. He did not. From him, I did not expect anything other than, well, a lift home.

There *had* been one occasion in which he had intervened. A gang of boys climbed the trees behind the back garden and began screaming homophobic insults into the house. He went out and told them to stop, and they stopped. But the reality was, they had been shouting for a long time, over an hour, before he took it upon himself to do something. And when he came back in, he did not come upstairs to see how I was, or to ask me what that was all about.

Is this something that happens regularly? Is there something I can do to help?

Were these words ever on his mind as he drove me home? Did he ever think of reaching out and touching my shoulder and saying, *Are you okay?* Or were such actions outside the bounds of the thinkable for him? Gestures that just did not even occur to him to perform?

Such inaction cannot, I think, be classed as passivity. My father had vigour. At school, he had been a sportsman, and he had not let himself go since; now, in middle age, he remained fit and active. Nor was it pacifism. For he was capable, I suspected, of violence; in fact, I knew he was. Although he had never laid a finger on me, although I had never seen him even raise his hand in warning, I had seen with my own eyes the nastiness which coexisted with his gentleness, which hid behind it, which, in certain unguarded moments, caught fire and briefly shone out.

As a young child, during one of our rare holidays, I had been allowed to invite a friend from the estate to come on the trip with us, and one day we, my friend and I, were riding on separate horses on a rural trail. When I say *riding*, I mean that the owners of the horses were walking beside us, leading the animals by the reins, while we clung to the saddles, gripped them with our quivering thighs, for fear of being thrown off. The road was uneven, the leather of the saddle was hard, my arse was aching; I was counting the minutes until I would be able to dismount. My friend was having an even worse time. On glancing back over my shoulder, I saw that he was crying, quietly. Alarmed, I turned to my father, who was walking a pace behind my horse's owner. *My friend is crying*, the tone of my look said. *Shouldn't we stop?* But my father misinterpreted me. He thought I was seeking a colluder. Giving me a horrible wink, he whispered: 'Bit of a sissy, isn't he?'

Bit of a sissy.

From where it is only a small step to: *You look like a freak.*

Words which, in the mouth of a grown man, do not stop being those of a schoolyard bully.

'He had no self-esteem,' my mother once said about my father. 'He thought he was *a nothing*.'

And I think she is right. He had an extremely lowly opinion of himself. But a point I think my mother misses is that self-hatred does not imply the death of the ego. Rather self-hatred is the ego's most fertile feeding ground. *I am nothing* is nothing but an ingenious mental trick, one which creates the illusion that the ego has been flattened into non-existence when in fact the ego is gorging itself on damnatory thoughts of itself, bloating ever bigger. A man who thinks nothing of himself is dangerous because his ego is so strong that it would rather eat itself to death than expose its true strength.

Bit of a sissy.

Only a man capable of great violence—a bully—would be able to say such a thing to a child, about another child.

For this brief moment, however, alone in the kitchen—the newspapers covering the entire surface of the table, my bare legs stretched out unimpeded underneath, no space for anyone else—I was getting a taste of what *home* felt like minus a self-hating father and a deserting mother. In my imagination, I was busy demolishing the cell in which I was trapped with such parents. My liberation, I could feel, was imminent. I had vowed to myself not to become part of that class of neurotics whose condition is determined by their having failed to get away. Those who, by staying close to their parents, by visiting their parents every Sunday, by looking after their parents as they get older, are constantly being reminded—*simply by breathing the same air, they are reminded*—of their own deaths. Watch me turn my back on such a death-in-life. Watch me being born again. Give me two, three, five years, then watch me—

Through the window, a flash.

Skin, hair, the top of someone's head.

My heart jumped, then sank: *they're back.*

The rattle and creak of the backdoor opening (no lock).

Suddenly aware of myself, exposed, I closed the front of my dressing gown and tied the belt. Drew my legs back in. Closed over the papers to clear some space.

Nothing lasts. Never a minute to myself.

Through the textured glass (style: Arctic) of the kitchen door, I saw a dark figure—it was a man, though I could see now it was not my father—entering the utility room. His bulk undulated behind the glass, as if made of water.

Frozen, cold, a hand holding closed my dressing gown, I watched him come through, turn solid.

A decade unseen, but still the same, by and large. And still: mad.

—

What are we going to do about N?

It was no surprise to anyone when N left school at fifteen. For the next couple of years, he moved from unemployment to low-grade jobs and back. The conundrum was: how to find him work that would make use of his considerable artistic skill? The solution: *get him on a course.* An expensive design programme at a private college, paid for by a loan taken out by my father—for, suddenly, paying for an education was no longer taboo—landed N a position painting cells for a Japanese animation company. Sounded sexy, but he hated it. A conveyor belt, really. I think he believed himself above it. He skived off. My exasperated father fielded phone calls from N's manager wondering where he was. He lasted a year.

(My greeting now: 'N, what the fuck are you doing here?')

He hung out, at that time, with a gang of boys for whom my mother felt considerable distaste. When they knocked in for N— *'Howye, Mrs McCrea, is N there?'*—my mother would be unable to conceal these feelings. *'I hate these young fellas calling to my door,'* she would say to N as a way of telling him that his friends were here. Whether oblivious or immune, these boys appeared unaffected by her contempt. While waiting for N to come downstairs, they sat at the table and made conversation with her, and seemed genuinely to admire her. Perhaps they thought she had a kind of class—a hippiness, an artiness—that was lacking in their own mothers. *'Now, Mrs McCrea, if you want those hedges cut, I'll get someone up for you. No need to be doing it yourself.'* I do not know what N got up to with this gang. Drink and drugs. Nothing more extreme, I do not imagine, than what the average teenager, including myself, got up to in that suburb. But my father, the strait-laced teetotaller, was worried, and a plan was hatched to get N a visa for the United States. N's name was put into a lottery and, unexpectedly, improbably, it was picked. The solution had been found. America.

(My greeting: 'Are you here on holiday or back for good?')

A few weeks before he was due to leave, he was arrested at a house party for possession. A block of hash. Possibly a pill or two (for that scene had just taken off). At N's court appearance, the judge decided not to put the crime on his record, for it would have prevented him from emigrating. The Americans would not have let him in. And, when all was said and done, was America not the best solution for him?

(My greeting: 'Did you even tell Mum and Dad you were coming?')

We did not hear much from him over the years. A phone call here, a postcard there. A rumour would reach us that he had moved out of New York City to upstate. Then: he was working in a bar and living with a gang of Irish lads, just like those he had left behind. Then: he had moved back to the city, alone, and was working as a doorman at an upmarket apartment complex. Then: we got a call from his girlfriend telling us, '*N should come home.*' I do not know how seriously my parents took this warning. Not very, I wager. I do not remember hearing any conversations which took the possibility seriously. And now, on their return from their seaside walk, I do not remember them being particularly happy to see him.

What are we going to do about N?

A line was quickly formulated. He was back in Ireland only temporarily. *To do a course.* Once he had his diploma, he would return to America. Whatever happened, the visa could not be allowed to expire. He had to go back.

But, of course, he was not going anywhere. He was here to stay.

So began the darkest years. N moved into the room we had once shared, and I went into one of the box rooms. At night—at all times, actually, but with added vehemence at night—he would pace from one side of the room to the other, as I had once done. I would lie in bed and, through the wall, hear him at it, and it was as though I was being visited by the ghost of my former self. Except that N's step was much heavier. *Thump-thump-thump-thump.* And instead of wagging his finger, which had been my compulsion, he would clap his hands together and rub them loudly; that is, at the start of a pace he would *clap*, and then he would *rub-rub-rub-rub* until he had reached the wall; turning around, he would *clap* again, then *rub-rub*, and so on, for hours at a time, sometimes till daybreak, all the while releasing his famous cackle, which he now punctuated with a single word:

'Ah-ah-ah-ah-ah-BABOON-ah-ah-ah-ah-BABOON-ah-ah-ah-ah—'

The baboon, I would later learn, was an Irishman with whom he had had some kind of falling out in New York, and whom N believed to be coming after him. I did not doubt that the Irishman existed and that he might, at one time, have been a threat to N. But, using the bits of information I gleaned from N's utterances, I worked out that the baboon was, in N's mental schema, a symbol for something much larger than this one man. The baboon was a figure to which N's entire paranoia complex attached itself.

'Look at you, you big BABOON, ah-ah-ah-ah, you're a BABOON, ah-ah-ah-ah—'

The baboon was anyone who, at any time in N's life, had crossed him, been mean to him, looked down on him, shamed him. The baboon was anyone in a position of authority who had disciplined N for his work or his attitude. The baboon was anyone who did not see, as N saw, the truth about how society worked. The baboon was anyone who had accepted their fate as an ordinary person of average means, and who, despite this, had the audacity to believe themselves better off than N. The baboon was usually, though not exclusively, Irish. (On the flipside, the baboon was never an aristocrat, or a recipient of inherited wealth, or a self-made tycoon, all of whom retained N's absolute respect.)

The baboon functioned in N's mind as an easily conjured target for his scorn. In turn, this scorn—aggressive, attacking—was a disguise for a deeper-seated dread of the activities of the world in which he, as a misunderstood genius, felt unable to partake. N's mental assaults on the baboon were merely the outermost manifestations of, and a distraction from, the fear he felt about being overwhelmed by a world he did not understand—or understood too well. N's fear was that of being humiliated by personalities who were a mystery to him, precisely for their being too familiar. Shouting at the baboon, in the safety of his own room, was a means of keeping dangerous relationships—dangerous because they were wholly ordinary and known—at bay.

This thing of darkness I acknowledge mine.

Meanwhile, external to N's head, the baboon manifested as a large tattoo on his upper arm. I saw this tattoo for the first time when I crossed

N on the landing as he was coming out of the bathroom with just a towel tied around his waist.

'Cool tattoo,' I said, though to be honest I found the baboon image to be black and menacing.

'Ack,' he said, 'don't get a tattoo.'

But then, a few days later, he declared:

'I want to be a tattoo artist.'

My father, sitting at the kitchen table, teacup in his hand, gaped at him, completely at a loss. 'Tattoos?' he said, as if pronouncing for the first time a commodity only recently imported from abroad.

'There's nothing wrong with tattoos, Dad,' I said, trying to be the voice of reason and to give N the benefit of the doubt. 'He could make good money.'

'Giving tattoos to corner boys?'

'Well, yeah.'

Once, while still at school, I had stuck a temporary adhesive tattoo onto my arm, a skull-and-crossbones affair, and showed it to my father as a joke. His response had not been anger; it had been stupefaction, followed by veritable despair. His face—and around it, his entire framework of values—had collapsed, and I had regretted the gag immediately. *Don't worry, Dad,* I had said, feeling terribly sorry for him, *'it's fake, don't you see? it comes off...'* Just as I felt sorry for him now, when I saw how the idea of N as a tattoo artist defeated him, how it went against everything he had been taught to expect from a son, and how he blamed himself for this, how this self-reproach showed in every line of his face.

Since N had come home, my father's anxiety, which had been kept for a long time at a low simmer, had begun visibly to bubble up. Whenever N was around, he became agitated. He wrung his hands. He adopted worried expressions and shook his head. He looked around at the rest of us in search of an explanation; when none was forthcoming, he moved his gaze off into the distance. When called upon by my mother, he tried to implement some version of discipline, sometimes forcefully so, though I think even he was aware of how old-fashioned, how inadequate he ended up sounding. Overwhelmed, he simply got up and walked out of the room.

About N becoming a tattoo artist, though, he need not have worried. For the next week it was:

'I want to be an architect.'

And then the next:

'—a graphic designer.'

And then:

'—a computer animator.'

This last idea, perhaps because it sounded similar to what N had worked at before, was fixed upon as a workable solution. What would have to happen to make it a reality? N would have to *do a course* (of course). For which he would need to create a portfolio. For which he would need to get a computer. And no ordinary computer. But one that had been built from scratch according to his precise specifications. The money was found, I do not know where—my father died with a pile of secret debts—and a huge hunk of beige plastic appeared on the desk in N's bedroom. An application was then made for a four-year degree—four years? were *we* mad?—at a reputable technical college, and, on the strength of his portfolio, which was messy and weird but which clearly contained the germs of talent, he got a place. Which meant:

'I need paper.'

'—pens.'

'—books.'

'—lunch money.'

'—a printer.'

'—a desk chair.'

'—a motorbike.'

'—a car.'

Many of these things he got. But some he did not. And he did not like to hear 'no'. Faced with any kind of resistance, he threw tantrums. Stormed around. Ranted and raved. Cursed. Insulted. Threw objects. Made threats. Manipulated. Stole.

'Gavin's at university, isn't he? He gets everything he wants. Everyone here has had every chance. Now it's my turn. Why are you being so fuck-ing mean?'

Like a deprived child, from whom nourishment had been denied, he was demanding that our parents acknowledge an overdue debt to him. Rightly, he was counting on their guilt about him to get what he wanted from them. When they refused, or were unable to provide it, he associated their refusal with poverty, worthlessness, coldness, desolation—that is, he associated it with *Ireland*—which he contrasted with the wealth, the abundance, the worth that he believed to be elsewhere, usually the America that he had just left (a belief that grew with time to fantastically idealised proportions, uncorrected even by his own direct experience of penury there). He displayed a desperate yearning for what others had and he lacked, a frantic envy of all that did not belong to him, which he had learned to articulate in a manner which was, for him at least, eminently reasonable.

'In America, I wouldn't have to get the bus to college. I'd have a car of my own. You people live like paupers.'

How familiar his sentiments were to me. Even if, at the time, only just out of my teens, I was, as yet, unable to put a name on them. The belief that I was exceptional, deserving of special treatment, destined for high rewards. And the hope that, if I distanced myself from people, my longing for connection with them would remain concealed. For me, as for N, this concealment was paramount because any such longing was experienced as a weakness. Giving in to this weakness was my—our—greatest terror.

'What are you studying?' he would ask when he found me bent over a book. Sighing, I would lift the book up to show him the cover. 'Yeah,' he would say then, 'I read the first bit of that. Remember, that's all you need to read. The opening few pages. No need to go on once you've understood the style.'

I have heard it said that, in madness, one feels like one is in a position of checkmate. One cannot make a move, or indeed stay still, without being beset in the mind by contradictory pressures and demands. Every posture, every situation seems untenable. Right is wrong, left cannot be right; one cannot win. I recognise this double bind, having been caught in it, as in a prison cell, for whole stretches of my youth. *What did they—the world, my family—want from me?* I was to speak correctly, pronounce my t-h's, but I was never to look down on those who did not. I was to work hard and succeed without, however, displaying any signs of materialism. I was to be aware of injustice in the world—Northern Ireland, South Africa, Israel, the American South—yet I was to be stoic in the face of any unfairness suffered by me, right here at home.

In our approach to N, we as a family imposed a similarly paradoxical set of expectations. We were ready to admit that he was mad, yet we continued to treat him as a responsible person. He had, in our view, legitimate grievances that deserved to be aired, but this did not stop us writing off his utterances as products of spite and ingratitude. We wanted to give him the trust to which we thought he was entitled, while, equally, we did not want to be taken in by his game. He was, in our eyes, gentle and soft-hearted; then, in a blink, he would appear abject, foul. Our approach to him, mind, was not born out of any wish to torture him. Rather, we were ambivalent because what we felt for him entered our consciousnesses in ambivalent forms.

In line with this, N's moods swung wildly. There were days when it seemed as though he was bursting with power. On these days, he would close himself into his room and work late into the night on his projects for college. Drawing. Designing. Drafting. Cutting. Building. The room would fill with smoke, the smell of which would invade the whole house, and for a spell the abundance he longed for would seem to be within reach. *He was going to do it. He had what it took, after all.* But then he would go to bed, and stay in bed until the afternoon, a habit which my mother tried her best to be liberal about, but, having her own history, her own trauma, there were limits to how liberal she could ultimately be. So she would go in (no knock) and open the window and pick up the overflowing ashtrays and shout at his still-slumbering body that *she was NOT A SERVANT*. Then, when he eventually got up, he would discover that the energy from the day before had dissipated, and that in its place had grown a counter-attitude of disdain or disgust or indifference for his work and for himself. In contrast to yesterday's fullness, he would feel that he had nothing inside and was lifeless. It was useless to do his coursework, to please his teachers, to get good grades, to pass; useless to strain for the rich, vivid life he believed to exist elsewhere, for at the end of the day that other life was far away, over there, never here. In this room, in this house, in this country, life always ended up being empty, worthless.

Which is to say, being committed to a real project, with a prescribed outcome and an actual deadline, made N suffer agonies of humiliation. He considered himself special, a colossal talent, but he was unwilling to subject himself to the shameful necessity of proving it, to himself or to others. Participation without the loss of his being was impossible—and also not enough. So he clung to his isolation. His separateness. His closed routines. His mental circuits that involved only himself. It was better, easier, less disappointing to preoccupy himself with his fantasies, which could not be directly observed by or directly expressed to others, but in which anything was possible. In his mind, he could be anyone, anywhere, do anything, have everything. There, he could establish the highest standards for himself and always attain them. There, and only there, he was all-powerful and free.

(*There* was a place I knew well, and now, looking back, I ask myself: if my writing had not taken off, if I had never found a subject for it, or a form to put on it, would I still be *there* today, in the same cell?)

All of this became plain to me one evening when we were watching television together. The ads were on. I was in the armchair, with my feet up on the cushion, my knees pulled into my body. He was sulking on the couch. Glaring at the screen. Pulling the hairs out of his hands with his teeth.

'You people live in poverty, you know that?' he said, speaking from his usual script.

As a rule, I ignored his provocations. Responding was not worth it. But this time, for some reason, I took the bait.

'I'd hardly call it poverty,' I said.

'Look at how you're living. In a barn at the bottom of a hill. Peasants, the lot of you.'

'Oh?' My tone was sarcastic, unkind. 'You made a lot of money in America, did you?'

'You don't understand anything. Where I worked, they had *Picassos on the walls*.'

'And were they yours, these Picassos?'

'You don't get it.'

'What don't I get?'

'The people I worked for, their apartments—'

'What did you work as again?'

Low. I knew what his job had been. Opening and closing doors for rich people. Carrying their luggage up.

'You should've seen it. Real art everywhere.'

'So?'

'So, you're fucking nothing here. Ants. And you don't even know it. Over there, I knew the most powerful people in the world. Jewish. Friends with everyone in Hollywood.'

'What do you mean you knew them?'

'God, shut up.'

The film came back on. But I was not really watching it. I was watching him watching it. And he was not really watching it, either. His mind was obeying other things. Wrong things. After a minute, he said:

'I did that.'

'Did what?'

He pointed at the telly.

'I gave them that idea.'

'What ide—?'

'Ah, Christ! You're so bleeding thick.'

'All right, explain it to me. What was your idea?'

I was speaking calmly. Rationally. For I had decided that I was going to help him realise that the fact that he did not think there was anything the matter with him was one of the things that was the matter with him.

'You know the film *Fight Club*?' he said, keeping his gaze fixed on the moving images, which were not those of *Fight Club*.

'Yeah,' I said.

'You know the pink soap?'

From the publicity posters. The *Fight Club* logo carved into a pink bar of soap.

'Yeah.'

'I gave them that idea.'

'How?'

'Don't be so—. They were the most powerful people in the world.'

'Who?'

'The owners of the apartments. I used to talk to them.'

'They invited you in? To talk?'

'They'd see me drawing in my pad and would ask to see my work.'

'And what was in your pad?'

'My sketches. My ideas.'

'The pink soap?'

'You don't understand. They knew everyone in Hollywood.'

'They took your ideas and sold them to Hollywood?'

'They had everyone's number. They could call anyone.'

'A bit far-fetched, don't you think?'

That N preferred the imaginary to the existing mediocrity, that he had chosen the imaginary state as his vital force, was undeniable. More difficult to determine was whether he was aware of this preference, or whether, in fact, these imaginary feelings and actions had chosen him.

'You're a fucking idiot,' he said.

Later, after I had, like a good boy, given her my report, my mother asked him: 'Are you receiving messages from the television?'

'What are you talking about?' he said.

He was at the table, eating at a speed that, merely by watching him, gave *me* indigestion.

She was standing over him, holding a tea-towel like it was a weapon.

'Do you hear voices?'

She was cross. Accusing him of a misdemeanour.

He laughed, mockingly: 'Leave me alone. I'm eating.'

'Tell me straight, N. Do you hear voices in your head?'

'No. That would be mad.'

———

At my graduation dinner some months later, as soon as N sat down at the table, before he had even been given a menu, he called the waiter over and ordered himself a coffee. This act was fundamentally unacceptable to everyone else at the table. We wished it was not happening, though outwardly we each displayed a different degree of tolerance to it.

I did what came naturally to me: I looked over at my mother, whom I knew would be unwilling and unable to hide her feelings, as I was doing.

Her jaw had tightened, and she was gazing fixedly at an uncertain point above our heads. Over her eyes, there had formed a glaze. Inside her were beating the drums of war: *say it, don't say it, say it, don't say it—*

'N,' she said then, turning back to him, 'you can have a coffee with your dessert.'

'What's the problem?' said N.

'We've just sat down,' she said.

'It's not a big deal,' my brother R said. 'Let him have what he wants.'

'It's a habit he picked up in America,' I said, as if N were not there. 'From those diners, you know? Where they bring you a coffee immediately?'

My father wrung his hands nervously over his plate, on which his napkin was still folded.

'It's eight in the evening,' my mother said. 'What does he need a coffee for?'

'Fuck sake,' N said. 'It's just a coffee.'

And true enough, when it came, it was just a coffee. But it was not about the coffee, was it? It was about N showing up here in smelly clothes, looking dishevelled, and doing whatever the fuck he liked.

The first course arrived, and N began to do what he always did around food, which was shovel it in, wash it down, then return to the trough, wholly unconcerned with how he looked or sounded to those around him. And my mother did what *she* always did, which was to overcome her feelings of mortification about N by criticising him and trying to control him.

'For God's sake, N. Eat slowly.'

To this, N said, 'All right,' like an obedient child, though he did not alter his behaviour even a little.

'N, what did I say? Leave some for everyone else.'

'Leave him alone, Mum,' I said, even though I, too, thought he was being a slob.

Wanting to finish it, my brother R made a gesture indicating that we should just ignore him, as we were so practised in doing. Meeting his cryptic statements with silence; shaming his outrageous outbursts by pretending to have heard nothing; reaching over him, around him; talking behind him, through him: how easily all of this came to us when we worked together.

Between courses, N contributed little to our conversations and was sometimes mute for long periods. Either he sat back in his chair with his arms folded and peered down his front, as if curious as to why his own leg was jigging so furiously. Or he slouched forward with his elbows on the table, his fists at his temples to support his head, and stared down at the blank tablecloth. From time to time, in a superficial effort to include him, we directed a question to him, but his response was to grunt, or say 'Yeah' in a manner that suggested that he had not really heard or was not really interested. Then, the next minute, out of the blue, he became over-excited, and interrupted our discussion about a different subject entirely:

'Did you see that Spanish film in the IFC?'

'Which one?' I said. 'The Almodóvar?'

'Yeah,' he laughed, 'it was funny.'

Before receding again into his cell and closing over the gates.

And it seemed, again, that he had dropped out. That once more there had occurred in him a radical diminution of curiosity concerning that which was passing before him. Until more food arrived and he pounced on that. But even then, if I looked closely, I could see he was not really interested in the food, either. The privation he felt, which he tried to counteract with food, was obviously and entirely mental. In evidence while he ate was the split he felt between body and mind, and his absolute identification with the latter, the part of him which felt unembodied:

paradoxically, as he ravenously crammed food into himself, he appeared to lack a sense of having substance, of taking up space, of being biologically alive and real; the food was immaterial; it was feelings he was after.

The plates were taken away, and, with nothing to feed his mind off, he withdrew once more.

Then, from nothing, he erupted again. This time picking up on something that he had heard, minutes ago, in the course of our exchanges: an ironic broadside my brother R had made against German folk culture.

'What the fuck is wrong with Oktoberfest?' N bellowed.

The table went quiet.

Flashing in our minds: the memories of the past occasions, too many to count, when we had responded to his vicious attacks with equally vicious, though cooler, more composed, counter-attacks. When we had refused to make the effort to see some sense in his point of view, whether it was right or wrong. When we had struggled to concede that there might be validity in his tirades. And when there had, therefore, been carnage.

'Someone answer me. What's your problem with German folk?'

Of course, there was actually nothing wrong with German folk. And, in fairness, R had not explained why he loathed it so much. Assuming our assent, he had simply made a remark about it and rolled his eyes, and we, understanding the spirit in which his remark was made—more than anything it was an aesthetic point, which, thinking about *Lederhosen* and *Dirndln* and *'Im Wald und auf der Heide'* and *der Schuhplattler*, was hard to oppose—nodded and laughed along.

'You're ignoramuses,' N said.

Which put an end to our sneering.

For a moment, we looked into our glasses and felt embarrassed.

If it had not been German folk, it would have been something else. Monarchies. Or tax. Or abortion. The subject itself did not matter. For all he was doing, in actual fact, was saying what it was forbidden to say in our family. Channelling the unspoken, the silenced, the suppressed view, which was—he could depend on it—the right-wing view. The passion with which he spoke was short-lived; it had no source in conviction. His aim was simply to cut through the smug consensus. For where had this consensus got him? (Nowhere but a *barn at the bottom of a hill*.) And what had the smugness made of him? (Nothing but *a pauper*.)

Ultimately, he was fighting not to win an argument but to preserve his existence, but for us that was neither here nor there, because, in truth, we wanted him to disappear.

'All right, N, all right,' my mother said, as if soothing N, though in fact she was stabbing him with her tongue.

'What do *you* know about German folk?' he said.

'Don't start now, N.'

'What's the matter with you all?'

'N, don't speak to your mother like that,' said my father.

'Christ almighty,' said N, immensely frustrated.

'That's enough, N,' said my mother, 'we're trying to have a nice meal.'

To me, it felt exposing to have N challenge us in this manner. Unable to accept his real disturbing presence, I felt angry with him and wanted to punish him. Put him back in his place. I did not allow myself to do this, though. Instead, I said, 'Mum, leave him alone,' for when she treated him like this, I hated her, as well.

As I hated the rest of the family for how they treated him, and as they hated me for the same.

It was like an elemental force: acting out of shared helplessness, we were destroying ourselves.

In many cases, when there is illness in a house, the family has to turn itself into a nursing home or a psychiatric hospital, in order to contain the illness and to support the child who is ill. Whereas many families are able to do this, others are not. Some, like mine, cannot stand the presence of illness. Our own bonds, those connecting the rest of us, were not strong enough to surround him, hold him, keep him safe. We did not have the wherewithal to turn ourselves into a regenerative cell. Instead of stimulating the family's protective qualities, and triggering a collective response on that basis, the illness provoked hostility, in-fighting, and eventually wore down the family structure. As a consequence of trying to *do something about N*, we came unstuck, one from the other, and, having done nothing about N, eventually floated off in separate directions.

—

Usually, N saved the worst of himself for the hours when our father was at work. Our father was an anxious man who believed himself unworthy of true respect, but it was not the case that he possessed no authority in the house. His physical presence, which was imposing, the opposite of wimpish, had the effect of containing N's most belligerent impulses, of blocking them and driving them inwards. Which is to say, when our father was home, N, as though following his example, became quieter, less crazed, more gloomy, more discouraged. Together, at least until one of them spoke, or N had one of his outbursts, they tended to resemble one another. Although distinguishable by their respective expressions of sadness, and by a long chalk not equally likeable, when on the opposite side of the same room, trapped inside themselves, they were unmistakably father and son.

Apart, however, they turned into different beasts. While our father was out putting on a rickety performance of responsibleness at a job he resented, N, stuck at home, let fall all pretence of personal responsibility, put aside any sense of measure, and thus liberated gave vent to his grievances: the injustices he believed had befallen him, which, whether perceived or real, functioned as justifications for attacking our mother, at whose door he laid the blame.

'Why do you fight with her so much?' I remember asking him.

'Because I hate the woman,' he replied matter-of-factly.

Because, I think he meant, he had never been able to make her love him.

All his life, he had watched her share her love with everyone except him, and still now she seemed intent on denying his demands for it; even when he begged her, as though for a salve, she remained cold to him. There seemed to be nothing he could do, except the one thing he knew how to do, which was to spoil other people's enjoyment of her love by poisoning its source.

'Listen to you, putting on the poor mouth,' he said to her once, while she was entertaining the family with a story from her working-class youth. She was, by general assent, at her best during such performances: bright, sharp, funny, self-ironising. N's interruption—'poor mouth'—put a fast end to her show and was, to my ears, worse than any obscenity he had ever thrown at her.

But it takes two, this tango of love's denial, and my mother, on account of her own withholding of love from herself, danced for her life. Far from floating free of the whirl, she was implicated in each and every movement; oftentimes she was the one who stepped out first, who led; she could not help herself. By finding fault with him. By nagging him. By saying his name in an admonishing way. By throwing disapproving looks to others, about him. By commenting on his eating habits as a means of criticising his body weight. By reminding him of who he was, as opposed to what he thought he was, or would be, or could be. Always in the knowledge that, by these actions, she was perpetuating their affair (of the heartless) and showing her readiness for an open clash.

Otherwise, on those days when she appeared to have chosen the higher path of devout acceptance, he manufactured opportunities to draw her into combat. Having woken up in the same dismal place as yesterday, with no immediate prospects of change, dependent on his parents for the basic necessities, and in desperate need of an outlet for his unspent fervour—I am speaking here about a man 'in his prime'—he clomped around the house, opening and closing the doors, checking that our father was not there before charging at her.

'Give me a lift to work,' he might say (for he had dropped out of his course, having lasted only a year, and was now packing shelves at a home-and-garden warehouse alongside teenagers and students, supervised by well-meaning half-wits, which, unsurprisingly, made him delirious with rage).

'You can get the bus,' she might reply (for, as the crow flew, the industrial estate in which the warehouse was located was not a great distance away).

'I've missed the first bus,' he might say to that (for, despite the proximity of the industrial estate, he had to catch two irregular buses to get there; it was an operation that had to be properly timed and executed, and he had purposely left it late; which is to say, as a rebellion against the indignity of having to take public transport, when everyone else in the world seemed to be cruising around in spanking new cars, he had purposely left it late).

'That is not my responsibility,' she might say then (for, despite being neck-deep in his affairs, she was eager to display some independence from them).

'Come on, Mum,' he might respond (for he found it absurd, the height of injustice, that he should have to take the bus, when there was a functioning car parked outside), 'just give me a fucking lift, will you? It'll only take a few minutes.'

'Where's your bus card?' she might say to that (for, although she resented doing it, she got him a weekly ticket because it saved her having to constantly hand out change from her purse for his fares).

'Didn't you hear me?' he might say (for he found the repeated rehearsal of this routine immensely frustrating, *why doesn't life ever just flow in my direction?*) 'I've missed the bus. I'm going to be late.'

'I can't do anything about that,' she might retort, again putting on a show of disinterest, though she must have been aware of the futility of this. The instant she had seen him standing in her kitchen, just back from New York, unannounced, she must have understood the problem that she now faced, and that this problem had no fast solution. N was not going to rush to get a job and move out. On the contrary, he was going to bed down and cling on and demand and demand, until, in the end, she would have to have him forcibly removed.

'What's wrong with you?' he might say then, enraged, the gang leader of his own self. 'What made you so fucking mean? Have I done something wrong?'

'N, don't start,' she might say—pointlessly, given that the start had come and gone a long time before.

'Start what?' he might say, for in his eyes nothing had ended that needed to be started again; he was just picking up where they had left off; it was a tortuous path they were both on, but one he would be able to put up with as long as it kept going; what he could not bear was reaching a dead end. 'I'm only asking for a fucking lift.'

She might ignore him then. Give him a dose of clean air.

In response to which, he might start thundering around. Picking objects up and putting them down. Sighing loudly. Marching out, slamming the door, then striding back in.

'Take me to the bus stop, then.'

'No, N. That's not the deal. If you like, I can pick you up this evening.'

'Come on, Mam. The bus stop is just down the road.'

'You'd be there by now, if you'd just left the house instead of starting this.'

'For fuck's sake. You won't even give me a lift to the bus stop? Why the hell not?'

'The exercise will do you good.'

'What do you have a car for'—here he might actually tramp out through the hall and fling open the front door, in order to reveal my mother's crappy little Mazda squatting idle in the driveway—'if you don't bloody use it?'

'Leave me alone, N.'

'What are you even doing right now? Reading the fucking paper? Jesus Christ! Why won't you help me?'

So, at this point, she had a choice. Either she could dig her heels in and refuse to give N what he wanted, in which case there would erupt a vicious fight, one which threatened never to terminate because N's craving for contact was impetuous and insatiable, far exceeding what he needed and what my mother was able and willing to give, until my mother would threaten to call my father at work, or, if the threat was not enough, would actually call him, and my father would ask to speak to N—but by this time N would already be gone out the door, pounding down the road of the estate like a bull released from its pen.

Or—the equally hopeless alternative—my mother could acquiesce to N and drive him down to the bus stop, in which case she would take advantage of the sullen silence he would adopt for the duration of the short journey (an outcome of the shame he would feel about using coercion to get his way) in order to make it known to him that she was acting under duress, going against her own wishes. 'You're bullying me,' she might say, 'you're abusing me, and I'm going to tell your father about it when he gets home,' thus treating N like the child that he so desperately wanted, once and for all, to be.

That evening, then, when my father did get home, exhausted as usual, my mother might say to him, 'You need to speak to N,' in response to which my father would not ask why, for he knew without needing to be told. And anyway it was impossible for my mother to explain. Her trouble with N was not the nature of the requests he made—if one listened dispassionately, he was not asking for anything extraordinary—but rather the mass of unspoken desire which was contained within his requests, which she was unwilling or unable to acknowledge, never mind satisfy. N, it seemed, still believed that our mother was omnipotent and that it was up to her, if not to make him happy outright, then certainly to prevent all evils, whether from internal or external sources, from touching him. What N was asking from her, really, was permission to project some of his bad self into her, and to take some goodness out of her; this, she was never going to grant him, for it would have meant signing up to the principle of lifelong mothering, which was nothing less than a denial of herself as a whole being.

When confronting N, our father was unequivocal in his allegiance to our mother. Her status as the injured party was presumed, her right to redress accepted without question. Our father deeply disliked and carefully avoided being emotionally upset, so he rarely got angry with N. Instead, he gave him a stern speaking-to. Impressed upon him—in the most general terms, using the loose-fitting language of a bygone version of discipline—the necessity of *doing what your mother tells you*. And, more often than not, N would not fight him. 'All right,' he would say, before shuffling off to apologise.

Which makes me wonder whether, in his attacks on our mother, he was actually urging our father to protect her from him. Searching for a paternal authority that could and would put a limit on the actual effects of his impulsive behaviour. A strong hand that would hold him back from acting out of the visions that came to him when he was in a state of agitation.

Occasionally, though, when he felt cornered, N did rail against our father, too.

'Why the fuck did you sell the house?' he might say, referring to our father's family home with the piano and the apple orchard and the toilet on the top floor, which had been sold to pay for the psychiatric care for my father's sister, and which represented for N the privileged life that he, by rights, ought to be living. That house was his inheritance, his due. It was something good that he had, which was now gone, and its loss was the reason he was not getting on. If he were living in that house today, he seemed to believe, everything would be well. 'We should have hung on to that house. Selling it was the biggest mistake this family has ever made.'

On the occasion I am thinking of, N and my father, were, for a reason that escapes me, in the hall. When my brother started shouting at my father about the lost house, my mother came out of the kitchen and joined them. From the sitting room, where I was, I could hear everything that went between them—or, rather, when I turned down the volume of the television, I could. My brother was hysterical (over nothing, over everything). My mother, with a resolve she lacked in my father's absence, was berating him (about nothing, about everything). My father, who did not know how to cope with tempers, was silent; I imagined him to be standing between them (lost, in the middle of nothing, everything).

Listening to them, my skin was cold, my heart pounding. And in my mind, there was a muddle, for I found it difficult to ascertain with whom my loyalties lay. N was the most obvious person to hate, and there is no doubt that I hated him, first and foremost. But this was not the whole picture. For it was clear to me, even as I hated N, that there were reasons for his behaviour. So much of what he did lay outside his consciousness and therefore beyond his control. He was a person whose capacity for love was insufficiently developed. Throughout his life, from infancy onwards, he had become progressively more and more inhibited in love, and consequently more and more alienated from others, more depersonalised. He had now reached the point of being unable to have feelings in relation to others, except to inflict violence on them. And—the muddle—I could not help blaming my mother and my father for this. N's bitterness about the shortcomings in his environment and his ingratitude for any assistance he received came from a belief that they, his own parents, were not truly on his side. They had been unwilling or unable to clear away the frustrations that littered his path and against which he reacted so strongly, and were therefore not good people. My parents had not earned N's trust. They had not proved to him that they were benevolent figures who wanted the best for him. And, accordingly, I hated them as well, on his behalf.

I have since learned, the hard way, that hating everyone in a situation is really just the experience of being trapped in pain. What I call 'hate' is merely the illusion of a way out. Predictably enough, though, when I burst into the hall—my way out—it was N, and only N, that I assailed. It was not often that I got involved in N's skirmishes with our parents. I preferred to slink around on the peripheries and eavesdrop. But, in this instance, overwhelmed by hate for all three of them, I could not think of anything else to do than give that hate to N, heap it all onto him, let him carry its weight.

I was overwrought. In a frenzy. Wisely, after only a few seconds spent in my searing radiation, N retreated upstairs, and I collapsed across the lower steps and wept.

'He has to be stopped,' I said, 'before he kills us. Before he kills *you*.'

On *you*, I took my hands from my face. My parents were standing two paces away, and a pace apart from each other. Neither of them moved to comfort me. Neither spoke. Rather they just stood there, peering down at my prostrate figure. My mother's face was like a wall. My father's, by contrast, was ashen and limp. Scared of me, he appeared. As though he had just discovered that I, in fact, was the killer.

It was Gavin in the hall with the terrible words.

In my Big Dream, I am looking at my mother who is holding me in her arms. My infant self is wearing a red dress, a fact which causes me intense embarrassment, yet I cannot take my eyes off myself. I am fascinated by this feminine figure whom I know to be me. At some point I realise, or perhaps all the time I have been aware, that I, the perceiver, am not merely myself. I have a second personality, which is my father, perceiving me. Which is to say, I am present in the scene as my father, and, simultaneously, I am my absent father, peering in from the outside, anxious about the state of affairs that has developed without him. As him, I see a spoilt boy who has been dressed in an elaborate fashion by his indulgent mother, the type of boy who plays with dolls and has fits of tears. I am ashamed by how my son has turned out, and I feel guilty also, for I am to blame for it. It is my lack of authority, my inattentiveness that has allowed it to happen.

And there is something else. In my father's eyes, the son is split, too. The boy in the red dress is not only the sissy Gavin; he is, at the same time, the mad N, kicking his legs in the air, demanding attention, demanding love.

Sissy and *mad*: much of a muchness: my failure as a father made flesh and blood: both of them *freaks*.

Too late to rectify now. The damage done. Stepping forward, entering, intervening, trying to fix, would only make a bad situation worse. *Everything I touch turns to shit.* Simpler, the only way I know, is to turn away (*a place I cannot see is a place I cannot ruin*) and look for somewhere to lie down (*in sleep at least I can tread the backward path to innocence*).

Conveniently, there is a mattress lying on the floor behind me, *half in the room and half out, the near side lit by the lights, the far side in shadow.*

This is my bed for the night.

On Good Friday, a few weeks after the family altercation in the hall, my father got into bed. On Easter Saturday, he did not get up. And on Easter Sunday, regardless of there being no sign of movement from him, we went ahead with the family lunch.

Assembled round the dining table, in the room directly below his drugged and unconscious body, we ate salmon steaks and roast potatoes, and my mother and N, on exemplary form, snapped and snarled at each other, in response to which my brother R and his wife threatened to stop bringing their young children to the house, for they no longer wanted them exposed to this sort of emotional violence—a convenient game of distraction for us all. No one was prepared, or had the courage, to bring up the subject of our father, to ask aloud the critical question of how his chair had come to be empty. No one appeared to be feeling any urgency or panic about his current condition. No one went upstairs to check in on him. No one inquired about how many barbiturates he had taken. No one suggested calling a doctor or—*alarm bells!*—an ambulance.

Dad is in bed: this was all we knew and wanted to know.

The consensus view, agreed upon by dint of an exchange of glances—knowing, jaded—was that the situation was unfortunate, though hardly surprising, given the stress he was under in his job. For the time being, he was best left alone. Let him sleep it off. The worst of it would pass without the need for drastic intervention. A holiday, then, would have to be organised, for that was what the man needed above all else. After that, we would have to start thinking about getting him a new job, or negotiating an early retirement package, or, or—

The following day, when he failed to rise once more, my mother finally took it upon herself to call the doctor, who—*sirens!*—immediately summoned her to a face-to-face appointment. My mother cycled to the clinic, and was, I think, a little taken aback at how grave the doctor believed the circumstances to be.

'How many pills has he taken since Friday?' the doctor asked.

On hearing my mother's estimate—more or less, give or take—the doctor did not hesitate to pick up the phone and call an ambulance. And, with that, a new term entered our lexicon. *Parasuicide.* An apparent suicide attempt, or suicidal gesture, whose aim is not that of killing oneself. The archetypal cry for help.

My mother got back to the house before the ambulance arrived. She went straight upstairs, shook my father awake, and told him what was about to happen. (*To* him or *for* him?) Then she came back down and began making preparations for his departure. Packing a bag. Ringing my brother R. And my sister. And a woman friend. And a reliable neighbour.

I was at the dining room table studying for my master's exams. My mother did not come and tell me what was happening, and I did not go and ask her. I already knew, and she knew that I knew. What was there to say? (But more importantly: *what does this say about us?*)

Above me, I could hear my father shuffling about. Getting dressed, I imagined. *Did he wash? Was he going to wash?* From the kitchen, behind me, came the sounds of my mother running things under the tap, needlessly, while she waited for him. After some time, he came down—and I could hear, as he entered the kitchen, that he was changed. The soles of his shoes were dragging on the floor, and his gait was slow and uneven, as though, after such a long period on his back, he had lost the power in his limbs and had to learn how walk again.

'What's wrong with you?' my mother said.

She was irate. Audibly seething.

My father mumbled something I did not catch.

'What?' she said. 'Speak properly.'

He went again: I could not hear the words he used, but I could hear that he was slurring them. I suppose he was making some form of apology.

'What's the matter? Stand up straight. Is this how a man behaves?'

It was a strange thing for my mother to say. Strange because she had never been overly concerned with masculine norms, except, on the rare occasion, to condemn them. (When I decided to join a gym for the first time, for instance, she gave me a grave warning: 'Don't pump yourself, I couldn't bear to see you with a neck like a rugby player.')

And yet now: 'Is this how a man behaves?'

i.e. *'Bit of a sissy, aren't you?'*

It was my father's own slight returning to him, his just deserts, which one imagines might feel satisfying to witness. In reality, it was anything but. I can remember few more devastating moments in my life.

When the ambulance arrived, my father climbed in, while my mother dashed around the kitchen, organising a few final things. I got up from the dining table and opened the kitchen door. Her back was turned to me. She sensed an unwanted gaze fall upon her and swung around. Our eyes met.

Not moving from the doorway, keeping my grip on the handle—a sign that this was not the start of a discussion but rather a fly-by—I said,

'You shouldn't have said that. Questioning his manhood is not going to help.'

She paused for a second, just long enough for the blood to pump into her face. Then she quickly finished what she was doing and left without saying a word.

My father was taken to St J——'s Hospital in Stillorgan. On admission, he was relieved of his belt, his shoe-laces, his mobile-phone cord, and his razors. He was assigned a bed in a shared room in a locked ward. (At long last, a lock.) He was not allowed out of this ward at any time. To get in, we, the family, had to wait at the door until a nurse came and, using a card key, opened it for us.

The walk: down a long corridor. To the left, windows that gave onto a nondescript, corporate-looking, easy-to-manage garden. To the right, doors, some open, some closed. Halfway down, the corridor opened out into a common area. A coffee table. A couple of couches. On which we sat while the nurse went to notify our father of our presence. When he came, we made room for him. Then we sat together for a while, saying very little.

This was visiting time.

In the walls surrounding the seating area were more doors, some of which were left ajar, allowing us, while we sat, to look in at the other patients. Men. Lying on angled mattresses. Or sitting in bedside chairs. Anything but secluded. Specimens on display. Which we—the day trippers, the onlookers, the seekers of knowledge and understanding— assumed into ourselves as points of comparison on our internal scale: zero for *all there*, ten for *out to lunch*. And let me tell you, it came as no comfort when we found that another man ranked higher, that is crazier than our father. *For what, then, was he doing in here, with them?*

The other patients, for the most part, left us alone. Only once were we approached. A young man, mid-twenties. In a state of delirium. We had heard him from a distance, laughing and calling out, making sounds not unlike those N made when alone in his room, only these were louder, looser, more unashamed, coming from somewhere over there, *better not to look, keep your eyes down*, but now suddenly he was amongst us. Out of breath from running up and down the corridor. Addressing my father by his first name. Telling jokes that did not convey any immediate sense. Whooping. Cursing. Putting us, it seemed, under test.

Were we reliable?

Were we worth destroying?

In the time it took for a nurse to come and lead the man away—an excruciating minute—my father, visibly humiliated, pushed his hands into the tight space between his thighs and, by moving his chagrined gaze across our faces, willed us to disappear.

Willed *us*, that is. Not the man.

For the man was where he belonged. As was my father. We were the intruders. What on earth had we come here to see? *Get out of here*, his silence seemed to be saying. *Leave me alone. Let me have my breakdown in peace.*

After this, the doctors forbade us from returning *en famille* for a while, as my father's condition tended to deteriorate after our visits. Understandable, given that shame seemed to underlie much of his pain, but not easy to hear. Or to obey. Not visiting equals not caring, does it not? Could we stand to be seen to be not caring?

Because of this rule, I did not see him again for a couple of weeks. By my next visit, he had been moved out of the lock-up. Judging him to be, quote, *low risk*, the doctors had transferred him into a double room in an open ward on the first floor. They had not authorised the return of his belt or his laces yet—low risk was not *no* risk—but at least he was free now to move around the hospital grounds. I found him sitting in the common room, which was located behind the reception area on the ground floor: through a double door, down a few steps into a large clearing containing a jumble of mismatched tables and chairs, and a counter selling tea and coffee and chocolate bars. I bought a pot of tea and some biscuits and brought them to the table where my father was sitting.

'Did you come alone?' he said.

'Yeah,' I said.

My university was walking distance, so I had come after class, and, from then on, this became my routine, three or four times a week. When my seminars ended, or after I had finished studying in the library, I would walk to the hospital, sit with my father for an hour, then get the bus home. Or if my mother was here, get a lift with her.

'You don't have to come,' he would say.

'I know I don't. I want to.'

Then we would sit, mostly in silence, exactly as we had once done in the car when he picked me up from the library.

And I would take him in.

And he would take me in.

And we would look around and take this place in.

And sometimes there seemed to be only a small space between us, and sometimes a chasm.

After a while, I would go to the ward to visit my schoolfriend O, whose room was just down the corridor from my father's. I would spend a few minutes with her, remembering past times, trying to make sense of what had gone wrong. There was so much I wanted to say to her for which I did not yet have the vocabulary. And, anyway, she was so heavily medicated—her pupils appeared even more dilated than my father's—that it was hard to make meaningful contact. That would have to wait.

'You don't have to stay,' my father would say when I came back downstairs.

'I'll go in a few minutes,' I would reply.

The doctor responsible for my father did his rounds once a week. He came to my father's bedside, accompanied by his trainees, and asked my father a few questions about how he was adjusting to the medication. Any side effects? Any improvements or deteriorations of mood? My father's answers would be noted down in his file, and his doses would be adjusted if necessary. Then my father would spend the rest of the week waiting for the doctor to return. He was offered no individual talking therapy. No counselling. No couching. No mentoring. No group sharing. No cognitive analysis. No organised system of peer support. No focus on the breath, no philosophy, no yoga. No living in the present. No stillness. No questioning of stressful thoughts. No twelve steps. No affirmations. No positive thinking, no negative thinking, no thinking about thinking. No screaming rooms. No pillow-beating. No heart circles. No non-judgemental listening. No self-forgiveness. No Gestalt. No Vedanta. No TM. No Vipassana. No Family Constellations. No NLP. No reiki. No Enneagram. No Ayurveda. No flotation tanks. No reflexology. No acupuncture. No aromatherapy. No colour therapy. No Bach flower remedies. No homeopathy. No micro-dosing. No fucking tarot cards. Nothing. Except a Catholic chapel—*Mass celebrated daily, 5 pm weekdays, 10 am weekends*—and pills, pills, pills.

To put it bluntly, the system was categorically disinterested in what my father had to say. It was concerned neither with his mind as a generator of consciousness, nor with his body as an experience of consciousness, nor with his voice as a conveyor of consciousness. It did not care about his human personality, his individuality, his stories; it lacked all curiosity in what he believed and how those beliefs might or might not be causing his pain. The doctors' only business, as they saw it, was to identify, using certain narrow tests and criteria, specific symptoms in my father's behaviour, to describe those symptoms, and, with this information, to make a cut-and-dried diagnosis. Create a label to pin to the file. A rubber stamp for the records. On the basis of which a cocktail of drugs could be legally prescribed. And that settled the matter. My father's psychology played no role whatsoever in recognising its own patterns of suffering, in comprehending its own motives for perpetuating them, or in making its own repairs.

In this system, my father was simply, in a medical sense, diseased. His behaviour was a sign of this disease; his emotional state expressive of its existence. As such, the doctors could claim to have a thorough knowledge of something concrete, a psychopathology, when, in fact, calling him diseased was a way of not understanding him. An excuse not to have to listen to him.

Listening, in this sense, did not mean scanning the first words of his phrases and believing that this was enough to make a judgement, medical or otherwise. It did not mean finishing his sentences for him. It did not mean knowing, always already, what he was about to say. It did not mean ticking boxes on one's chart. It did not mean putting words in his mouth. It did not mean telling him, based on these presumptions, who or what he was.

Rather, listening meant being with him. Which meant opening to him. Which meant being absolutely vulnerable. Willing to have one's own beliefs challenged. Willing to have and to acknowledge one's own emotional responses. Willing to be hurt and disturbed. Normally, for this, one went to a watch a film in the dark, or to read a book in private; one did not like to be in such a vulnerable state at work, on the hospital ward. It was unprofessional, one claimed, but really one was afraid of being overwhelmed. One did not want to have to deal with oneself in this way, with the result that one could not deal with him, the desperate man in the bed, my father.

But who am I to talk?

I had not learned to listen to my father, which meant I had never *been with him*, either. Not really. Why should I have expected a bunch of strange doctors to do something that I, his son, had failed to do?

'Is there something I can do to help?'

In the car with my father, or home alone with him, had I ever thought to say such words? Did I ever think of reaching out and touching his shoulder and saying, 'Are you okay? If there is something on your mind, I am here to listen.' Or were such actions outside the bounds of the thinkable for me? Gestures that just did not even occur to me to perform?

My father's suffering took the form of doubt about his capacity to be a husband and father. Over many years, he had built up a false self of extreme degree: he was, he believed, a deficient provider, which caused him to overwork at a job that did not suit him. When this false self collapsed—as all false selves must, at one point or another, however briefly—he must have experienced, amidst the anguish and the confusion, a distinct sense of relief. A weight lifted off his mind. By *being with him* at that moment, by seeing the vulnerable child standing in the rubble, by hearing his cries, by showing him, somehow, that I could discern his relief, and that I was relieved that he was relieved, would I not have helped him to understand that it was only as this relieved child that he would ever know love?

The year in which this happened was 2000. I completed my master's exams on Thursday 18 May. That weekend I spent socialising in town, which consisted of taking ecstasy and dancing and sleeping at friends' flats. I got the bus home on the evening of Monday 22 May. The weather was bright and warm. I was unwashed and tired, self-conscious under the light. My skin, I felt, was pale and spotty, my hair greasy. I urgently wanted to be inside where no one would be able to see me.

I arrived at the house just as my mother was leaving for the hospital.

'Do you want to come?'

The fast answer was no. A stronger instinct told me: go.

At the hospital, we sat with my father at a table downstairs. He had received good news. His request for an individual room had been granted. Tonight, for the first time, he would be sleeping alone, without a snoring man in the next bed. And he had been given back his belt, shoe-laces, and mobile-phone cord. (My father had not called this 'good news', but, naively, that was how we received it. A sign of progress. Evidence of improvement.)

When it was time to go, he walked us out. Through the double doors at reception, then out the main entrance. We said goodbye and walked to the car. Got in. Glanced back the way we came. And what we saw was like an old-fashioned film reel: man at the entrance of an old stone house; breeze lifting the strands of his fine grey hair; sun on his face; his arm raised and now waving.

On the way home, my mother said, 'That's good about the room.'

'Uhuhn,' I said.

'But he was very quiet. Did you notice that?'

'Yeah.'

'Distant. He was distant.'

The following morning, early, the phone rang, waking me up. As soon as I became conscious of the sound, I understood that I had been waiting for it. My mother answered. Spoke a few words that I could not hear. Then she came up to me. N, who was older, was sleeping in the other room, but she did not go to him; she came to me.

'I have to go to the hospital,' she said.

'All right.'

She dressed quickly and left.

And I lay in bed, waiting.

Amongst the many memories that came to me as I waited was the summer's evening—how old was I? nine or ten—when a bumble bee, hiding in the folds of my duvet, stung me on the hand, and I, shocked, began to scream. Hysterically, to scream. Uncontrollably, to scream. In a manner disproportionate to the injury and inappropriate for my age, to scream. And as I did so, I heard, coming from downstairs, as though from the bowels of the earth, the noise of my father knocking over a chair and flinging open a door and pounding-pounding up the stairs: deep, rich, resonant sounds that reverberate within me still. Then, before I knew it, he had me in his arms, pressed against his chest, where I could hear his heart pounding-pounding; it had been so long since I had been embraced by him like this, the sensation was of tracing something newly discovered back to something known.

'My God'—he was heaving great sighs of relief—'you gave me a fright.'

'Sorry,' I said, 'it was just a bee,' and I put my arms around *him* then, so that he would also be safe.

INTERLUDE: PARIS, 2013

My mother has two photographs of my father on display in the flat, both from a trip they made to Paris in 1996: in the first photograph, my mother and father are leaning on a stone balustrade outside the palace at Versailles, both of them have their left leg resting on the ledge, foot hanging in the air, bodies facing in the same direction rather than towards each other, my mother's back to my father, her backpack forming a buffer between them; in the second photograph, my father is alone, seated on a public bench on the Esplanade des Invalides, it is spring because the trees behind him are budding, above the buildings in the background cirrus clouds streak across a blue sky, the sun is in my father's face, making him squint; he and my mother have recently left the Musée d'Orsay and are now having their packed lunch: my father has a morsel of bread in his hand and is chewing on the bite he has just taken, my mother is behind the camera, and I am sure she can see how handsome he still is at fifty-eight—his skin virtually wrinkle-free, his cheekbones prominent, his jawline strong—just as I am sure she does not tell him this, nor does he in his turn tell her she is beautiful, ever, the understanding being that these things have been said in the past, in some form, and are now understood, and I suspect that at the time of this photograph they were no longer making love to each other, either, that they had become companions more than lovers, and my mother herself admits that theirs was not, in her words, *an extraordinary marriage* and that the only reason it lasted was because my father made her laugh, that with a single understated remark he had the capacity to overturn her bad moods, to defuse her temper, indeed sometimes she found him so hilarious that she would be brought to tears or to wetting herself: I have a number of memories of my mother in this state, gripped by a fit of laughter, unable to speak, tears coming down her face, one leg crossed over another in an effort to stem a flow, and as a witness to this scene I usually could not help laughing myself, which was strange because I did not find my father particularly funny, in my eyes my mother was the funny one: she did not possess my father's quick wit, she did not deal in sarcasm, she was never consciously cruel; her humour, rather, operated as a sort of mode of being: she was a bit eccentric and believed certain rules did not apply to her, so she would cycle around the neighbourhood on a bike with a big basket on the front, smiling and waving at everyone she passed, and would not hesitate to cut through the park where cycling was prohibited, and smile and wave at the park-keeper when he shouted at her to dismount; and sometimes she was downright outrageous: one summer evening, totally sober and for no special reason, watched by me and my friends, she did a jig in the sitting room of our family home, wearing her swimming costume and a pair of knickers on her head; and as a boy I was never sure when this outrageousness might express itself, so being with my mother in public was for me an experience laced with danger, there was always the chance she might do or say something that would embarrass me, but equally there was the possibility that we would end up laughing together and by that means feel truly close to one another, and today this ambivalence about being in my mother's company remains, I am still on guard against her capacity to mortify me, just as I still hope to receive her gift of cheerfulness, to share in her joy, and I wonder, does she feel the pressure of this when she is with me? does she change her behaviour in order to meet or to thwart my expectations of her? do I confuse her by sometimes criticising the same parts of her that on other occasions amuse me? and perhaps an answer lies in the trip I take with her in 2013 to Paris, where I find myself being especially attentive to her conduct with the Parisians, the way she approaches them and communicates with them, and in particular the way she speaks about them to me afterwards—her hypotheses about their personalities and their relationships and their daily customs—and I sense that, as much as she envies them their flats and their streets and their bakeries and their monuments and their museums and their cafés, as much as she regrets never having had the opportunity to experience their style of life for any significant length of time, she is thankful for the life that she has had, every bit of it, without exception, from the hardship and the scrounging and the loss, to the friendship and the solidarity and the solitude and the peace, she is grateful for what all of this has taught her, the depth it has granted her vision, the wide spaces it has opened in her mind: which is to say, she is happy where the Parisians we meet are not; I lose count of the times I witness her good humour dissolve their hard fronts, and I am unable to refrain from contrasting the ease with which a smile comes to her face, a smile that is genuine, a smile devoid of malice, a smile that does not come at the expense of others, with the difficulty they have in arranging their face in anything other than a scowl; which is to say, she is a cultured woman, in my estimation more cultured than any of the Parisians that seem to impress her, if by culture we mean the ability to be comfortable with all types of people and to have insight into the circumstances that determine human behaviour and to turn to art for help in teasing out the contradictions therein, as opposed to the act of studying for a university degree or wearing nice clothes or buying food in a certain shop or reserving a box at the opera, which any moron with money can do; and it is because her happiness and her culture have been hard earned, achieved against the odds, that she takes both so seriously: she does not read trashy books, she does not possess a television and has never in her life viewed a soap opera or talent contest, she does not rush past art to get to the gift shop, she does not scoff at the abstract or the avant-garde, rather she lingers in front of it and appreciates it and tries to understand it—*this* is worth her time—which explains the air of solemnity she adopts where others might be tempted to snigger when we go to an exhibition of male nudes at the Musée d'Orsay and we find ourselves standing in front of Courbet's 1866 painting of a vagina, *L'Origine du monde*, beside which is hung Orlan's 1989 photo of an erect penis, *L'Origine de la guerre*, and in reverent silence she contemplates these two works, and I believe she understands, on some level, that there is no choice to be made between them, they are not a binary but an amalgam, that instead of aligning ourselves with one or the other, our task is to confront their mutual dependence—the ferocity of sexual intercourse, the trauma inherent in childbirth, the desire for possession that is the basis of separation and hate, the libidinous drive to war—and to see that in the place where vagina and penis overlap there is life and there is also death, and that death, when it is given life, is not always fearful; in our imaginations, it purposely adopts a form we can grapple with: for my mother and me, the form it takes is my father hanging from a noose, a picture of suffering but also of release, on his face a grimace and a smile, both.

CELL V

On a break from work, I am at the table in the living room, sipping from a cup of herbal tea and feigning to read the newspaper while really watching my mother reading in her chair. She is re-reading a novel, which she is not against doing even when the bookshops and libraries are open. The intensity with which her focus is fixed on the page tells me that she is following the story as though for the first time. She has forgotten most of it, I imagine; those parts that are familiar to her, she savours and finds new meaning in.

Sometimes after visiting a house devoid of books, or after being in the company of people whose conversation never touches on books, or simply after finishing a book she found particularly gripping, she says in genuine disbelief, 'Can you believe there are people who don't read?'

'I can,' I say.

'Do they know what they are missing out on?'

'No, and they don't care.'

'But what do they do with themselves?'

'They watch television.'

'Some people have it on all day.'

'They do.'

'From the moment they get up. Can you imagine? I'd die.'

One year for Christmas, my mother got my father a book about Ernest Shackleton's expeditions to the Antarctic, which he got through, eventually, and said he enjoyed. And there were a couple of political biographies on the shelves that might have been his. But, other than that and the daily newspaper, he did not read. But nor did he interfere with my mother's reading, which had begun in earnest when she was home alone with young children, and had not ceased for a single day since; by all appearances, he respected it. Admired it, even. For Christmas and her birthday, he bought her books—and often only books, for that was all she wanted—from a list she made. One year, I remember, she asked for 'Brokeback Mountain', the Annie Proulx short story, which had just been published on its own. It makes me smile, now, to think of my father searching the tables of Hodges Figgis for that book, perhaps even asking an assistant to locate it for him, and then paying for it at the register, oblivious both to its content and to the fact of bookshops being fertile cruising grounds. His only concern, on getting home, was with how short the book was. How small. 'Look at this,' he said to me, 'it's tiny. I'll have to get her a few more. Go and ask her for some titles.' Because if it was not a pile of good-looking hardbacks, it was not love.

At the time my father gave my mother 'Brokeback Mountain', I was at university, living at home, and still on the receiving end of a lot of homophobic abuse in my neighbourhood. I had not heard of Proulx's story. I saw it by my mother's reading chair and picked it up and put it down many times before understanding what it comprised and how significant it was that my mother had got there before me. Once I had read it, I felt torn. Happy, on the one hand, to have a mother who would read such a book. Betrayed, on the other hand, by a mother who displayed more concern for the wellbeing of a pair of fictional cowboys in Wyoming than for her real gay son.

Two years after my father gave my mother 'Brokeback Mountain', he died. At that point, I was still at university, still living at home, and still on the receiving end of homophobic abuse in my neighbourhood, though it was beginning to peter out. Temporally, his death marks the final stage of the abuse. Emotionally, his death is bound up with the abuse. The anger I feel about the former is indistinguishable from the anger I feel about the latter. I am unable to divide the two angers out and examine them separately. When I recall one, I recall the other.

I will, when the moment is right, talk to my mother about the abuse, as I feel determined to do, after all these years. I will tell her to put her book down and listen to my anger and take the portion of blame she deserves. But who is to say that, in telling her to put her book down and listen to my anger and take the portion of blame she deserves, I will not also be talking about my father's death?

The phone was in the hall, at the end of the stairs. I did not put on my dressing gown to go and answer it. I went down—*did I rush?*—in the clothes I had gone to bed in: a T-shirt and a loose pair of boxer shorts. As I stood with the receiver to my ear, I could feel on my bare legs the draught coming under the door from the fallen-down playroom.

'Gavin? You have to come to the hospital.'

My mother's voice, its tone, was describing an event that was unsayable, one that had occurred in a space that no word had ever penetrated.

'Is he dead?'

'Yes.'

In that instant—*what was I was feeling? nothing beyond the satisfaction that arises when something expected simply and straightforwardly takes place*—I noticed, through the frosted glass flanking the front door, two figures loitering on the step outside. I opened the door to two women, my mother's friends. Their faces were pale and wore expressions which declared the gravity of what was happening *to me*: around their eyes, where normally there was brightness and exuberance, I saw extreme caution (*'Does he know yet?'*); their eyebrows were worried (*'Perhaps he does'*); their lips, which would in other circumstances already be engaged in vigorous activity—salutations and jokes—were sealed closed (*'We'll wait for him to speak first'*). I was awfully confused. *What did they think I was feeling?* I certainly did not feel like the person they were reacting to. From the receiver, which I was still holding to my ear, the crackling sound of nothing being said merged with the sound of people gazing at each other; it was in the midst of this unusual quietness that we stood—*was my mother also on her feet?*—waiting for someone to speak.

Finally, coming down the wire:

'My friends will give you a lift.'

'All right. They're already here.'

'Get N up. Take him with you.'

I hung up and brought my mothers' friends through to the kitchen.

'I need to have a shower. I'll be ready in twenty minutes.'

Upstairs, I shook N awake.

'Wake up, Dad is dead.'

I said this with a brutal matter-of-factness. As though I were saying, *Wake up, you're going to be late for work.*

'What?' he said.

'You heard me.' A pitiless energy pulsed through me. My heart was hard against him. For a stranger, even for my worst enemy, I would in this moment have been able to muster some softness, some compassion, but for my own brother I had not a shred. Partly because I was incapable of being soft with him, having never seen what that might look like; partly because I believed—*that is, before my father had even died, I believed*—that he was implicated. 'Come on, get up. We've to go to the hospital.'

Under the shower, very hot, I felt giddy. It had happened, and now that it had happened, it seemed like it was always supposed to have happened, exactly this way, and I was excited to tell my friends about it. I anticipated their sympathy. I looked forward to receiving their phone calls and their cards. Already the news would be travelling around the neighbourhood; perhaps in this precise instant, as I stood here with the hot water hitting my back, I was being pitied, cried over. Someone in me—a version of myself, no less real than any of the others—gloried in this. As a child, in bed, in the minutes before sleep, I had often visualised my own funeral to see who would come and how they would behave— like Sicilian widows, as it happened, beating their chests and falling on top of the coffin—and now, just like that, I got to have such a funeral without even having to die myself.

Overwhelming ovations.

My name shouted out.

My body covered with flowers.

I was not thinking sensibly. Or I was being sensible in a situation in which thought was by force irrational. Either way, right now there was no distinction in my mind between the wished-for and the real: my father was dead as a result of my own desires. More than once during the period of his confinement at St J——'s Hospital I had had the thought, *This is all so pointless, only death will put an end to his torment*, and now it felt as if, by entertaining this possibility, I had helped to bring it about. I had wanted him gone, and now he was.

(I had willed his death—let the true facts be known—not because I hated him, as other sons hate their authoritarian fathers. No, I loved him. I wanted him. In my fantasies, I cherished him as a model of masculine sexuality. But, likewise, my feelings of internal personal failure, of lacking substance, of being nothing, which often dominated me and led *me* on occasion to envisage my own death, came, I believed, from his influence. He was the eternal lost cause, hanging heavy around my neck; for my own sake, to obtain freedom for myself, I had to renounce him. This renunciation, which culminated in his death, would be the great trauma of my youth, and the end of my youth; it would also be the beginning of my independence.)

By now, the bathroom had filled with steam, making it hard to see and to breathe, and, as a result of a sudden shift in my inner fault planes—*on one side, the belief that I was loved; on the other side, that I was abandoned*—I began to choke on air, and then, the planes shifting again, felt I was about to be sick. I clasped a hand over my mouth and said silently but firmly, *No.* Which stopped the vomit from rising up but not the panic: the fearful conviction that things escaped me, that people separated themselves from me, underneath which lay guilt for having separated myself from them, and out of which came wild despair, a terrible and impotent rage, anguish that wept aloud, misery contained within a simper, sorrow that was numb: in a few short seconds, every possible mood of suffering.

That morning, like most mornings in Dublin, the roads were choked with traffic, so it took us a long time to get to the hospital. My mother's friends were ideal company. They had put themselves at my service, though I asked nothing of them. They did not pose questions or wonder aloud about how or why, as so many others would over the coming days and weeks. Everything they said was kind and related to the present task of getting to our destination, and I think we even managed to share a laugh.

At the hospital, they stayed downstairs while N and I were led to a room on the first floor where our family was to gather. My brother R was already there. My sister was the last to arrive, as she had to travel from outside Dublin. I do not remember having any physical contact with them, or with any of the staff. After a while, my mother entered, accompanied by a few staff members, I cannot remember exactly how many. These staff members immediately left the room to allow my mother to tell us in private how precisely our father had done it. (*On his first night in the single room he had requested, with his shoe-laces and belt, from a rail in the wardrobe.*) At this news, R cried out and began to sob, the only time I have ever witnessed him expressing emotion of any kind. My sister wept. N sat in dumb silence, as did I.

My mother? I cannot say anything about her state other than: she was distressed. My focus was squarely on her. I was eager to know what condition she was in. Yet my memory of her expressions, her gestures, her tone is extremely vague. Maybe it was the shock, maybe the strangeness of being in this room with its gaudy furniture and its ridiculous pictures of waterfalls and lakes, but my mother's figure in the chair—she had sat down to speak to us—appeared insubstantial, like a shadow, the space between us without depth. By contrast, my own limbs looked solid, dense. My head felt heavy. It was as though everything had been turned inside out; interior thought exploded outwards; exterior material collapsed inwards. That was what made it strange.

A matter of seconds, then, and two staff members came back in. It was disturbing to me how little time we were given to be by ourselves. To do whatever we needed to do, as a unit, with this new information. A minute, maximum, was what we were allotted. Barely time to visualise the various parts of the scene—*shoe-laces, belt, wardrobe*—before they piled in on top of us.

One staff member was a hospital manager, possibly a nun, though my only evidence for this was her demeanour, which resembled that of the nuns who had taught me in secondary school. (You know what I am talking about: the arrogance dressed up as modesty, the violent whispering.) The other staff member was the hospital chaplain, who was obviously so used to receiving the unquestioned respect of strangers wherever he went, in whatever circumstances, that he believed he could say and do what he liked without repercussions. He was, in a word, one of those men who blunders through life, totally unaware of the damage he himself is causing, and who therefore exists in a constant state of wonderment as to why everyone else is so angry: *Lord, what has made them this way?* But the poor man—I say *poor* but of course I do not have a whit of pity for him—had not yet met my family, had not yet met me.

His first error was to choose the empty chair beside mine. He pulled the chair round so that it faced me, before settling into it, his arms resting on the armrests, his feet planted on the ground, as puffed up and as uptight as a tin-pot dictator on his ceremonial throne. Watching him, pictures of my father—*how had a man so tall and so sturdy managed to suspend himself from a wardrobe?*—faded away, to be replaced by the questions: *Who is this fucking creep?* and *What the hell does he want?* The chaplain, clearly unhappy with the silence in the room—a silence which he had played the predominant role in creating—peered around himself at the people gathered, as if expecting to be addressed, as though *he* was what mattered now. And the excruciating thing was, he *did* matter to me. He mattered so much that he was all I could see; my one and only desire, right then, was to do violence to him; if I could find a way to hurt him, I thought, I would be relieved and happy.

Unable to stomach his grinning moon-face any longer, I channelled my ire at the Permanent Pioneer badge on his lapel. (For those who do not know, this badge is a gold shield with a sacred heart and a crucifix at the centre, surrounded by sunbeams bursting out. It is worn by those who have taken a pledge of total abstinence from alcohol for life, that is by those who need others to know that they have taken such a pledge, for it is on the higher moral floor that the Pioneer gets his kicks.) And I kept my gaze there until—unable to resist his own allure, drunk on the belief that his presence was a boon, his voice a salve—he addressed me.

'So what's your name?'

I did not answer except to jab, jab, jab, jab an imaginary spear into his sacred heart.

'Are you in college?'

In all the world, it was only him I hated, and those who let him live, function, and prosper; I would willingly have watched him die.

'What are you studying?'

What am I—what? Is this the sort of thing they had taught him to say at the seminary? Had 'What Are You Studying?' been one of the lessons on his Higher Diploma in Pastoral Theology (Health-Care Chaplaincy)? Had 'What Are You Studying?' been written somewhere in the required reading for the compulsory module 'Caring and Spiritual Accompaniment in the Community'? Had it been part of his reflective journal? A key element of his synthesis paper? Had it got him his full five credits?

'What are *you* fucking studying, you abject weasel?' I should have said. But instead—for my deplorable Catholic education had left me completely unequipped for direct confrontation with any apparent authority—I got up and went out to the corridor. Standing in the open doorway, I looked left and right: no one to be seen. I felt suddenly lost. I did not know what I was doing there, or what I wanted, or who I was looking for. So I started to scream.

'Someone! Somebody help! Please!'

I was whirling about myself. Flinging my limbs out. Stamping my foot.

'Help!'

Possessed by feelings for which I do not have a better name than psychotic. *Bring the strait jackets. Load up the Valium. We've got a live one.*

'Help!'

No member of my family came out to me; none of them tried to calm me down. Neither the chaplain nor the hospital manager moved from their seats. I was totally alone, totally at the mercy of myself.

'Please! Somebody!'

Around the corner, at last, came a familiar figure. A neighbour from the estate. The husband of one of the women who had driven me here.

'Who are they?'—I gesticulated madly through the open door into the room—'What are they doing here? They need to go! Get rid of them!'

Reaching me, the neighbour put a hand on my shoulder and said, 'All right, it's all right,' which was all he could say, for he did not know what I was on about.

'Get rid of them! Please just get rid of them!'

Get rid of what? he might have been wondering. *The feelings?*

The child psychologist D.W. Winnicott—it is never too late to get help—tells us that there are four kinds of crying. Crying is either the release of bodily tension (satisfaction) or a signal of distress (pain) or an expression of anger (rage) or a plaint (grief). Satisfaction, pain, rage, and grief: Winnicott does not expressly say it, but what I take from his schema is that any given bout of crying contains varying concentrations of these four elements. Because I cried only a handful of times in the days following my father's death, it should not be too difficult to demonstrate how this might be the case.

Crying at the morgue:

A plain building in grey brick. A long ramp designed for wheelchair users. A door. Through which I was expecting to find a reception hall or an anteroom. I was not prepared to come upon—immediately, no warning, as soon as the door opened, no barrier, no curtain, open to the world, plain to the eye—the trolley with the body lying on, a sheet to the neck, the head bare, and the face, well, the face was simply the face, was it not?

My legs weakened, and I collapsed on the ramp. A neighbour, the same man who had talked me down from my psychotic fit at the hospital, pulled me up onto my knees. He held my arm so that I would not fall down again. With my free hand, I clung to the railing. In that position, low to the ground but light in the head, man-some and child-some, I wept, screaming as I did so: 'No, no, no, no—'

It was a tantrum. I was crying in anger. Maybe it was a healthy thing to do, a means to get to know the extent of my rage. Maybe it was normal.

Harmless. But it did not feel healthy, and I did not feel harmless. For the few seconds that I knelt there, I really intended to ruin everyone and everything, and I did not care if I ruined myself in the process. Yet the people around me remained calm and unhurt by me. My family moved quietly away from me, into the room; together, no fuss, they ignored my feelings and went to meet the facts. My neighbour, meanwhile, stood patiently beside me, waiting for me to comprehend that my crying was nothing more than a hopeless demand for change, and that the change I wanted was not coming, and that what I believed to be happening—'No, no, no, no'—was not what was actually happening, and was so much more frightening.

At which point, my crying abruptly stopped, and I stood up unaided.

Walking slowly, cautiously, I followed the others inside.

Yes. Yes. Yes. Yes.

Crying at the wake:

The body, coffined, was brought back to the house and laid on top of my parents' bed, right in the middle where I had once slept between their warm flesh. The room had been prepared by a group of women from the estate. The floor had been hoovered, the surfaces dusted, the windows cleaned. The mattress was covered in a clean white sheet. A bunch of flowers and a candle placed on the dresser. No pictures needed to be taken down, no clocks covered, for the walls of this room had always been bare. Looking in through the open door, at a time of the day when the light was fading outside and the glow of the candle was beginning to show on the preserved skin, it was a simple and beautiful scene. Into which I entered and from which I left, in and out, alone or accompanying others, with an increasing sense of ease, until I was quite comfortable with it, indeed liked it.

The body was dressed in a simple work suit. The hands were interlaced and resting on the stomach. At one point, a set of rosary beads appeared, looped around the fingers—planted without our permission—but these were quickly and easily removed. In the morgue, the mouth had been contorted, with the lower jaw separated from the upper, and set at a slight angle, so that the lips formed a grimace and seemed to be on the verge of opening, threatening a rupture. Now, though, the bones had been set back in place, and the breach glued shut, the surface made impermeable once again.

Alone with the body, I laid my palm on the forehead, and ran it over the hair. On a couple of occasions, I kissed the nose. And once, overcoming my trepidation—feeling it safe to do so now—the lips. It was my last chance, which I was glad to have taken, but the sensation was such—something flowing that suddenly comes against unyielding matter—that I did not feel the desire to do it again.

'Why's B in a box?' my young niece said when she saw him. She had always used his first name, B, never 'grandad', so the music of her phrase, the alliteration, was sweet to hear, and funny. I laughed, and then, before I knew it, I was crying. Out of sadness, this time. Contrary to my tantrums, it felt like a stepping *towards* the world. A request for a place in the community of people. A sorting out of what I was responsible for and what I merely felt responsible for. An admission that I am hurt, and so an earning of the right to keep good relations with others. A kind of gratitude and, equally, a kind of repentance. A melancholy from which I would, I knew, spontaneously recover, and from which joy could, if not forced, emanate.

My niece would grow up to be an opera singer, a mezzo-soprano, the rarer kind. A source of tremendous pride for my mother. One night at supper, she says:

'It's terrible he never saw her sing.'

And—hand on heart—it is okay that she does not, and will not say, *It's terrible he never saw your books.*

Crying at the church:

Unprompted, on the spur of the moment, the neighbours formed a procession behind the hearse and followed it the whole way down the road of the estate, past the petrol station, to the church. An impressive gesture. Poignant. And one that took my family by surprise.

Inside the car, N tapped the driver on the shoulder and said, 'Speed up there and we'll give them a run for their money.'

Which sent me into convulsive laughter.

I loved N for that.

There was a large crowd at the church, most of them friends and acquaintances of my mother. As per tradition, we sat in the front row for the show. A schoolfriend of my father, a priest, joined the entire local clergy on the altar: there were so many of them up there, wafting around, bustles brushing, petticoats flaring, trains catching—*was he going to trip?*—that it resembled the Pride main stage. I found it amusing. Another schoolfriend of my father's gave the eulogy, during which he told the story of the mirror in the bathroom that never made it onto the wall. That was funny, too. I laughed aloud, and the laughter did not feel all that different from crying; it certainly was not its opposite; rather the two seemed to be closely related parts of a larger exercise of the emotions. A kind of mutual reassurance, one soothing the other, at a critical time.

At moments, though, the desire to laugh felt like a divine test. For the duration of the condolences—you know that absurdist spectacle in which the congregation queues up to shake one's hand, *sorry for your loss, sorry for your troubles*—I had a giggle in my throat, lurking just beneath my voice box, which, whenever I was called upon to say something, *thank you, thanks for coming,* would rise up and threaten to burst out. It took a lot of energy to keep it from the brink and gulp it back down, but I managed. Until my schoolfriend O appeared in front of me. She had been released from St J——'s Hospital for the day and was here accompanied by her distraught-looking mother. High on anti-psychotics, she was dazed, disconnected, with a distant look in her eyes, as though viewing the world from within a transparent cell. As soon as I had her in my arms, the giggle finally came out, transforming first into a wail, then into a plea:

'Get out of there. Promise me you'll get out of there.'

After the service, outside the church, in the midst of a large crowd—*are you going to the grave? will I see you back at the house?*—I was approached by L, a woman whom I recognised despite not having seen her for about fifteen years.

'Bless your heart,' she said, handing me a photograph.

Or rather: she handed me the photograph, *then* she spoke.

That was the order of events.

I looked at the picture. Then looked back at her. Then looked at the picture again. If one enters a state beyond disbelief, a domain of *über*-incredulity—where one lacks credence of one's lack of credence, because one had now seen everything—what does one do: laugh or cry?

L was the matriarch of the K family, born-again Christians from the United States—well, let us be accurate, from *Florida*—who came to Ireland in the early eighties to spread the word, *their* word, and who chose as their base the house directly opposite ours. L was married to T, who was now hovering behind her, in a similarly coloured tracksuit top, an expensive camera hanging around his neck, smiling the same unnaturally white smile. Together they had three sons with whom I sometimes played as an infant. The photograph was from the wedding of the eldest.

Pause: *the photograph was from the wedding of this woman's eldest son.*

'You used to play together, remember? That's his wife. Isn't she beautiful? Oh, he's just so happy.'

The K family moved back to the United States when I was seven or eight, but they did not let us forget them. They sent us regular missives, keeping us abreast of developments in their evangelical mission, which of course began in their home, with their own children: *our eldest son continues to deepen his relationship with God and feels called to start his own mission; our adopted black daughter has at this time fallen away from God but we continue to pray and trust that she will return.* The height of entertainment—when they were not alarmingly dark. On one occasion, we received a book in the post, some badly written tripe about whatever, at the back of which was a template letter, which we, the readers, were encouraged to photocopy and send to our local schools, warning our teachers and our principals against teaching our children anything (positive) about homosexuality or The Gay Lifestyle (as if lessons, positive or negative, about these subjects were even a remote danger in Ireland at that time), for fear of the wrath of God, who in this case would manifest on earth as a defunding campaign headed by L herself.

195

(*Know Thy Audience*: the long-lost Eleventh Commandment.)

And now, by chance, they were back in Ireland on a visit. The coincidence of being in the country at the same time as my father's funeral was, for them, a happy one. Everyone in one place! Like a big old reunion! Determined to get what they came for—which, as far as I could gather, was our approval—they waited outside the church (they refused to enter during the Mass) and pounced on people, anyone they recognised, as they came out. Mingling, beaming, they passed around pictures of their family, and boasted of their religious achievements, and, as if that were not enough, asked people to go round the side of the church for photos, exactly like a wedding. As a special thought, they presented my mother with a brown envelope containing two (more) books: *The Prophecies of Heaven* and *The Prophecies of Hell*. Which, by all reports, my mother accepted with a smile, before passing them to the person nearest her and saying, 'Get rid of these.'

Bringing us to the present moment: me, standing mere metres from the hearse into which my father's coffin was in that instant being loaded, holding a photograph from their son's wedding.

Laugh?

Cry?

Between *The Prophecies of Heaven* and *The Prophecies of Hell*, what was there?

Nothing less than everything I could see around me. The church wall. The hearse. The coffin. The people. The black tarmac on which we stood. All of this lay outside the moral world. This was a place where laughter was never purely happy, crying never purely sad. A land, my land, a no man's land, made rich by ambivalence and doubt, whose civilisation—built out of love, in recognition of hate, without recourse to prophecies—remained blessedly unseen by the voyaging zealots.

They will not read this.

They do not know me.

I have been spared.

———

Crying at the graveside:

Back at the house, the funeral directors had had trouble getting the coffin round the bend in the stairs; at one point, I thought they were going to drop it. Now they were lowering it with extra care, it seemed, into the hole. In unison, deeply concentrated, attuned to one another, they fed the leather straps through their hands, and then, as a single body, stepped away. And so it was done, what Freud calls 'the most important event, the most drastic loss, in a man's life'.

The crying I did over this—the finalisation of the event, the state of its being done—had a special quality. It was the crying of apprehension. The experience of coming to know, definitively, that in certain circumstances I must expect pain. Happenings would end. People would leave. That which was going would stop. And while this would never stop hurting, it would no longer take me by surprise. Henceforth, I would be newly watchful for signs of imminent endings; perceiving any, I would feel all sense of security drain away—that would be inevitable—but then, as a means of recovery, I could always journey back in memory to this graveside, and reanimate this loss, and learn once more its lesson, which is that the only safety that exists is the awareness that safety, that is, invulnerability, is a fantasy, and not an especially desirable one.

Don't be too careful, a wise friend once said to me, *you might hurt yourself.*

Yet apprehension was not the whole picture. Freud also says that 'grief over the loss of his father cannot suppress the son's delight at finally obtaining his freedom', and in my case he is right. My father had not been particularly strict with me. I could not accuse him of having been domineering. Nevertheless, he had not been free of the impulse to drag me down, to pull me back to his time, the olden days, from which I was desperately trying to liberate myself. So I was crying, also, out of happiness: no longer would I feel that weight on me, that terrible drag backwards. My father's possessions—the ancient moral good and the ancient moral evil—had been buried with him, and, as of now, I had the freedom to do what he would have considered wrong, or even what *I* would consider wrong, if my own ethical decision required it. I had no further reason to succumb to his worn-out standards. Gone, the arbiter. Gone, the pardoner. Gone, gone—and the question now would be: how much of my freedom would I squander searching for new external rules? How much anxiety would I spawn hunting for replacement authorities to guide me away from that very anxiety?

As innocent as grieving is—as blameless, as inescapable, as worthwhile—it is, if you ask me, a sadistic pursuit. It has the capacity to be pleasurable. Unlike the suicidal depressive (my father), the griever is able to be depressed about *something*, something that has some sense in it. The griever's guilt, far from being diffused and unnameable, possesses a face and a body; it has a voice and a story, which become the implements with which the self-punishment is performed. Whereas in suicidal depression the attacking ego has the person's entire sadistic arsenal at its command, in grief it is limited in its weaponry to those thoughts and images associated with the lost loved one, with the result that the level of suffering in the ego can be contained and the potential for pleasure released. Which is not to say that self-punishment in grief cannot be severe, or that it does not have the capacity to tear the ego asunder. The point I am making, rather, is that the pain experienced in grief, up to the point where it becomes suicidal, allows of a searching round for satisfaction, for enjoyment, for gladness, for delight.

This, in any case, has been my experience. In grief, deep within the agony of it, I have found pleasure. All in all, just as much as I hated the funeral, I enjoyed it. I disliked having so many strange people packed into the house during the wake, I was uncomfortable having my space invaded in this way, and at the same time I liked having everyone there. I liked the atmosphere. The bursts of laughter from the drinkers downstairs, and the quieter though no less expressive giggles of the pot smokers, myself amongst them, upstairs. It was nice to have my friends there, and to notice, painfully, which of them *were* there and which of them were not; I was glad to see the different ways that they responded to the situation, and to begin the excruciating mental process of reconfiguring my future friendships on the basis of this information.

In the weeks that followed, when I bumped into acquaintances on the street, or met mates socially, I was upbeat and convivial, which was not so much a denial of my inner turmoil as an accurate rendition of it. I was high. Which, far from being happy, was just a specific point on my emotional swing, as confusing and as stressful as being low, and always on its way back down there. In response to people's expressions of sympathy, I never failed to provide a smile and a thank you, and I impressed even myself with my skill in judging whether my interlocutor was genuinely keen to talk about what had happened, or whether the onus was on me to move us into safer terrain. When people—usually, I have to say, my friends' parents—said stupid things, I did not get upset or feel the need to educate them; rather, I stored their words in the same repository as my anger and vowed to put them both—the anger and words, together— to proper use, in the service of beauty, in the future.

With a similar kind of energy (*what to call it? torment enraptured? a glee that aches?*) I threw myself back into my studies, marshalling a fierce new assiduousness—a diligence, a punctiliousness, dormant since my primary-school years, which now returned with a vengeance—in the writing of my master's thesis. I wrote on Nabokov's *Lolita*, a book about fatherhood and its perversions, and it was thrilling to realise— what? Well, it was thrilling to realise the amount that one can realise when one focuses the mind. It turned out that I could pity Lolita and want better for her while also yearning to take her place on Humbert's lap. That I could condemn Humbert, abhor him, at the same time as I desired him. That having an emotional response did not mean capturing a single feeling in its pure state but rather experiencing patterns of often contradictory feelings in their living state. That in adopting a position, be it moral or intellectual or aesthetic, I was not proving myself incapable of adopting, simultaneously or at another time, its opposite. That in fact the idea of opposites was deeply problematic, and that it was literature that could, better than any other art, exemplify this. In a word, I was hooked. I wanted in. The decision about what to do with my life had been made.

My master's thesis would be my first labour of love: a love which came out of grieving, if indeed it was not my grief in toto, though it appeared in my system in disguise: as impertinence, as boldness, as doggedness. The resulting text, no doubt, bears the marks of these things. I expect it might be embarrassing, as defiance tends to be when reflected upon in retrospect, though I have no intention of ever re-reading it to find out. Suffice to say that the feelings I felt while composing it, I still feel; they make up the same drive that propels the writing of these words now.

What entered me was a fearlessness of the same sort suffered (for it *is* a kind of suffering) by those who are compelled to explore dangerous regions or jump out of planes or go to live in caves. It—I am talking about the fearlessness it takes to become a writer—must have started in my unconscious as an inaccessible urge, which then became apparent in my thoughts as a fixation on an unreachable standard, which was felt in my body as motivation, which was indistinguishable from anger, which corresponded to my feelings of abandonment, which themselves carried the apprehension, in both senses of the word, of death: the anxiety that death would come before I had had the chance to reach my unreachable standard, and the appreciation of (or even the wish for) death as a result of my attempts at reaching that standard.

In short, it was a kind of suicide: the killing of that false, fearful self that in the past had held me back from calling out in pain, and that, if allowed to live on, would hold me back from writing down the pain.

(Today when people fear me, which sometimes happens, it is this fearlessness, I think, that they fear. They worry about what would happen to them if they found themselves in its direct path, if they got in its way. And they are right to worry. They would not stand a chance. Those I am most intimate with know that it is best to keep the course to my unreachable standards clear.)

Of course, I am sure that, to many, it did not look like I was grieving at all. Or that I was fleeing grief by throwing myself into my studies, into future plans, into romantic visions of a writing life. And I can see why people might have thought this. It is unquestionable that repression was at work in me. That I was turning the face of my father away from me, keeping it at a distance, denying it entrance into my conscious thoughts. After the excitement of the funeral had died down and familiar routines returned, I rarely brought my father up in conversation. In private, it occurred to me to think of him only occasionally. For a long time, I did not cry about him again. But I insist, nonetheless, that this did not represent 'not grieving'. Rather, this was my grieving. The whole of it. None of it left out. The repression that was taking place was not hindering my father from continuing to exist in my unconscious, from organising himself into bigger and more complex forms, from creating idealisations of himself, from putting out feelers and establishing connections with other unconscious material—or from appearing to me, later, in my dreams, more vivid to me than he had ever been in waking life.

I know what this apparent 'not grieving' looks like from the outside because my mother was engaged in it as well. At the funeral, she did not beat her chest and call out my father's name; she was not a wailing widow. In all, I saw her cry only a couple of times, and then with great restraint. More often, I saw her comforting others. Anyone who asked for it, at any moment. Even people with only the feeblest of links to my father; even people I had never seen before in my life.

(A memory: in the bedroom, by the coffin, a woman, unknown to me, clinging to my mother, her head on my mother's shoulder, weeping, while my mother rubbed her back as though soothing an overwrought infant, *there, there,* and in her face she was glowing, my mother was, with the glow of someone who had already submitted to whatever of life was left after loss, and who in this submission had found transcendence, and I can safely say that, in that moment, and around that period, she was at her most beautiful.)

Today when she speaks about that time, she does not express sorrow. Instead, she says simply, with no audible rancour, 'The rug was pulled out from under me. I had to fend for myself.' My father, an uneven provider at the best of times, had suddenly stopped providing altogether, so now she had to do it for herself, without any help from others. To this end, she left her job as a nurse's aide in a convent, in which she had been demeaned by her employers and bullied by a co-worker for years, and sought employment elsewhere: the work would be the same, she would still be wiping arses, but maybe her value would actually be acknowledged, and a more decent wage paid?

In an interview for one of these positions, the man behind the desk asked her to 'run him through her CV'. My mother—I can just picture it—was appalled by the question, doubly so by the haughty manner in which it had been posed, and refused to answer. *Her CV?* She had been taken out of school and put to work while still a child, and had been on her feet ever since, hoovering and catering and serving and caring, 'women's work', and was now sixty years old, with three difficult children, and a fourth with 'actual problems', and a husband still warm in the ground—*that* was her CV.

'You didn't say anything at all?'

'I sat in silence and stared at him until he moved on.'

(And she wonders where she got *us*?)

She eventually found a job in a respite care centre for people with MS. Here, too, a co-worker bullied her. (It is a pattern: people who have undergone ordeals and yet manage to be radiant are threatening to many. Their example will always show up the smallness, the pettiness that surrounds them, and for this reason they must be torn down.) Despite this, my mother found a lot of meaning in the work. She got on with the patients. Became attached to them. Had an enormous reserve of patience and sympathy for even the most demanding of them. Perhaps because they had met a fate that even she, who did not fear death, had a dread of. MS was, she said, 'the worst disease of all' because, unlike dementia or Alzheimer's, the mind of the MS sufferer remains intact, a helpless witness, as the body progressively breaks down. She brought home many stories, the most common of which, and the most heart-rending, were those of the patients, both women and men, whose spouses had left them after their diagnoses, or, worse, after the patients' attacks had become regular and severe enough to require constant care, leaving them to live out the inevitable deterioration alone; that is, leaving them *to fend for themselves*. Unsurprisingly, it was at this time that my mother began to school us on our obligation to 'turn off the machine' if she ever became incapacitated or fell into a coma.

After a few years at this job, and as her legal retirement age approached, she did a course that trained her to become an exercise coach for people with MS. This then became her vocation, for which she travelled in her little car, packed with a portable stereo and a large bag of balls and sponges and plastic juggling sticks, to a number of different respite care homes, where she would help to transport the patients from their various wards to a common room, and together they would exercise to music. The motility of the patients varied greatly. Some could kick their legs out or raise their arms to catch a ball. Others were in wheelchairs. A number were barely able to move. Depending on who was in the class, my mother would adapt her routine. She might start with the fingers, then move on to the wrists, elbows, and arms. The neck, the head, and down through the body to the legs. After that, with the introduction of the props, things were liable to get raucous. A gentle ball game might quickly descend into a free-for-all. My mother often spoke of a young man, mostly paralysed—his mind, remember, unimpaired—who would call out (in joy? in despair?) whenever a ball landed on his lap. And of a woman who would always want to take a prop away with her, which meant my mother was continually making trips to toy shops to buy replacements.

'I basically work for free.'

And often, literally, she worked for free. When the budget of a particular centre was cut, or if the normal budget did not cover the summer months, she would continue to show up regardless. At a swimming pool in Tallaght, for instance, where she helped the patients to dress and undress, and to get in to the water, and to kick their legs, and to dance about, she kept going after they had ceased paying her for it.

'They'd miss it if I didn't go.'

Meaning: they would miss *me*.

My mother cared deeply for these people. She cared for them with an ease and a grace that had not been possible in her relationships with her husband or the rest of us. And she was not ignorant of her importance to them, either.

'It's the highlight of their week.'

I do not think this was a delusion of hers. I believe they did indeed look forward to seeing her, and that they loved her with a love that, unlike that which came from her husband, from us, her family, could not be mistaken for anything else.

This job she did until the pandemic put an end to it. In other words, what neither old age nor deafness nor the onset of dementia had been able to do, the new virus did. And she was distraught.

'I don't think I'll be going back to work after all of this ends,' she says sadly now, several times a day, as though trying to come to terms with the loss, trying to drum the reality of it into her head.

'This might be the moment to stop, all right,' I say. 'You're eighty, remember.'

'They'll miss me. No one else will do what I do.'

Because no one else will be grieving quite like her.

My mother has not had another romantic relationship since my father's death, nor has she shown any interest in forming one.

'She's fond of the men,' she says of a similarly aged acquaintance who has had a few dalliances since her husband died, and who still goes ballroom dancing and picks up dates. 'She'd like to meet someone. Can you imagine?'

'Yes,' I say (in the tone of a man in his forties living with his mother). 'Wouldn't you like company sometimes?'

She looks at me, horrified, as though I am suggesting she get into leather and kink. 'Another relationship would be death. Who would come up to your father's sense of humour?' Then she thinks for a second. 'Well, maybe to go to the cinema every once in a while. But other than that, no way.'

Another relationship would be death.

Meaning: *her next relationship would be with death.*

Meaning: *anything else, before that, would be suicide.*

I spoke earlier of feeling that my father, in life, had been a drag on me, and that his death had brought a sense of release from this. I would be surprised if my mother had not also felt this, or something like it, when he died. I wager that, in her private moments of mourning, she took some pleasure from the idea that being husbandless implied, as well as more responsibility and more difficulty, a new state of freedom. A freedom that would consist, if not in doing whatever she wanted, then certainly in doing far less of what she did not want to do: less cooking, fewer hospitals visits, that sort of thing. I do not think freedom is conferred, nor do I think it can be thought about uncomplicatedly, but I am convinced that immanent in my mother's grief was an awareness that with my father she had been trapped, or at least prevented from finding out the exact degree of freedom she was capable of, and that now it could be different. Here was a chance simply to be an individual, a woman—a mother and a grandmother when called upon, but the rest of the time a follower of her own rhythm, a keeper of her own habits.

The tragedy is that, in reality, what my mother got after my father's death, far from freedom, was an enforced second marriage, this time to my brother N.

Exit father, enter son.

Left alone in the house with N, with me as an unwilling witness, she, like a bride in an arranged match, launched into a duel-to-the-death with N. Converging on the empty space created by my father's absence, they charged at each other, and clashed, and fused together. The tragedy of this was that it disqualified my father's death from standing *as* my mother's tragedy. Rather than being the devastation out of which alternative modes of living sprouted, his death turned out merely to have cleared the ground on which a long, drawn-out campaign of conflict was waged—in the name of family, of love, and for that reason the true calamity—between two of the surviving forces.

In one camp, the son:

After my father's death, N got *worse*. (And maybe that was the case for all of us: that in whatever ways we were *bad* or *mad* before, we fell to an even lower standard.) The quantity of depression that could be contained in him without himself and others being severely hurt, N surpassed, doubled, trebled, and he was now unable to curb it. He was, on most days and most of the time, furious. He had come home from New York to be helped, and he was not being helped. Far from it, everyone was working against him, making things harder for him, *and now what, a suicide?* how could he ever achieve success in these conditions? His concerns were, by any external measure, valid and serious. Feelings of frustration would be, for anybody in a similar position—deserted at precisely the moment he needed support the most—natural and justifiable. Yet, even so, N's expenditure of anger and malice seemed to be in no proper relation to the subject itself. Not even grief could explain the magnitude of his rage. Nor was our father ever mentioned in his tirades. In point of fact, his outbursts were caused by trifles. The smaller the cause, it seemed, the larger the explosion. Suggesting that the whole bulk of his fury had already been present to begin with; only by chance did it happen to settle on one matter or another as a pretext for breaking out.

By insulting my mother, by browbeating her, he was boasting, actually, of his own wretchedness. Humiliating her with it. Making her a party to it. Blaming her for it. He suffered, therefore she would suffer. His hell was that of wanting the breast but being torn by guilt for hating the breast at the same time. She was his beloved mother—and openly, now, he despised her for being precisely that.

N's was a loathing so wild that it would not let him rest. At all times of the day, he strode to and fro around the house, stamping his feet, glaring, laughing, shouting, responding to voices, until he was infused with enough spite for another round and would burst into the kitchen—

'N, I don't want a fight,' my mother would say, pre-emptively, but it would already be too late.

He was in the grip of what Freud calls 'the omnipotence of thoughts'. A state in which the consciousness is overwhelmed by a frenzied cycle of eruptions, irruptions, and interruptions: words and images piling into the mind and demanding attention and appearing to have great importance, before being swallowed up by different words and images that appear to have even greater importance, though in fact they are merely more of the same. By going to our mother, by constantly setting on her, he was probably trying to find an escape from this mental barrage. Perhaps he believed she could provide him with something that would stop it or settle it down. When she could not, it meant more disappointment and frustration for him, more chaos and confusion, for which she, now, could be held liable.

As far as I could see, from my admittedly skewed position on the sidelines, this was all he gained from his attacks on her: the right, according to his own unconscious logic, to blame her for his own attacks. To keep her as his scapegoat. Other than this, she seemed to have no real function for him. When she was not needed by him in this capacity, she disappeared from his view, became irrelevant, and he was alone again with his voices.

The voices that addressed him.

The voices that were inserted into his mind.

The voices that came from different places in the room.

The voices that came from different parts of the world.

The voices that had nothing to do with him.

The audible voices.

The arguing voices.

The persecuting voices.

The voices commenting on his actions.

The voices influencing the feelings in his body.

The voices transmitting other people's thoughts through him.

The voices that needed to be answered.

The voices he obeyed.

The voices he disobeyed.

The voices with whom he could relate.

The voices that prevented him from feeling togetherness with others.

The voices that kept him from feeling at home in the world.

The voices that he could not share.

The voices that kept him safe in isolation.

The voices that stopped him from doing anything spontaneously.

The voices that only he understood.

The voices that, if spoken out, would be misunderstood.

The voices that ruptured the link between intelligence and feeling.

The voices that set the highest standards for his life.

The voices that, nevertheless, pushed him closer and closer to the edge of the ravine.

With these voices, thanks to them, he was living on the lip of insanity. Yet at all times, in the background, behind his abstruse utterances, there remained a personality which could not be called anything except sane. This personality stood looking on, so to speak. And occasionally it moved to the foreground and made altogether sensible remarks and objections. Which, because they marked such a departure from the meanness and the senselessness of what came before, made him seem almost wise.

'Sometimes he speaks more sense than the people in wigs going into the Four Courts,' my mother would say about these apparent moments of clarity.

Nevertheless, engaging him on his ideas, devoting attention to the meaningful connections in his speech, orientating oneself to him in such a way as to leave open the possibility of understanding him, as my mother occasionally tried to do, rarely achieved much. More often than not, N refused to be held to what he had said. He did not like to be tied down to a position, even one he had only just propounded, for this was tantamount to admitting that he possessed a discrete, unified personality, one that could be comprehended, apprehended by others, and *that* he had to avoid.

In the time it took my mother to get a conversation with N up and running, he was already interested in something else, and felt annoyed with her for being unable to keep up with his mental movements. And it was *his* mental movements that were of supreme importance. He was so self-absorbed that what my mother was thinking, beyond anything relating to his enrichment or nourishment, was immaterial to him—and how *could* he care for a world outside himself when the world inside was in disorder?—with the result that she stopped sharing her honest thoughts with him and learned only to defend herself from him. And, predictably enough, her first line of defence was attack.

In the other camp, the widow:

Towards N, my mother was capable of showing restraint. Several times I witnessed her giving him the leeway to behave erratically when another person, another mother, might have felt compelled to shut him down. She understood that it was terribly hard for him to stop being the way he was. He had no choice, for he could not bear the world, and she could genuinely see why he might feel this way. (She had, buried within her, an artist's mentality, which incorporated an admiration for people who went beyond the bounds of everyday consciousness and sought out the irrational. Moreover, as a leftist, she was aware that the more that critical reason dominates, the more impoverished life becomes, leaving the way free for political absolutism and fascism to rise. 'Under the dominion of overvalued reason the individual is pauperised,' as Jung says.) She was, in a word, sensitive enough to grasp that N's accusations against her related to his failure to become an artist, or his failure even to want to be an artist, in spite of his potential, which was the same as failing to become a person. Without a vocation, a *métier*, an art, an interest, he was lost. And having been lost for so long now, he was desperate, devoid of hope. Long gone was any chance of being loved, and he was quickly forgetting what it was like to be liked.

Even knowing this, she could not bring herself to like him. For liking him equalled *being like* him, being the same as him, hence losing herself to him, in him. At the end of the day, hating him, and being hated by him, was easier for my mother because it threatened less of her identity. Perhaps, after all, there was such a thing as persistent depravity on which kindness and forgiveness were wasted? Goodness was getting her nowhere. Giving him advice, giving him money, giving him whatever he asked for: none of it was bringing about any change. On the contrary, the giving itself—because it rarely came fast enough or generously enough—served only to provoke or aggravate his madness. When he got out of control, for example by taking the framed pictures off the wall—his own paintings which had she made a point of putting up—and throwing them around, she would call my brother R, who, acting as a surrogate for my father, would come to the house and scold N and tell him enough was enough. Any more of this and he would be thrown out and the locks (what locks?) would be changed.

But in N's eyes, our father had only ever been a paper tiger. The authority that R was trying to replace had been an outward show only, lacking substance. As a result, for N, there was always more.

At first, he would, in apparent good faith, make a display of contrition. To which my mother would listen without ever, I do not think, accepting. (I certainly never saw her apologise to him in return, for her own part in the struggle.) But then, sometimes in only a matter of minutes, the antagonism between them would again seep, break, burst out. And for as long as they lived under the same roof, it was—simply *was*—going to be this way.

After a few months of useless combat, my mother called St J——'s Hospital, thinking that they might be able to help (and believing, I think, that they owed her a favour or two). The whole family was called in for a group session. On arrival, we were brought to a small office, where a young woman, a doctor of some kind, who had obviously been briefed about what our father had done in the ward upstairs, asked us some questions. *How can I help?*

My brother R spoke first and went on the longest. My mother and my sister made some shorter interventions. I did not open my mouth. I had chosen silence, for, on stepping into the room, I had instantly seen the absurdity of our being there. One group session, offered by the hospital authorities out of a sense of obligation and quite possibly as a measure to avoid litigation, was not even going to scratch the surface of the problem; in fact, it risked making it worse. *The problem?* I am talking about N, of course. He, and not my father's death, was the reason we were all sitting there. He was the subject of the conversation. As much as R and the others, with their considerate tone and careful choice of words, tried to make it sound like they were not ganging up on him, it was clear that he was the conundrum they wanted the doctor's help in solving. N, sensing this, lashed out by calling us, the whole family, 'pathetic' and 'poor'. R, who needed no more provocation than this, pounced on him: 'What are you talking about, *poor*? Do you even know what being poor means? Let me tell you, it means having no options. *You* have options.'

I closed my eyes and pinched the bridge of my nose. R was trying to help. But he did not live in the house with my mother and N. He did not see what they were doing to each other on a daily basis. Therefore he did not, could not comprehend just how poor they actually were. How poor we all were. Our options had long run out.

At around this time, if not at this very meeting, it dawned on my mother that N's problems—his madness, his badness—were not going to resolve themselves spontaneously, just because we willed them to. She began to see that his problems were nothing less than his identity, one based on defending himself against a hostile world, which he was not going to give up without a savage fight. By demanding that he change his (problematic) identity, she was effectively demanding that he open himself up, that he become vulnerable. And, as long as he fought against this demand, as long as he struggled to maintain the integrity of his defensive walls, she would be stuck in the role of the sieging army, the sacker, the dispossessor. The siege would be endless, there would always be more to sack, more to dispossess, and he would remain *her* problem forever. The conclusion she came to, gradually but irrepressibly, was this: if she was ever going to get N some proper help, by which she meant some other place for him to live and someone else to dispossess him of his insanity, she needed to get him diagnosed.

Which is to say: she needed to get an official stamp certifying the existence of that part of N which she hated. The part of him which she had for so long tried to deny. The part of him which she believed to be false but which, for her own sake, she now desperately needed to be true.

Honestly, I do not think my mother believed that N *had* an illness, like having a cold. She used to say that he was 'unwell', but by this I do not think she was implying that he had 'got' madness in the way that one might have a material possession, or a virus. She understood, rather, that he had come to experience and behave in the world in ways that were strange and tiresome and incomprehensible to most people, including himself, and that, at most, this experience and behaviour fell into certain broad categories of mental dysfunction. (She was probably even aware that to get anywhere with him, to bring about any change in him, he would have to be known in relation *to her*: that what N was to her determined considerably what she was to him, and hence his actions.) But my mother, who knew N better than anyone, also knew that he was on course to destroy himself (to prove that he was really alive) and that, if she allowed him to stay close to her, he would destroy her, too. In seeking a diagnosis, she was not hoping for a cure for N. She was not naive enough to think that a diagnosis would increase her, or anyone's, understanding of him. All she was doing—and I admire her for it—was trying to save herself.

From then on, she was a woman on a mission. She sent letters. Made phone calls. Knocked on doors. Queued up in wards and government offices. To anyone who showed the slightest hint of interest, she set forth her plight, and was sure to ring them again afterwards to drive home the case.

'I can't die and leave this problem to you,' she used to say to us, N's siblings. 'This has to be sorted before I go.'

When eventually the diagnosis *was* sorted, and N put on medication, her assignment then became to get the newly labelled 'disabled' N onto benefits and, crucially, onto the housing list. *Independent living* emerged in her vocabulary as a favoured turn of phrase. Used synonymously with 'the promised land'.

'He'd have his own little flat. But someone would come and check up on him. Make sure he's taking his meds and not living in his own filth.'

I doubt that N believed he had a disease, either. Even after his diagnosis, he did not form any lasting attachment to the terminology of the medical condition assigned to him; he rarely used it to describe himself. I can remember him doing so on only one occasion, and even then he sounded unsure of the words. It seemed to me that he was merely testing them out. Seeing what impact they had on himself and others when spoken aloud. After that, I never heard him use those words again. I do suspect, however, that he internalised the idea of himself *as a problem*. That because we, his family, approached him as a problem, he, too, began to conceive of himself as such. Nothing else explains why he, the raging bull, so willingly accompanied my mother to the medical appointments and the social-worker visits. Or why he signed whatever forms needed to be signed to be officially classed as disabled. Or why he went on the agreed date to collect his meds, and took them, even though he did not like the effect they were having on him. (Increasing his appetite and making him fat. Dulling his mind. Robbing him of his creative impulses.)

Sure, he had his moments of rebellion. Every so often, he would come off the tablets or adjust the dose. And he refused to give up smoking dope, even though this was strictly prohibited by the prescribing doctors and later got him thrown out of more than one residence of independent living. But this does not take away from the fact that, during the process of getting a diagnosis, in the face of assorted familial and bureaucratic commands, he did what he was told. He got with the programme. In short, he was docile.

N was, and is, more than anything else, simply human. Yet at that moment he was pathologised, turned into a problem greater than that which he or his mother or his family could be expected to straighten out by themselves. A problem so great, so extravagant that science has not yet found an answer to it. Which released us from the obligation to know him, for all we could really know about him was that he was unknowable. From now on, we were, in good conscience, able to refuse to adapt to him, to withdraw from him, to make a start, that is, on our own road to *independent living.*

The third front, the daughter:

At this time, my sister, too, became unwell. She developed a syndrome whereby she would get severe cramps whenever and whatever she ate. Initially, she blamed the elements of her diet themselves and, on the advice of alternative medical practitioners, began to eliminate certain of them. But this changed nothing. Anything at all that went down her gullet, regardless of its composition or its consistency, caused her pain. Already thin, she lost weight at a dramatic rate, and within a matter of months she was being fed through her nose in the anorexic ward of St V——'s Hospital.

This—the not eating—was my sister's cry. She needed to cry, and to do so at this volume—that is, a deafening silence—because we, the rest of us, were refusing even to whimper. In our weakness, we were acting too strong, and she had to bear the brunt of this. As well as for herself, she was crying for all of us.

So little did I appreciate this generous gesture of hers that I refused to visit her. I had done enough hospital visiting for my father, I thought. I had no intention of doing the same for her. She had a duty, we all did, to hold herself back from this sort of self-inflicted, added suffering. (Yes, such holding back was itself a kind of suffering, perhaps the only kind that can truly be avoided—yes! yes! I realised this!—but at least, and this was not nothing, it did not expect succour from others. It left people well enough alone. Suddenly, a regime of repression seemed highly desirable. I would gladly be its enforcer.)

After some days and much goading from my mother, I relented and agreed to go to the hospital. By my sister's bed, also visiting, were an uncle and a neighbour. There were not enough seats, so I sat a little apart on the windowsill. The visitors made small talk while my sister sat in the bed, with the tube taped to her nose, and peered around, too feeble to contribute, and I think at some point she cried. I cannot say for sure because I could not look at her. I had caught a glimpse of her on entering, but I immediately defended myself against this mental picture; indeed, I defended myself so well against it that, sitting by the bed, I could not take my sister's predicament as seriously as I might have liked to, could not feel the deep feelings I might have felt. I could not take the risk involved in comforting or supporting her: the risk, that is, of 'catching' all this madness like a cold.

The final frontier, me:

By this point, I was already making my concrete plans to leave Ireland. I did not deny to myself or others that my planned leave-taking was anything other than the rage of rejection taken out on my surrounding environment: the place I was born, its culture and its people, especially my family, most of all my mother. My rejection, my rage, when it was not spewing over all of this, was aimed at *her*, or rather at the idea that this particular mother was the only one I would and could ever have. Within me, I felt a sort of diffusion of desire: in going abroad, I would lose her, but by spreading my bets and finding others to take me in, I would ultimately gain through being well insured against feeling this abandonment again.

While waiting for my savings to rise to a level that would cover the costs of my departure, I watched this intra-familial war unfold, as though experiencing a dream. What I saw had an unreal quality to it. As though what I was witnessing were an already vanishing past. These were people and events that might once have had something to do with me, but they no longer did, for I belonged to a future time. All of this, now, was a bad memory.

But this sense of dreaminess, far from unreality, was in fact the very real outcome of my belief that I was merely an observer on the periphery and not an active participant. That things were happening around me, terrible things, in which I was not a factor. I was not, I believed, inflicting any damage, nor, thanks to my first-rate defences, was I being damaged. Like N, I was totally identified with my mind and therefore lived under the illusion that my body did not take up any space in the world. And, like my father, I actually thought that by staying out of a fight I was not adding to it, or by walking out of a room, or leaving a country, I was free-ing myself from the difficulties it contained.

What a lie this was.

A lie that I continued to tell myself even as I fought wildly with my mother, and with N.

Even as I openly disdained my sister.

Unthinkingly, I was becoming unthinking, in other words taking after the men in the family, which as an orientation was mistaken; it would lead to dangers. Moving in that direction, I would cause a lot of hurt to myself and to others. It would take me many more years to finally get the message. The warning. That perception implies involvement.

In my Big Dream, I am looking from the edge of a room at a family scene. Because the room has only two walls, nothing inside is hidden from me. I am party to everything that takes place. Yet I remain separate, on the margins. It does not feel like my presence is having any influence on what I see. Contrary to the maxim that the observer changes the experiment, it seems that my being there, as far as the course or the outcome of events are concerned, is the same as my not being there.

So I turn away—*what difference does it make?*—in search of somewhere to close my eyes. (Whether I am looking or not looking, awake or unconscious, seems to be of no consequence to the world.) Now with my back to the room, facing into blackness, I discover a mattress lying on the floor, half in the light and half in the dark, and I lie down on it.

Here it is comfortable, but I do not find rest. This is because the mattress is filled with water, so that every small movement I make creates a wave underneath me that rolls down the entire length of my body. In defiance of my craving for stillness, I am kept in motion, always on the move, never stopping.

At a certain point, I notice that the mattress, too, is floating. My bed is doubling as a raft. But it is not going anywhere. Although there are no walls preventing it from moving out into the darkness, it is not setting sail. Rather, it is staying here in this in-and-out place, anchored exactly halfway between light and dark. And I cannot be sure whether the panic I feel about this derives from my inability to get away, or from my knowledge that this *is* away.

I went to Kyoto first, the furthest possible distance, but, feeling undernourished by the culture there, at turns too restrained and too blaring, I soon came home. What I found on my return was a situation even worse than I had left. I had known, on leaving, that my mother and N should not be allowed to live alone together. That they would be the end of each other. Any social worker looking at their situation would have demanded an immediate separation. Something had to be done. But I did not have any solutions, and I was not going to stay around to try to find any, nor did my mother want me to.

'Go and live,' she said.

As soon as I had saved enough money, I did. This time to Rome. There, although I learned the language quickly and well, I did not find the love that I presumed to be waiting for me, I mean I did not find it *quickly enough*, and I was desperately lonely. Most of my time was spent working at mind-numbing freelance jobs to survive, leaving me little time or energy to do the great writing that I had moved to the city to do. I contemplated returning to Dublin and on many occasions was close to doing so, until the thought of being in the house with my mother and N filled me with dread, and I put a halt to those plans.

I did not call my mother often. At most, for a couple of minutes, once every couple of months. By not telling her much about my life, I was trying to stay out of hers. I wanted to get her, everything about her, out of my head. If I was failing, it was because I had never broken up with her properly. So, at Christmas, on one of my irregular visits, I left her a note. After witnessing a particularly bloodthirsty altercation between her and N, I went to my room and wrote down what I really thought of her. (Her, not N, for these words were bent on returning to the source.)

I'm not coming here again, I wrote. *It's not healthy. You are hard and cold. Your behaviour disgusts me. You're NOT MY FAMILY.*

And, instead of holding on to it, keeping it for myself until it was time to burn it, I put it on the kitchen table as I was leaving for the airport early in the morning.

As bad and as mad as anything N had ever done.

Back in Rome, unattached now, I lived an outwardly healthy life. I took long walks and went to the gym and ate well and got the sun. I grew my hair long and changed my style of clothes. I read and finally began to write. In bed at night, however, after another day spent without speaking to anyone else, I binged on pastries and chocolate until I was sick, after which I fell into long, uneasy slumbers. I would wake in the morning as though coming out of a void, with no memory of where I had just been.

Until one night my father came. The dream was, and remains, so vivid, and holds such significance for me, that I consider it my first Big Dream and the source of my other Big Dreams.

We are in the car driving down the road of the estate, away from the house. He is behind the wheel, of course, and I am beside him in the passenger seat. At the exit of the estate, a T-junction, he stops the car. There is no reason for him to stop, because there are no cars coming on the main road. Without looking in the mirror, I feel secure in the knowledge that there are no cars behind us, either. We are alone in the world.

The sun is shining and this feels like an opportunity.

I turn to him. He is wearing beige, as he often did. His face remains in profile. He does not turn to face me even though he can feel me staring at him.

I put a hand on his shoulder. The sensation of this—the material of his coat and, under that, the tautness of his muscle— is real. I have no doubt, in the dream, that I am in the material world and this is happening.

'Dad,' I say.

He does not acknowledge me.

'Dad,' I say again.

He continues to look out through the windscreen, squinting against the strong light.

'Dad,' I say a third time—and now finally he turns to me.

Our eyes meet. By the expression on his face, I cannot tell if he is happy or sad.

'Dad, are you okay?' I ask then.

And as I wait for the answer, which never comes, I can feel that I am crying.

I woke up crying from this dream. That is, I was already crying when I came into consciousness. The crying, tears and all, began while I had my eyes closed and was still asleep, which was something that had never happened to me before and has not happened since (and today I wonder if it is even a physiological possibility). I lay in bed and continued to weep for a long time: a complete experience, one that allowed nothing other than itself.

When it finally wasted and I got up, I found myself to be in an altered state. I felt hung-over, except instead of dullness in my mind there was a kind of curiosity. In the bathroom mirror, I saw myself, as though for the first time. I saw the skin and the flesh. And the hair. And the eyes. I saw the volume of me. And, seeing that, I felt my weight.

I pulled at the flesh of my cheeks. *I am a body*, I thought. *I am cells that take up space and can be seen and think they are me.*

I glanced away from the mirror, then glanced back.

And for an instant I saw myself, I think, as my father in the car would have seen me.

There was no hiding it. I was here. Not on the perimeter, because there was no perimeter. Not at the centre, either, because where would that even be? What it was, I was simply in. And there was no out.

In the weeks after my father's death, a lot of people had asked me, *why did he do it?*

Soon after I had left the note for my mother, my sister called and asked me, *why did you do it?*

These were not questions that the face in the mirror thought to ask me now. Not because they were silly questions, or ones not worth asking, but because they were questions that I was not yet equipped to consider; they were question for later years.

For now, baby steps.

Fatherless, motherless: one foot in front of the other.

Are you okay?

INTERLUDE: HORTA DE SANT JOAN, 2013

Outside a village called Horta de Sant Joan (population one thousand) in the Els Ports mountain range in Catalonia, in a farmhouse at the foot of a dramatic peak called Santa Bárbara, I lived with J, a man twenty years my senior, cultured and worldly and wealthy, whom I esteemed as a mentor and protector, and whose company, in that paradise, felt like an exquisite revenge for the years of unhappiness in Ireland and the pitiful education I believed I had received there: in the mornings we took the dogs to the top of the peak or to the nearby ravine for a river swim, then in the afternoons we separated, each to his own little office, where I worked on my first novel, which by now was close to completion, and in the evenings, when we came together, we would eat by the fire and read and watch films; a simple life, special precisely because it was so ordinary, so unselfconscious—natural beauty was simply what was there, culture was simply what was done every day—and I almost could not believe, after years of constant agitation to get away to this ideal place, that I had arrived at it; yet underneath the new calm, layered over the new happiness, coming after the new melancholy, threaded through the new writing, was anxiety, which forced me to acknowledge that to be remote from others, even when I desired it, necessarily constituted a loss, and that when I wrote, I was doing so in order that, one day, I might be read by the same people I was supposed to have rejected, that contained within my writing was a rebellion—against certain systems, against certain ideas, against certain tribes—but also a plea for belonging; but for now my writing, as yet unpublished, had only one reader, J, whom

I had come to rely on as a patient relies on his therapist, as someone uniquely positioned to understand me and to return this understanding to me, a situation which was further complicated by the fact that, while we were still affectionate with each other, J and I no longer made love, our connection now being more psychical than physical, which was no small thing, the intensity of the experience was not dampened as a result, our relationship seemed only to get more pressurised as we both tried to wring what goodness we could out of each other's minds, which gave me some insight into why some people describe relationships as a sort of brainwashing: since I was hearing only one voice for weeks and months on end, it became hard to distinguish between what I was thinking and what I was hearing, between what had come from me and what had come from him, and maybe ultimately there is no difference, maybe the idea of owning a thought is a delusion, but this wisdom was only available to me in hindsight, after our vicious rows, our violent attempts at disentanglement and our equally violent attempts at re-entanglement, had ended, and in the aftermath of these battles, when my throat was raw from screaming and the poison collected in my brain had seeped down into the rest of my muscles, I fled the house and rushed to the mountains, hoping that I could rediscover there a part of myself that was uncontaminated, still pure: I walked and walked, and sometimes I thought that this—the walking—was all I truly possessed, that if I lost everything—relationship, dogs, farmhouse, ambition—it would be okay because I would not have lost the capacity to walk; with just a glass of water and a few morsels of rice in my stomach, I would be able to follow this path and climb this slope and reach this summit and look out across the plains to the west and the crests and gorges to the east, and there would be nothing stopping me, either, from approaching the edge, and allowing the sensation of vertigo to overcome me, and, if on a certain day I saw no reason to go back down the mountain, I could even succumb to the desire to step off: but before that could happen, I had to get through a visit from my mother, whom I felt impelled to convince that I had found my place in the world, that I had *arrived*, but she was not persuaded; as much as she enjoyed the mountain walks and the river swims, as much as she adored the dogs, as much as she appreciated the good food and the warm weather, as much as she liked J and believed he was good for me, she could also see the amount of mental work I was expending in keeping all the components of this scene in place and upright, she did not believe the life I was showing her was going to last, she suspected that sooner or later I would tire myself out trying to turn a dream into a feasible situation, at which point I would do what I had always done, I would run away; and, God, how I hate that she could see through me like this, how it hurt to know that in her eyes I had not changed, that I was still her child, and the only thing that consoled me was the thought that, if indeed I had not grown up, if I had failed to thrive on my own terms, then she must have been partly to blame—*if I was travelling the world looking for a home, was it not because she had failed to create a proper home for me? if I was so afraid of people that I felt the need to live apart from them, was it not because she had not protected me from them when they were being cruel to me? and if I was working this hard to build a beautiful setting in which to play out my life, was it not because the setting she had built for me as a child was so ugly?*—so after a pleasant week in her company, on the day of her departure, in the car on the way to the airport, I could not stop myself from punishing her for all of this, 'When you were saying goodbye to J,' I said to her, 'you didn't invite him to Dublin, you didn't ask him to visit, that was very rude of you,' and the truth was I did not care whether or not my mother had invited J to Dublin, and I did not believe she had purposely been rude, my purpose was merely to jab at her weakest spot, to hit her where I knew it would hurt (on the face of it, I was merely calling her forgetful or thoughtless, but in her mind I might as well have been calling her a whore) and she was quick to defend herself, but I did not back down, the opposite, I intensified my attacks, which she parried with what sounded to me like further provocations, and in no time we had returned to the past, from which there was no exit except through the fire: a departure hall of a small regional airport, throngs of holiday-makers, blaring public announcements, screaming children, and ringing out above it all was my mother's voice, 'You have hurt me, do you hear me, Gavin? *You have hurt me,*' as I walked away from her, out the door, into the heat of the car park, and on the drive back to paradise I felt no remorse, as far as I was concerned my actions had been justified, she had had it coming for a long time, I did not care that this rupture I had caused would probably take months to heal; my only concern, now, was to get to the house and change into my hiking clothes and go with the dogs to the top of Santa Bárbara, where I would sit near the edge and feel the breeze on my face, and maybe, if I felt brave enough, look down.

CELL VI

It is after midnight, and I am washing my face at the bathroom sink. My mother comes to stand at the open door. She has been sleeping for a couple of hours, so her cheeks are puffy and creased.

'Did you just come into my room?'

'No.'

'Look at me. Did you?'

I am topless and have a towel tied around my waist. With my mother's gaze on me like this, I become conscious of my thinness and the tattoos covering my arms and running onto my torso.

'No.'

'Look at me in the eyes and tell me.'

I take a small towel off the radiator and press my face into it. Then I turn to meet her eyes. There is, I see now, genuine distress in them.

'No.'

'I could have sworn you walked across my room.'

'Well, I didn't.'

'I could have sworn.'

The next morning, coming into the main room, I find her at the table with a pen in her hand, its nib hovering over an old envelope. *When there is confusion, make a list.*

'You all right, Mum?'

I ask her this because she is staring blankly at the wall.

'I'm becoming confused,' she says. 'I don't know what's a dream and what's not.'

'What did you dream?'

'My childhood friend. You know, the one in the nursing home?'

'Yes.'

'I don't know—. Is she dead?'

I am not entirely sure. There have been phone calls from the friend's daughter, but when my mother relays to others—to me or to her other friends—what she thinks she heard on these calls, she gives conflicting accounts. To one person, she says her friend is sick. To another, she says her friend died last month.

'You sent a card to the family yesterday, didn't you? Was it a sympathy card? Or just a card saying you were thinking of them?'

'I'm not sure.'

'You don't remember what kind of card it was?'

'No.'

'Or what you wrote.'

'No. I dreamt I was going to visit her in the nursing home but was unable to get there.'

'Well, that's true. You can't enter a nursing home these days. You're not allowed.'

'But is she dead?'

'Yesterday you told me her daughter had called to say she'd died.'

'That's right.'

'Did her daughter really call you? Or was that a dream?'

'I'm not sure.'

I take the list from her. 'Look, don't worry about it now. And forget about buying any of this. I'm responsible for the shopping, all right?'

She goes for her walk and comes back with a single bag of shopping: bread, blueberries, yoghurts, a block of cheese, a bar of dark chocolate, the newspaper. Nothing that is needed. Certainly nothing that would amount to a meal.

'Good timing,' I say, bringing a pot of proper food to the table. 'This is ready.'

'I didn't walk fast today. I feel as though I've barely exercised.'

'You've been gone for four hours.'

'More of a ramble, really.'

The bright morning has turned into a dull afternoon, and her clothes are wet from the rain. As she removes them and divides them amongst the different rails for drying, she says, 'People have gone awful neurotic. They're nervy. They see me coming and dive off the path onto the road. Like I've got the virus seeping from my pores. Thank God I'm not like that.'

She has a shower and changes into dry clothes. We eat, and afterwards she sits in her chair with a cup of tea and looks out at the rain: 'It's great not to have to go out in that now.'

She reads a little and then does the crossword until, overcome by tiredness, she puts the pen down, folds her arms loosely across her abdomen, puts her head back onto the headrest, and closes her eyes. When she wakes up, about an hour or so later, the rain has stopped and an evening sun is shining. She gets up, arranges a few things in the kitchen, goes in and out of the bedroom a couple of times, then the bathroom, then back into the bedroom to change. Finally, she comes out dressed for a walk.

'I'm going out to get the paper.'

'You've got the paper. There, look.'

I point towards the chair she has only recently vacated.

'That's yesterday's.'

'You bought it this morning. Check the date.'

She does not check the date. Instead, with a perplexed expression, she peers out the window.

'What time is it?'

'Seven in the evening.'

'That's impossible. I've already been to bed.'

'You had a nap sitting in your chair.'

'So this day isn't over? I've to live through the rest of it?'

'Afraid so.'

When I get up the next morning, I notice that her breakfast things are still on the kitchen counter, untouched. My mother likes to prepare her breakfast before going to bed at night. She pours muesli into a bowl and covers it with a piece of kitchen towel. Then she washes some blueberries and puts them to dry on the draining board. A teabag in a cup. A clean plate and a knife. A loaf of bread, covered in a tea-towel, on the board. When she wakes up, at six or seven, she goes to retrieve these goodies. Adds yoghurt to the muesli. Wets the tea. Makes toast. Brings it all back into bed, where she eats sitting propped up by pillows and reading a novel.

I pop my head into her room and see that she is still asleep. This is unusual but not something that worries me. I leave to exercise and do the shopping. When I get back, the breakfast is still there and she is still in bed—alive, I can hear her breathing—but frozen, it seems, in the identical position.

Her eyes open.

'Hi Mum.'

'Hi love.'

'Are you all right?'

'Just a bit tired.'

'Well, stay where you are, then.'

'I just overdid it, I think.'

'Have a rest.'

I make lunch.

'Are you going to eat something?'

'I don't think so.'

'Are you feeling fluey?'

'A little.'

I bring her a Lemsip and a big glass of water.

'Sit up and drink this.'

'There might be something going round.'

'No shit.'

'What do you mean?'

'I mean the pandemic, Mum.'

'Oh, that. All I have is a little cold.'

'We should get you tested.'

'Don't be ridiculous.'

Surreptitiously, whispering on the phone so my mother does not hear, I order a test. I am given an appointment at a test centre on a requisitioned naval ship docked on the quays.

'How am I supposed to get her there?' I ask the woman.

'Don't you have a car?' she says.

'No.'

'Oh.'

'So?'

'Well—'

'She has symptoms. I can hardly put her on the bus.'

'No.'

'And will a taxi take her?'

'Maybe.'

'*Where are you off to? The test centre on the quays, please.*'

'I see what you mean. I don't know what to say to you. Is there no one else that can give her a lift in?'

In the end, my brother R rents a car. I put a mask over her face and fresh surgical gloves on her hands.

'Don't touch anything. Keep your hands on your lap. Let R open and close the door for you. And keep away from people. All right?'

'Are we going to need money?' she says.

'For what?'

'The test.'

'Jesus Christ. The test is free. Have you been listening to what I've been saying?'

On her return a couple of hours later, she describes the experience: 'We couldn't even stop for coffee on the way home.'

She stays indoors for the next few days while we wait for the result. Physically, she is feeling much better. She hoovers and waters the plants. Eats well. Does lots of reading. But I can tell she is nervous. That she will not be able to feel fully well until she has been told that she *is* well.

Finally, I get a call with the result.

I find her at the sink in the bathroom, rubbing cream into her face.

'They called.'

She stops rubbing and turns to look at me. Her eyes shiver. She is not breathing.

'It's negative.'

After days of presuming, still it comes as a great relief to hear it said: 'Oh, thank God.'

Six years ago, on a bright May morning in 2014, I received an email from my agent, R, telling me that she had received an offer for my debut novel. It was a respectable offer, she said, from an excellent editor. She would iron out the details and call me later in the day. 'In the meantime, plan your celebrations. You are now an author.'

I read this on the toilet in the little shower room attached to the bedroom I shared with my then boyfriend, Y. Y had taken the shower-room door off the hinges, making it possible to communicate between the toilet and the bed. He was still under the covers and was going to be late for work. I had already showered and was about to leave.

'Y,' I said. 'I sold the book.'

His head appeared from under the duvet. On one side, his grey curls were standing high off his scalp; on the other side, they were flattened. Squinting, he blinked a few times but did not say anything.

'Did you hear me?'

'I heard you.'

'My agent is going to call me later with the details.'

'Uhuhn.'

He flopped back down onto the pillow and disappeared under the covers.

I left the flat in a state of exhilaration that even Y could not undermine—for it was my own, completely and utterly and indestructibly my own—and set off on my walk. From Haggerston along Regent's Canal to Angel. Through Myddelton Square Gardens and Percy Circus. Across Grays Inn Road into Bloomsbury. There, I had a choice of places in which to spend my day because an academic friend had, quite illegally, loaned me a card that gave me access to all the University College libraries. At first, out of a fear of being found out, I had stuck to a specific building which had an automated entrance gate, but soon, gaining confidence, I was breezing between different buildings, saluting the security guards, and acknowledging with a nod those students and lecturers whose faces had become familiar. When I got bored of one spot, I went in search of another—somewhere with less noise, older rooms, more character— though I returned most often to Senate House because the tables there were separated one from the other, cut into little alcoves facing the windows, offering both seclusion and interesting views over the city.

That morning, I entered Senate House by the Russell Square gate. An hour had passed since I had left the flat and I still had not figured out how I was going to celebrate, though I had made a mental list of the people to whom I was going to tell the news first. *Would I call my mother or send the news through my sister?* Just as I was approaching the door, my phone rang: an unrecognised number. Presuming it to be someone or something related to the book deal, I answered.

A woman's voice: 'Gavin McCrea?'

I was excited: 'Speaking!'

Serious: 'I'm calling from the M—— Clinic.'

Blank: 'From where?'

'The M—— Clinic. You did a sexual-health screen with us two weeks ago.'

Did I?

'Oh.'

It was true. I had. On Y's insistence, we had gone together. Personally, I had not seen the point of it. We had exchanged negative test results at the start of our relationship and had made a pact of monogamy. Nevertheless, Y had been resolute, it seemed he needed the extra reassurance, so I went along.

'You need to come to the clinic, Mr McCrea.'

I need to what?

The earth had begun to spin. I thought I might faint. I found a wall nearby and fell back against it. I was a good gay. An upstanding gay. An integrated gay. A gay on the make. A romance-and-poetry gay. An

'I-don't-go-to-saunas' gay. A gay-marriage kind of gay. Gays like me were not supposed to be *called in.*

'Is it HIV?'

'Do you want me to tell you over the phone?'

'Go ahead.'

'Yes, it's HIV.'

Suddenly the world stopped spinning and the objects of the world appeared extremely distinct and impossibly close. The grey bricks of the Senate House tower were stacked in perfect lines, thousands of them, reaching into the sky; each and every one was within touching distance.

I don't understand. How—?

'How?' I said.

'I'm sorry, I—'

'No, *I'm* sorry. I don't know why I asked that. Of course I know how. I'm on my way.'

Without pausing to collect myself, I powered through the doors of Senate House. Instead of heading left to the lifts, as I normally did, I went straight through the other doors on the opposite side, bringing me out onto Malet Street. Turning right, and walking fast, I passed the Royal Academy of Dramatic Art—where in another life I might have gone, and where this would not be happening—then came onto Torrington Place, then Huntley Street, then Capper Street, and was at the clinic and sitting in front of a doctor in under ten minutes.

'Is it possible there has been a mistake?'

'No.'

'Is there anything I can do?'

'Based on our analyses, you contracted the virus within the last three months. You've been diagnosed early, which is good. But it's too late to take post-exposure prophylaxis. For PEP to work, you have to take it within seventy-two hours of possible exposure.'

'In the last three months did you say?'

'We can't be completely precise. But, yes, it's a recent infection.'

I collapsed forward onto my lap: 'Oh, Y. What have you done?'

'Who's Y?'

'My boyfriend.'

'Well, it's not *his* fault, is it?'

'What do you mean?'

'You can't blame anyone else. You're responsible for your own body. You took the risk.'

Live a little. Take a chance. Stop worrying. Relax. What are the odds? Nothing ventured. Try your luck. Bend the rules. Get away with it. Have the nerve. Take the leap. Be in the moment. Don't be so—

Yes, there was all of that. But also:

Do it to show you can. Do it to prove you will. Do it to ensnare him. Do it because you want to trust him, even though you don't. Do it because you are the exception. Do it because there is no better protection than monogamy. Do it so as not to be so—

Love as prophylaxis.

I had met Y only a year previously. After finishing the novel, I had left Horta de Sant Joan—and J—to take up a teaching post at a university two hours from London. I had been signed by my agent, R, and now, in the evening after my classes, I was doing some final edits to the manuscript with a view to making submissions to editors in the near future. I was, I felt, finally on the cusp of a career, though I did not say this aloud, and I did not give myself permission to relax. A debut was, after all, merely a debut. It proved little. A second book would have to be written, and promptly, and needless to say it would have to be good. With this in mind, I was already gathering materials and making reading lists and planning a means of supporting myself financially for the next couple of years. At the same time, and with the same sense of urgency and determination—for it was, to my way of thinking, part of the same larger project of sculpting a rounded life for myself—I set about researching the best way to find a new boyfriend in the fast-forming digital age (an age to which, during the previous years living with J in rural Spain, I had been more or less oblivious).

MANAGE YOUR FILTERS

I decided upon a desktop-based dating website, as opposed to one of the new-generation phone apps (*filter #1*). The site came with a hefty subscription fee (*filter #2*) and was linked to a left-leaning newspaper (*filter #3*). It required you to write a detailed self-description (*filter #4*) and encouraged you to publish several photos (*filter #5*). In addition, it asked you to provide information about your personal preferences regarding age, geographical location, desire for children, and so on, which it used to create a pecking order in the system: those men who answered the questions in the same manner as you were brought to the front of the queue (*filter # 6*). To make contact with one of these men, you were expected to compose him a message in which, I supposed, you introduced yourself (*filter #7*) and gave some indication as to what drew you to him (*filter #8*). If the man liked what he saw (*filter #9*) and read (*filter #10*), he could respond to your message, preferably, I imagined, in a way that made plain why he was attracted to you also (*filter #11*), thereby creating an open channel of communication between you both. If at any moment, for whatever reason, either party decided he wanted to shut down the exchange, he could do so simply by clicking a button marked 'block' (*filter #12*). 'Blocking' a man meant they disappeared permanently from your screen. If it so happened that, later, you came to regret your decision to 'block' him—perhaps you had been too hasty in your judgements, perhaps initially you had set your standards too high, perhaps you had misinterpreted his jokes, perhaps he deserved another chance—you could press a button marked 'unblock', though there was no guarantee that, having been 'blocked', he would be charitable enough to give *you* a second airing.

Concealed behind our veils, we danced. The hope? To end in nakedness.

After a few false starts and awkward blunders, I managed to start a dialogue with a handsome Italian with a full black beard and receding hair, a human-rights lawyer. We wrote to each other about books and life in England and the difficulties of being gay in Italy. Our communication, which switched between English and Italian, was mature and, it seemed to me, evenly pitched. Not too long-winded, not too blunt. Not too hot, not too cold. Not too heavy, not too light. Step, step, step, step, step. Point. Hold. Stretch, contract. Be light. Show strength. Reveal, then conceal again. Lift, lift, jump, lift, lift. *Can he carry me?* I sensed that he could. *Does he have the spine?* I felt that he did. *Would my mother like his technique?* She probably would. I was confident that we should and would meet in person. There was a Chapman Brothers show at the Serpentine: *perhaps we would meet there and afterwards have lunch in the restaurant next doo—*

Did the computer make a noise, like a bell or a bleep or a ping, when a man responded to your contact request? I cannot remember. But I do remember the thrill I felt—right in the middle of writing to the Italian lawyer—at seeing a missive come in from Y. Y had been one of the first men I had contacted, a couple of weeks before. I had not been surprised to hear nothing back from him. My appeal to him had been an act of wild speculation. A long shot. I disbelieved, actually, that I had the capacity to lure such a man to me, and I continue to disbelieve it. For he was—anyone who saw him could not deny—extremely handsome. In his face a comingling of Daniel Day-Lewis and Manu Chao. In style, louche. Vintage clothes that were one size too small and a generation too young. The delicate limbs of an ex-hippie. A round little belly like an ex–rock star. Equally appealing to women and men, and himself attracted to both: the text of his profile said that he had been married to a woman who had died young of a rare congenital condition.

In contrast to my dialogue with the Italian lawyer, that with Y was hot and fast, and lacked all gracefulness and balance. He came at me hard, and swung me around, and pulled me this way and that, until I was dizzy and teetering, and I was so flattered, then, when he stopped me from falling that I did not care that he had been the one to trip me up, nor did it seem strange that I had given him permission to do so.

'Hey Gavin,' the Italian lawyer wrote a few days later, 'I have not had a response from you. Are you still interested in being in touch?'

'I'm really sorry,' I wrote back. 'I have made an appointment with someone else. I'm not comfortable juggling several dates at once, so I am going to pursue that. You're a fascinating and handsome guy. To be honest, I didn't think you were that interested.'

Fucking liar. I knew well he was interested. But in this dance—the steps of which I had rehearsed for so many years with my parents—unless a man is brutal with me, unless he rips the veils from my body and tears them with his teeth, I will not trust, and certainly will not value, his attention.

Y met me off a morning train at Liverpool Street. He was there on time but had not showered and was clearly hung-over. His hair was standing on end. His clothes smelled of stale smoke.

We kissed on both cheeks.

Because he was Venezuelan, I spoke to him in Spanish.

He responded in kind, but hesitantly. He was nervous. Maybe even a bit overwhelmed. That surprised me.

'You look like your photos,' he said.

'Oh,' I said.

Climbing the escalator to Bishopsgate, I saw there were black stains on the seat of his second-hand trousers.

Get out of this, my mother's voice in my head said. *Don't be rude, be kind, but get out of it.*

At the Chapman Brothers exhibition, Y was less interested in looking at the art than in regaling me with stories of having sex in this specific gallery space with an ex of his who had worked as a security guard here.

'What art was showing?' I said.

'Huh?'

'Whose work was on view when you were having sex?'

'Oh. I can't remember.'

Get out of this.

In the restaurant next door, where we went for lunch, it was very bright. The light coming in through the large windows was merciless, permitting no shadows or contrasts or blurred edges. Everything was visible. Across Y's cheeks and nose ran an archipelago of angry red blotches, which I took as a warning about the state of his general health, though I was not put off by it, for, far from taking away from his looks, it added a careless, disreputable quality to them. He had a shake in his hands, too, slight though definitely neurological. This, along with the slenderness of his fingers and wrists and arms, made him appear vulnerable. Which he sought to overcome with overly confident gestures: the seductive laying of his palm on my knee or the playful squeezing of my shoulder. I had a sushi platter and water. He had—actually, I cannot recall what he ate, but he drank white wine: one glass and then another.

I paid, as my mother had taught me always to do at a first meeting, even—especially—if you were never going to see that person again.

'Oh, that's a good sign,' he said in lieu of a thank you.

Which immediately made me regret it. For it gave the wrong impression. As good-looking as he was, as unconventional in fashion, as exotic in background, I was not that taken by him. In fact, I thought he was trouble. The act of reaching for my credit card, far from a show of interest, had come from a desire to call time on our meeting and put permanent distance between us. *Pay*, my mother was telling me, *and get out*.

Afterwards, we walked along the lake. I led us in the direction of Marble Arch, my sights on the Bond Street tube.

'What are your plans for the evening?' he said.

'I'm staying with a friend in Islington. I'm going to have dinner with her there.'

At this, abruptly, he put his arms around me and kissed me.

His embrace was unexpectedly reticent, his caress coy. Perhaps he sensed that my feelings for him were cold.

'Change your plans,' he said.

Get out get out get out get—

Icily, passionlessly, I pulled his body closer to mine and rubbed my cheeks against his stubble and prised his thin lips open and pushed my tongue into his small mouth.

'I suppose I can spare another hour or two.'

We went to Soho and had beers and ceviche at a Peruvian restaurant, then cocktails in a flashy bar on a parallel street, where Y, sitting on the couch beside me, reached his hand down the back of my chinos (fresh and pressed) and put his middle finger into my arsehole (waxed and moisturised).

'Stay with me tonight.'

'If I do that, I'll never see you again.'

Did I even want to see him again?

'Sleeping with me tonight doesn't mean it has to end there.'

'No?'

'No. I like you.'

'Well, I'd prefer to wait for my feelings to catch up.'

'Catch up with what?'

'I don't know. What I'm saying is, I don't want to rush things.'

'Are you playing by the rules?'

'Rules?'

'Do you think holding out for a second or third date means you're not a whore?'

'It's not about being a whore. It's just—'

A heterosexual couple at a nearby table were glancing in our direction. They had noticed where Y's hand had gone. Shamed by their gaze, I stopped gyrating my hips. Y's finger went still but stayed inside.

'My friend is expecting me.'

'Call her.'

'I don't know. It seems rude.'

He pushed his finger in deeper.

'Call her.'

I sucked in some air. He was far inside now, tickling my prostate.

'I won't call her. I'll go and speak to her in person.'

I had supper with my friend in her kitchen and told her about Y.

'He invited me to sleep at his place,' I said. 'Do you mind if we change our plan?'

'You like him, don't you?'

Did I?

'Yes.'

'Go, then. But be careful.'

I rejoined Y in Bloomsbury, where he took me to an illegal party in an occupied office block. The party itself was nothing to write home about. At its core, in what looked like the office kitchen, was a jamming session—acoustic guitars, a bongo, clouds of pot smoke—and leading off from that, a warren of empty rooms with video screens and flashing lights and thumping music. To me, the place felt underpopulated, the people too stoned to kick anything off. The entire night, I did not have a single interesting conversation. As a matter of fact, I do not think I engaged in anything resembling a conversation at all. For there was very little talking going on. Instead, a lot of standing around, alone, together. An exchange of smiles when a bottle or a spliff was passed on, but then an immediate return to one's own cell, the general social idea being stoicism: be unmoved or at least appear to be.

Looking back, I can say that what I felt in that squat, amongst those hip people, was an overture for how I would feel throughout my relationship with Y. I had left Ireland in search of a home; I had left wanting harmony, security, synchrony, sameness. Yet I was also aware—my father's lesson—of the repressions and violence that make such a home imaginable, and I was trying to escape those things, too. My desire for a safe place was undermined by the knowledge that such security had to be struggled for, adapted, chosen, and was therefore inherently unstable. There would be no perfect fit. And maybe, ultimately, there was nowhere to go: no home with a family for me. So I lived in fear of two fates: either that I might succumb to the comforts of convention and build a cheap replica of the home I had run away from, or else that I might end up as a lost soul, spiritually homeless, banging on a bongo drum in a disused office in some lonely city. Which is to say I was, at one and the same time, thrilled to be holding Y's hand in this alternative vision of togetherness and terrified that I would belong irretrievably to it if some passer-by merely looked at me and unconsciously associated me with it.

Y and I began to spend every weekend together. We took turns: one week he would come to my city and the next I to him in London. Y had an ordinary administrative job and was, he admitted, intimidated by the idea of meeting my friends and colleagues at the university. If this was true, it did not show. Helped by his awareness of himself as the beloved only child of two doting parents, and by his deep need to match up to privileged Europeans whose personal and economic development had not been stunted by the privations of a childhood under communism, and by the cocaine, of course, that he put up his nose, he came across as confident and charming. He was noticed. He made an impact. He appeared pleased with himself.

I noticed that heterosexual men, in particular, were susceptible to his modes. At a house party I organised to celebrate my birthday, Y did not have to move from his place on the sofa because a succession of besotted straight men brought him everything he required, from drinks to plates of food to lines of coke. The import or veracity of what Y was saying did not seem so important to these men; it was enough that Y, the child of a communist regime, had by some accident made it here, dressed as he was, high as he was, beautiful as he was, holding forth as he was; he made them feel like they were close to something that normally happened far away; he made them feel like they were touching history; what was mystifying, he demystified.

'Whenever there was an economic crisis,' he said, 'the shelves in the shops would empty out, and we would survive only on condensed milk.'

'He's still addicted to the stuff,' I said. 'His parents send him boxes of it from Venezuela.'

'How does one eat condensed milk?' a man asked. 'I mean, what does one do with it?'

'I think most people use it for baking,' I said. 'Y, though, just opens the can and drinks it straight.'

'Ugh,' said another man, his face hovering over a line, a rolled banknote held like a cigar between three fingers. 'That sounds—'

'Unhealthy?' I said. 'It's so sweet it smells metallic. Almost fishy.'

'Recipe for a headache,' someone said.

'Recipe for *diabetes*,' someone else said.

'To top it off,' I said, 'his skin always breaks out in a rash afterwards.'

'I can't help it,' said Y, enjoying our bourgeois disgust. 'It's satisfying. It makes me feel full.'

'Are you a communist?' someone asked him.

'Nah,' said Y. 'Communism suits some people. Psychologically, they can handle it, you know? They like the limits. The sameness. But it's not for me.'

That's for sure.

Later, while I was making tea in the kitchen, one of the men approached me.

'Your boyfriend is amazing,' he said.

'You think so?' I said, soaking up his approval, which by myself, *for myself*, I could never have earned.

'Fuck yeah,' he said, slapping me on the back, 'you're a lucky man.'

My female friends were more cautious. They could see Y's allure. But they could also see its dangers. A personality that so avidly sought to make itself felt in others was bound to be split.

'What is he like when you two are alone?'

It was a good question. One that was difficult for me to answer, for Y and I spent very little time by ourselves. When he came to visit me, I did my best to keep him close to me, to build screens around us, to enclose him in a cell of my making, but he fought against these efforts of mine. Left at home with just me, he was restless. He hated to stay in. He wanted to go out and be in a crowd. In public, he was affectionate with me, he was happy to be *seen* in my company, but when it was just the two of us, he felt a lack. I was not enough to satiate his appetite for attention. What he craved were the multiple diversions of the tribe.

In London, it was even worse. He always made sure to organise our days in such a way that we would be surrounded by others. Most of our alone time was spent on buses and tubes on the way to the houses and flats of his friends, many of whom did not seem especially excited to see him, and few of whom made any special effort for him. I lost count of how many sitting rooms and kitchens I sat in, being served tea or snacks by people who did not appear to be that close to Y, and who were mystified as to what we were doing there. *Weren't we supposed to be in love? Shouldn't we be elsewhere, doing romantic things together?*

One Sunday, we travelled to a posh house in Notting Hill to have lunch with Y's friend, a man he had met at a music festival some years previously. The wife of this man had an obvious dislike for Y—my guess was that he was an unwelcome reminder of her husband's hedonistic past—and at lunch she could barely disguise her disdain. (Noticing that he was wearing a T-shirt of mine, a simple designer piece I had picked up at an outlet, she said, 'You're looking well, Y. A step up from your normal.') Then, as soon as the table was cleared, she sent us all away.

'Sorry to rush you,' she said. 'But the children have a horse-riding class at three and, darling, it's your turn to drive them.'

'Of course, darling,' said the man.

'We'll go with you,' said Y.

I stabbed him with my eyes: *we'll do what?*

At the horse-riding centre, while the children trotted in circles and the men talked in circles (about times of yore: yurts and mescalin and body paint and the sunrise and the sunset), I thought I might collapse, right then and there, out of boredom and frustration. My heart was pounding, for I was angry, too. *What the fuck am I doing here? I could be anywhere in the world. I mean, I could be in the library making great works of literature! Instead, I am stuck in this hell-hole with these asswipes!*

That evening, on the way home, I said to Y, 'We need to talk.'

'What's wrong?' he said.

'About today. I don't want you to involve me in your plans without asking me first. I'm not spending another weekend, no, another *minute* watching your friends change their babies' nappies. I've had enough. If you want to spend time with these people, go ahead. But count me out. I will go to the library and do some work. We can meet up afterwards.'

'No. You're not allowed to work on weekends.'

'I'm not *allowed*?'

'Weekends are for us.'

'If that were true, Y, I would be happy. If I felt like you had any interest in spending time with *me*, I would gladly sacrifice my work. Writing would be the last thing on my mind. But the fact is, you don't want to be alone with me. You only want me as a plus-one for your boring social engagements.'

'Boring?'

'Yes, boring. *So* boring. I've never *been* so bored.'

'You prefer your work to people.'

'I prefer my work to *boring* people.'

'What you're saying is, you're antisocial.'

'You, on the other hand, spread yourself too thin.'

'You have no feelings.'

'I have plenty of feelings. You just don't see them because you're not paying them any mind.'

'Well, I have no family here in London. My friends are important to me. I want to spend time with them.'

What could I say to that? Nothing. But inside I was screaming: *Your friends don't even fucking like you! And I'm not sure I do either! (And yet I'm here with you. Which must mean I want something from you. Is it because I don't like you that I want you to like me?)*

I did not tell my mother about Y. When I called her—only once every few months, when I had something concrete to tell her, for neither of us liked small talk, especially on the phone—I avoided the subject of relationships, and she did not ask, either. I thought I might get away with never telling her about him: *maybe I'll introduce him to the family at her funeral?* In truth, I did not want her to meet Y because I knew that, in her orbit, following her gaze, I would be forced to see the reality of the man I had chosen.

While Y often brought up the idea of a trip to Venezuela to meet his parents, I failed to suggest the much easier and much cheaper journey to Dublin.

'Are your family conservative?' Y asked, sensing my resistance to the idea.

'Not at all,' I said.

'I have a friend from, what's it called, Donegal? His parents disowned him.'

'No, my family aren't like that. I'd just prefer to have you to myself for a while longer.'

So, on the phone to my mother, I left Y to one side and gave her updates about my teaching and the forthcoming book, the ins and outs of which she did not retain, so I usually ended up repeating what I had told her before. By now, ours had become a distant relationship, though what we represented to each other remained important for both of us, I think. She was proud of me, I could tell.

'How is N?' I would eventually ask.

'I don't want to start about that,' she would say.

But then, unable not to start, she would tell me about him, the salient points, before she would catch herself and say again, 'But I don't want to start about it.'

They had, at last, been separated. The family home had been sold. She had moved into a flat, while he had been placed in a house for *independent living*.

'For men with problems, you know? I'm terrified he'll get thrown out, though. He's still smoking hash and his room is a pigsty.'

'Do the doctors know about the hash?'

'I don't know. They give him his prescriptions anyway.'

'Do you see him often?'

'Well, I go and clean his room.'

'Is that a good idea?'

'He won't do it himself.'

'That's his responsibility. Let him sit in his own filth, if that's what he wants to do.'

'You should see the place. It's disgusting. I couldn't leave it like that.'

'You should avoid seeing it, then. Don't go in. That way, you won't know what it looks like. You could meet him somewhere else.'

'I do on Fridays. I take him out for his lunch.'

Unhealthy food, pub grub, which she would watch him eat, without eating herself.

'I have my own thing on the way home. I always need to sit down and gather myself afterwards.'

'And how is he?'

'He was in rotten humour last week. He ate the face off me.'

'Why?'

'He wanted money.'

'Did you give him any?'

'Not enough.'

'If he behaves like that, you shouldn't give him anything.'

'Oh, look, let's not start about it. I'm glad your book is going well. That'll be something to celebrate.'

The only times I felt seen by Y—I mean really locked in his sights—was when we were having sex. More often than not, our lovemaking happened in the morning or during the day, Y being regularly too drunk or high or tired at night. I did not object to this state of affairs. For in the light, with no shadows to hide in, Y's false charm was dissipated. Having my gaze on his body made him more thoughtful about mine. His eyes were expressive and followed me about. In a little voice, like a mouse, he begged me to penetrate him. Or rim him. Or grab his neck. When I did these things, he whispered my name:

'Oh Gavin, yes, oh yes—'

I led in bed. I initiated, I directed. I think Y's greater pleasure was to be underneath a man, dominated by him, but his ego also required him to demonstrate that he could be virile. ('I'm a homosexual,' the London gangster Ronnie Kray famously said, 'but not a poof.') Because this was a requirement of the mind, however, rather than a deeper sacral urge, Y was artless in his penetrations, mechanical, like a teenage boy following the abstract instructions of his peers. I had to teach him to be gentle in order to persuade me to want it rough. *Had his wife never taught him this?*

'Put on a condom,' I said when, without warning, he pushed the head of his penis inside of me.

'We don't need a condom.'

'Oh, yes, we do.'

I was informed enough to know that the test he had shown me, though dated just a couple of days before our first meeting, was worthless. It took three months for HIV to be detected in a test, and who knew what he had been up in the weeks before he met me. (At this point, naively, I was oblivious to what he might have been up to *while* we were together.)

'Oh God,' he said, 'it's so depressing.'

'What is?'

'Don't you ever think, fuck it, let's just get infected and go on the pills and be done with it?'

'Shut up, Y. Too many people have died in the past for us to talk like that.'

'All of this worrying, all of this fear, it has fucked us up.'

He was right. Ever since HIV appeared, we—men who have sex with men—have been unable to extricate our desire for pleasure, for intimacy, for union, from the terror of a painful and lonely death, and that *is* fucked up. Our experience of sex is at odds with itself: we long to be free, to feel skin against skin, for that is how we know we are living, yet at the same time we long to keep on living, which means protecting ourselves from the invisible forces that would take our lives away. We know the rules and want to enforce them, but we also feel immense internal pressure to break them, for we are not content with half-measures, we will not accept anything less than total liberty, and it can sometimes be that the risk itself—the risk of liberty—is what inflames us. (Perhaps our ultimate freedom is having control about how and when we die. Perhaps by affirming life through sex, our deeper desire is that we should, as Freud says, 'die only by our own fashion'.)

Saying 'no' to the risk is a radical rejection of life, out of a fear that that life, the evident health of the man we love, is really just a cover for a force of equal strength: death. How many men's lives have been saved, over the decades, by such radical rejections of life? Thousands. Millions. Including many personal friends of mine. I am so thankful that they were decisive, that they said 'no', and I do not blame those who could not, did not, for all they wanted was life, all they were doing was living.

With Y, I also said 'no' in my mind.

When he was penetrating me without a condom, I was thinking: *no, this isn't right. Make him stop.* My mother was telling me, *There's still time to save yourself.*

'Are you sure it's all right?' I said.

'I showed you the test, didn't I?'

'Yes, but—'

'Come on, live a little. Don't be so—'

'Promise me you haven't been with anyone else. In the weeks before the test, or since.'

'I promise.'

'If we do this, it means you have to be faithful to me.'

'Yes, yes.'

Yes, yes.

But in my head, in my heart, my mother still said, *No, no.*

And even so, I let him.

I did not trust him, and I let him.

He did not last long. He ejaculated quickly and collapsed on top of me, and I held him tightly, and played with his hair, and nibbled his ear, and he moaned and nestled into my embrace, a mouse once again. So beautiful I could die.

Y's father had once been a functionary for the Venezuelan government. He had worked in the Venezuelan embassy in Moscow, but, for reasons that were not made clear to me, he was no longer employed in this field. ('I am persona non grata,' he once told me cryptically.) He was the author of a single collection of poetry, which had won a national prize. He wrote articles and stories, but I did not understand how he earned a living. All I knew was that Y sent him small monthly remittances and medicines, and that there was a vague medium-term plan for getting him and his wife out of Venezuela and resettling them in Spain.

Y's father adored his son. He was emotionally invested in him. Curious about his life. Eager to be kept informed about it. As soon as he got wind that Y had a boyfriend—one of Y's Venezuelan friends in London told him, I think—he sent an email to Y asking him to describe what I was like and how 'the first phase' was going. Y responded with the basic information, laying stress on my job at the university and my ambitions to be a novelist, knowing that this would play well with him.

It was not long, then, before I was receiving personal emails from him, welcoming me to the family and expressing a desire to meet me in person. His greatest wish, he said, was that his son and I should succeed in building a family together. His letters to me, written in Spanish, often contained references to his literary work. He asked my advice on little bits of translation. He wondered whether or not it would be possible to get an English-language deal for his poetry, which he wanted me to read and get my opinion of.

I was enchanted. In my core, I believed I could not function without the protection of a father. And here was one. A real one. Instantly, I felt in need of his approval. Perhaps a good father like him would permit me to forgive, and then help me to forget, my one, the abandoning one. I wrote to Y's father telling him that I loved Y very much, and that, despite the problems and difficult moments, I intended to build a family with his son.

Subtext: *I intend to build a family with you.*

Tone: *pleading.*

Mood: *desperation.*

Mother: silenced.

In Y's father's responses, there was desperation, too. And, folded into that, notes of warning. On this earth, he said, he did not love anyone more than his son, but he was aware that Y was complicated due to the large number of feelings that often overwhelmed him. Reading this, I myself was overwhelmed with feelings. Intoxicated. Here was a man who would put his hands in the fire for his son. Or who, at the very least, would say such a thing as an expression of his paternal love. In the photographs that Y showed me, he appeared thoughtful and kind. Like his son, he was handsome. I wanted him—with a desire no less real than that which I had for Y—to adopt me.

This was a wish that Y's father himself, a seducer in his own way, readily granted me. Whenever he did not hear from his son for a few days, he would contact me and ask me for our news, which I would send to him in nicely wrapped word parcels; it touched me greatly how thankful he was to receive these, and soon he was signing off, 'Your father-in-law'.

He often spoke in the 'we'—'We are happy... We are anxious... We are hopeful...'—as though he and his wife were both sitting at the computer composing the letters together. Indeed, soon I began to wonder how much of Y's father's discourse came directly from him, and how much of it actually came from Y's mother. My sense was that Y's mother, hovering over the keyboard, wanted to say more, to reveal more, to give more advice, and that it was Y's father, the diplomat, who held her back.

Y's mother was a sexologist. Also a published author. I tried to extract information from Y about what kind of sexologist she was, and how a sexologist might earn a living in a communist regime, but he was not forthcoming with details, either because he did not know or because he did not want me to know. For a long time, she did not write to me separately, in her own voice, and I thought she might never do so. Until one day I received a long letter from her, which expressed her anxiety for Y to build a family of his own. Many good people had passed through Y's life, she said, but he had not yet found a person who could move him emotionally towards a solid and truly lasting relationship. She hoped I was that person. Would I allow her to write to me? Her aim, she said, was not to interfere, but rather to get to know me as well as possible, and support me so that I might achieve happiness with her son.

Here, returned to me at last, was the beautiful mother I had lost. Deep inside my heart, in its farthest regions, in the place fathers do not reach, she had been calling to me, and now I had found her. All my fantasies of men, of fathers, were tied to her. All my problems with my own mother were solved by her. And now she had a face.

> *I love your son* [I wrote to her] *and one day (I don't know, in two or three years?) I want to marry him. We have already talked about the party that we will organise—and of course we have totally different ideas. You already know who will win that argument! Please write to me whenever you wish. I'm always glad to receive the news from Venezuela and the secret stories from your beautiful family.*

And now *my* beautiful family. Summers in Caracas. Swimming in the Caribbean. Rainforests. The *tepuis*. Fried plantains. Condensed milk. *Batidos* and *chichas*. Political debates. The Bolivarian Museum. *Is it possible to buy a house there? If so, how much would it cost?*

By now, my teaching at the university was coming to an end. The weather was getting warmer, and my students were starting their final projects or heading into exams. Y and I had made our summer plans. I was going to move in with him in London and look for teaching work there. In July, we would go to Spain on holiday.

Y came to my city for one last visit, arriving on Friday evening while it was still bright out. I cooked dinner for him and my flatmate—scallops to start, followed by sea bream, I will never forget this menu—which we ate at the dining-room table with a tall candle at the centre. After dinner, we planned to go and meet friends in a pub, then head to a house party. But at dessert, I began to feel heavy-headed.

'I think I might be coming down with something,' I said.

In a matter of minutes, my knees began to feel weak.

'I might have a lie-down before we go out.'

In bed, I shivered. My temples pounded. My joints ached. Mucus poured from my nose. My eyes streamed. The onset of the flu was shockingly quick, its intensity tropical, I had never experienced anything like it before. I could not have known it then, but what I was going through was, in fact, the process of seroconversion: the moment, between three and twelve weeks after first contracting HIV, when the body recognises the virus and begins to generate antibodies to it. Some people do not develop any symptoms at all; most people get really ill.

Y came and lay beside me for a few minutes, but quickly became bored. He got up and went downstairs.

Alone, not quite asleep, not fully awake, I became an audience to vivid images from my past. My childhood. My mother. My dreams of love.

After a while, my flatmate knocked and came in. He was taken aback by the sight of me:

'Oh my God, you're really sick.'

'I need to stay here. Look after Y, can you?'

Y did not bring me a cold cloth for my forehead. He did not put a bucket by the bed. He did not bring me water or aspirin or anything else. He did not spend a single minute looking after me, or express any concern for me. On the contrary, he appeared put out that I had chosen a Friday night to become incapacitated. More than anything, he was terrified that I might ask him to stay in.

'Go if you want to, Y.'

'All right.'

The fever did not let me sleep. I tossed and turned, and could barely breathe because my throat was swollen and my nose was pumping out fluid at a perturbing rate. I moaned and called out. I wanted my mother, who, when I was sick as a child, would lay her hand on my forehead and smooth back my hair over and over: *would any man I met in this life have her staying power? would he sit at my side and not move from there, and keep smoothing back my hair, until—the cure taking effect—I was still and resting?*

I checked my phone at two.

Then at three.

Four. Five. Six. Seven.

No messages. No calls.

At eight, I crawled—quite literally—out of bed, pulled on a tracksuit and went downstairs. I made tea but did not drink it. Deathly ill, barely able to differentiate the objects of the world, I sat on the sofa and waited.

At nine, my flatmate came home.

'Oh, you're up,' he said. 'How are you feeling?'

He was high and therefore, emotionally, behind several panes of glass.

'Where is he?' I said.

He sat down. His expression was serious. In his drugged state, he was struggling to find coherence.

'Gavin, I—'

'Where the fuck is he? Just tell me.'

'I didn't see it happen. I was downstairs. I wasn't involved.'

'Involved in what?'

'Some of the people at the party went up. For an orgy.'

'Was Y with them?'

'Yes.'

I stood up, I do not know how, and went to the kitchen. Leaned on the lip of the sink. There came from me, then, a howl. A primal scream. The wailing of a newly born infant.

My flatmate was behind me:

'I'm really sorry.'

I pushed past him and went upstairs. Packed all of Y's things back into his bag and put them outside the door. Then I called a taxi.

'I'm going to a friend's house,' I told my flatmate. 'I can't be here when he gets back. Don't let him in the house.'

'I'm sorry,' he said again.

I could not look at him. I was furious with him. I had asked him to look after Y, and he had failed to do so. Some of this, maybe most of it, was his fault. (That is to say, just as I had blamed my mother for my bullies' actions, now I blamed my good friend for my lover's. I treated my friend shabbily. Transferred my anger onto him, and, in so doing, nearly lost his friendship.)

The flu passed quickly and I was back in the classroom on Tuesday. Y called me several times, over several days, but I did not answer. I wanted a confrontation, I was rehearsing everything I was going to say to him, but I also wanted to force him into a big gesture. It was up to him, now, to do something truly extraordinary to win me back. Anything less than an extravaganza and he could fuck off.

In the middle of the week, I received an email from Y's father containing a photograph of a yellow-flowered acacia, which Y as a child had planted in the verge at the entrance to their house, and which flowered around Y's birthday every year.

My heart was pounding in my chest as I composed my reply. The thrill of restrained, tactful, articulately worded revenge:

*Your message comes at a delicate moment—a sad moment for me.
I have left Y. I have realised that we want different things in life.
I want peace and quiet, whereas he wants only to party, and we
can't seem to meet halfway. Y finds it difficult to be alone. It drives
him crazy to spend too much time at home. I, on the other hand,
do not really like to drink and take drugs (in the past I drank quite
a bit and took lots of drugs but now they no longer interest me),
and most parties bore me. Above all, it makes me anxious to be
alone at home waiting for Y to return from his revelling. I can't
bring myself to trust him—a fact that causes me a lot of pain. I
love your son, and I am sure that he will find someone with whom
he can build a nice life.*

After this, Y's father fell silent, and his mother—I was not astonished
to see—took the reins. In another long letter, she told me that my news
had not surprised her but had profoundly saddened her. She had had
great hopes that her son had finally found the person who would make
him happy. Y's difficulties, she explained, were the result of years of living
alone as a single man. It was up to Y, now, to demonstrate to me that he
could change his style of life. Her only concern, she said, was to help us
start again. To this end, she felt a duty to tell me some things about Y
that might convince me to give him a second chance. Did she have my
permission to write again and tell me these things? And could I please
not tell Y that she had written to me?

That Friday, Y was waiting outside my classroom. The building was a
maze, I do not know how he found the way, yet there he was, dressed in
a white shirt with an unfashionably large collar. I opened the door and,
before seeing him, I could smell the musk of his perfume, and my chest
tightened, and a lump formed in my throat, and I thought, *he came, thank
God, he came.*

Some students wanted to speak to me after class, so I gave Y the key
to my office and told him to wait for me there. I do not think I heard a
word that my students said to me, my heart was pounding and my mind
racing so fast.

In the office, he was sitting in the chair that my students used when they came to see me. I sat in the chair by the desk, in front of the computer—the place of authority, of superiority—and waited for him to speak.

'I'm sorry,' he said.

'No,' I said. 'I'm not ready for apologies. First, I need to know everything that happened. Start to finish. Don't leave anything out.'

It was, he said, just a silly game. They got naked, yes, but it was just kissing and touching. No penetration.

'Men and women?'

'Yes.'

'And you were with both?'

'Yes.'

'But you didn't fuck anyone?'

'No.'

'Because everyone was too high? No one could get a hard-on?'

(I was hungry for the details. I wanted to be able to picture the scene. In retrospect, I think it is strange that I was so focused on this, the sex, when the larger question was really: why had Y abandoned me during my illness? Why had he left the house at all?)

'Yeah, it was just a silly game, honestly.'

'Did you want to fuck anyone?'

'No. I felt used actually.'

'Used?'

'Yeah. Manipulated into a situation that—'

'Bullshit. Don't try that with me.'

He went quiet, and we looked at each other in the eye for a long minute. He looked tired. And fragile.

Suddenly, my defensive walls collapsed, and I began to cry.

I put my elbows on the table, on either side of the keyboard, and my face in my hands, and bawled.

He reached out to touch me, but I slapped his hand away.

'Don't come near me.'

'Come back to London with me.'

'No.'

'We can spend the weekend together, just you and me. We can talk about everything. Sort it out.'

'No. I don't know who you are. I don't know what you want.'

'I'm your boyfriend. And I love you.'

'You don't want me. You want everything and everyone except me.'

'You're wrong, I want you. You're all I want in this world.'

Inevitably—I knew what was going to happen from the moment I smelled him—I went with him to London that evening. Why? What did I want? I had not forgiven him, so did I want to punish him by being unhappy with him, by showing him how unhappy he makes the people he claims to love? Would I have gone if I had known what I know now, about him and about myself?

Useless questions. I did not have the ability to delay my love, or indeed my hate for Y until I had studied and become familiar with his nature inside out. My feelings for him were impulsive. I knew enough about him to understand that he was a danger to my carefully constructed sense of self, but I was, in equal measure, ignorant enough about him to believe that he could, having broken me down, having made me naked, see me for what I really was, a child with an insatiable thirst for love, and that, having seen me thus, he would give me the love I demanded.

Y betrayed me; he refused to belong to me. Yet love, in my eyes, was the desire to give: it was to pity and to pardon. Sitting beside him on the train, holding his hand, I had the feeling that forming a relationship was the utmost that a human being could succeed in doing. We, Y and I, both of us, were badly prepared for this, but at least we were trying, we were not giving up. Jung says that companionship thrives only when 'each individual remembers his individuality and does not identify himself with others', and we had not got there yet. On the outside, we appeared independent and strongheaded, but in fact we did not have such a strong perception of our own individuality. We were, in our different ways, lost in our identifications with others: he would not be happy until he was the life of the party, I would not be happy until I was the talk of it. But we would get there; if we worked at it, we would.

Lying in his arms that night, relieved and uneasy both, I had found myself in the most banal of situations. In going back to him, I was being a cliché. In my actions, I was being faithful to a well-worn formula: if I show him enough comprehension, he will learn how to change, and in changing he will finally become mine. At the same time, I was living in the illusion that I was related to Y—exactly as he was now, unchanged—in a most special way, and that this was life lived at its fullest. The suffering of loss and the satisfaction of retrieval: both were necessary elements of entanglement. If loss were to disappear, if suffering were to end, would our bond not also dissolve?

Besides, the demands I had been making of him were—I was the first to admit it—unreasonable. I wanted love, ever more love from him. I was needy, I lacked something fundamental, and I believed he would be able give it to me once I had taught him how to recognise his ability to do so. (What this fundamental lack was, I myself did not know. It could not be represented in my mind. It eluded language. I was able to refer to it, to demand it only obliquely, as one points to the sun but does not look directly at it. And maybe that is the best way of thinking about it: as a body of needs around which my emotions never ceased to gravitate; as a boiling mass of energy, which, regardless of what he gave me, Y would never be able to match. My demands would always be for extra. I was constantly asking Y for proofs of love that were impossible, humanly, to provide. Which was why I pitied him. Why I pardoned him.)

A few days later, I sent my mother, that is to say *his* mother, an email:

> *We talked—well, we fought and fought, and then we talked—and we are together again. I cannot leave him. He is too precious. Too beautiful. Too generous. Right now I can't imagine a life without him. And—the most important thing—I know that he loves me. We want to build a life together and I have no choice but to take the risk.*

'Oh, Y. What have you done?'

'Who's Y?'

'My boyfriend.'

'Well, it's not *his* fault, is it?'

'What do you mean?'

'You can't blame anyone else. You're responsible for your own body. You took the risk.'

The doctor, a man, was about my age. How many of these interviews did he do in a single day? Too many. I was just another body on the conveyor belt. Just another unschooled mind that needed, quickly, in the time allotted, to be rewired.

'Yes, doctor, I understand it was me who took the risk, thank you.'

I would have to take responsibility for what had happened. I would get nowhere, psychologically speaking, by blaming someone else. I get it. I FUCKING GET IT.

But—I wanted to do him real violence, punch his smirking, know-it-all face—I had only just received the news, had I not? Should I not be allowed a reaction of my own? Without the life lessons attached? Until a few minutes ago, this had been the best day of mine. I had achieved something I had been working towards for years. At this very moment, I was supposed to be planning a celebration. But instead? *Instead I am here, listening to you. So excuse me if there are a few things I need to come to terms with before I can think about my part in all of this.* Starting with the breach of trust in my relationship. *The man I loved has lied to me.* It was this, not the virus itself, that was foremost in my thoughts, and that I was struggling to fathom.

BUT THANK YOU, DOCTOR, ANYWAY, FOR YOUR WISDOM.

'What you have to understand,' he said, 'is that you're going to be okay. The medication these days is excellent. You won't die of HIV. The last AIDS ward closed down years ago.'

'I have lost weight recently. Is that related?'

'No. Have you been stressed? Skipping meals?'

'Well, I was finishing a book. And there was some relationship stuff.'

'There's your answer.'

'So the HIV has had no impact yet?'

'Not really. It's a resourceful virus, but a slow one. It can take years for it to break the immune system down. But you'll never need to think about any of that. The medication will keep the virus at an undetectable level, meaning it'll be inactive in your body. You're going to lead a normal life.'

'Inactive in my body, but still there.'

'In reservoirs. But these only reactivate if you don't take the pills. Otherwise, they remain dormant, entirely harmless. You won't be able to pass the virus on. You'll be able to have a safe and fulfilling sex life.'

Bullshit. No one will want to be intimate with me.

I'm stuck with Y.

If I lose him, I'll be alone forever.

'Don't you think it's a bit twisted,' I said then, 'that we're incessantly told to protect ourselves against HIV, that HIV is a terrible disease, the worst you can catch, and then, when you get it, you're told that actually it's all fine, there's nothing to worry about, just take the magic pill and get on with your life?'

The doctor shrugged. The philosophical questions he would leave to others.

My phone rang: Y.

'Hi,' I said.

'—'

'I'm here. Are you on your way?'

'Yes.'

When he arrived, he had his own consultation. Then we were left alone in a room so that we could have our moment.

We hugged.

Then the first thing he said was:

'We don't need to talk about who gave it to who.'

And I thought: *So this is how he's going to play it.*

And then I thought: *It never stops. When you think you've reached the boundaries of what you can take, the scene shifts, and another layer is added. And the strange thing is, you don't faint, you don't die. Rather you store the new information away, to be dealt with in some fashion, at some future time.*

Just not now.

I did not want to face it—the lie, the betrayal—right away.

I wanted simply to see this day out, and tomorrow I would figure out how I would be.

We did blood tests and were told to come back the following week, when the next steps would be explained to us.

'Go and have some fun today,' a nice female doctor told us. 'Everything's going to be fine.'

We walked in silence through Bloomsbury into Covent Garden. Who was leading whom, it was not clear. Y phoned his office and took the day off. Then he wanted a coffee, so we stopped at an expensive place with artisan cakes and men in aprons. I got one, too, even though I normally do not drink it. Milky with lots sugar, like my mother used to have it.

We sat at the base of the column at Seven Dials and watched the people pass by. I ate the sugar out of the bottom of my cup with a disposable spoon. We did not talk. I felt like I had lost touch with time: the illusion that the past was behind me and that there was always tomorrow, always more to come. I was in shock, not because I was going to die—on the contrary, I had been told *I was going to grow old*—but because I had come so close to the edge. It was only by a trick of time, a chance of birth, that I escaped the fall. In the same predicament twenty years ago, I would have been watching my young dreams hurtle to the ground. (What was it that I felt for those who had died so that I did not have to? Was it gratitude? Admiration? Guilt? Was it shame, for having ignored their lessons to me?)

After a while, we set off again. Although neither of us said it, we both understood that we were heading back to the flat. We walked all the way. On Columbia Road, a few minutes from home, Y decided he wanted a drink, so we went into an old pub. We sat at the bar and ordered two pints. We drank in silence and looked around: it took us an amazingly long time to realise that the people sitting on the opposite side of the room were in costume, and that those in modern dress milling around them, holding various pieces of equipment, were a film crew.

'What's going on?' Y asked the barman.

'They're making a film about the Kray twins.'

Y and I looked at each other and burst out laughing.

Was there a chance that everything around me was false? Perhaps. That I was alive and suffering, however—that was genuine.

We were still in the pub when my agent called. I went outside to speak to her. Pacing up and down the path, I listened while she told me the details of the book deal. At one point, I looked through the window of the pub and caught Y's eye. He was staring out at me, with a stern, unsmiling expression, as though angry with me for having revealed his culpability. The look disturbed me. *Who was this man?* That I felt protective of him did not mean that I was not afraid of him.

I signed up for therapy, individual and group. I booked appointments with a nutritionist and a peer-support coach. I began the process of coming out to my friends. In the library, I read through all the information booklets, underlining anything I did not know before. *A Long Life with HIV. Starting Treatment. Changing Treatment. HIV Mental Health and Emotional Wellbeing. Health Checks. Transmission and the Law. HIV and Stigma. HIV and Ageing. Undetectable Equals Untransmittable—*

'What are you doing all that for?'

Y was on the toilet, shitting.

I was at the sink, creaming my face after a shower.

'Because I need help. I need to understand what has happened to me.'

'What's there to understand? We take the pill and forget about it.'

'That's not going to be my approach. I need to know a little bit about why I'm taking the pill. What all of this means.'

Y wiped his arse in an unusual way: holding the paper in his right hand, he fed his arm into the space between his legs, dipped under his penis and balls, and, beginning at the top of his hole, wiped down, back to front. He then brought the paper out and examined it carefully, before folding it over and repeating the process.

I watched him do this:

'God, I wish you'd wash your arse with water.'

'Like you do? After every shit?'

'It would save me having to clean you with baby wipes before we have sex. They're terrible for the environment.'

'You wash too much.'

He left the bathroom and started to get dressed, without having taken a shower or even cleaned under his arms.

I flushed the toilet, which—a habit of his—he had failed to do.

'I have my first appointment with the counsellor today,' I said.

He sighed: 'Oh God.'

'I think you should sign up, too.'

'Uh-uh.'

He picked a pair of underwear off the floor and smelled it. Threw it back down and went for another pair.

'You know I'm in the process of telling my friends, right? And I intend to tell my family.'

'Your choice. I'm not telling anyone anything.'

'What if we're out with a group of my friends and your friends, together, and my friends bring it up?'

'Why would they do that?'

'Why *wouldn't* they? It's a fact of my life, isn't it?'

'Look, Gavin'—he pulled on a pair of trousers that were wrinkled from sitting in a ball—'in a few years, I'll mention in passing to my friends that I'm HIV-positive, and they'll say, *When did that happen?* and I'll say, *Oh, years ago,* and that'll be the end of it.'

I shook my head, revolted, and went back to the mirror. Dabbed cream along the border between my cheekbones and the sunken troughs around my eyes, which were red from lack of sleep. When I came back out, he was buttoning up a shirt, one of mine. I hated when he put my clean clothes next to his dirty skin. I would have to spray the underarms before putting it into the wash later.

'At some stage,' I said, 'we're going to have to talk about how this happened.'

He met my eye and froze: 'You can never ask me about that.'

I was actually happy to hear him say this. It was progress. An admission of sorts.

'Why not?'

'Because I never want to talk about it with you.'

'I don't understand that attitude, Y. I don't care what you did.' (This was not strictly true, I cared a great deal, but my first task was getting him to speak.) 'I just need to know the truth. How can I have a relationship with someone who is unable to give me information that I've a right to?'

'You don't have a right to it.'

'Well, it concerns me, doesn't it?'

'Who's to say it wasn't you, anyway?'

Ah. His familiar retreat.

'You know bloody well,' I said, *my familiar temper*, 'that I didn't bring HIV into this relationship. In the years before meeting you, I only had one partner. We were tested regularly and I got tested three months after our relationships ended.'

Y was packing his bag. He was not saying anything, but he was listening.

'And if you must know,' I went on, 'I got in touch with him. My ex, I mean. I told him to get tested. And just yesterday he sent me a photo of the result. He's negative.' I was gloating, like a poker player who had just turned over his royal flush. 'The only person in the world who I could have got HIV from is you.'

Y was searching under the duvet and around the side table: 'Where's my phone?'

'Did you hear me, Y? The partner I had before you is negative. Entering this relationship, I was negative, too. Now I need to know how I became positive. I need you to tell me.'

'Can you call my phone, please? I can't find it.'

After the diagnosis, Y increased his intake of drink and drugs significantly; he got drunker and higher more often. Entering the relationship, I was aware he was a pleasure-seeker, and I made a promise to myself not to be controlling about his immoderation. I did not tell him to refrain. I did not say to him, 'You've had enough.' I tried my best (though I admit this bit was hard for me, and I did not always succeed) not to shame him the next day or during his midweek gloominess. And—I hold my hands up—sometimes I myself indulged, my preference being for drugs because drink did not quite agree with me: *up* felt better than *down*. But I was, by both Irish and London standards, a lightweight. I had a limit beyond which I did not like to stray. Out of vanity more than anything else—I feared appearing ugly or out of control to others—I contained my highs within certain recognisable parameters. After the diagnosis, however, and to a great extent in response to Y's binging, the harmful effects of which were so plain to me, I stopped drinking and taking drugs altogether.

It was not an aberration, therefore, that the last fight I had with Y was one between a drunk man and a sober. This imbalance, which existed before the diagnosis but became especially pronounced after it, was an important element of what brought our relationship to its finale; it was also what made it ridiculous and, on the minor scale of my personal affairs, tragic.

In the morning, we made love. He penetrated me. Afterwards, in my arms, he told me that what he needed when he was feeling bad, by which he meant *in pain*, was affection. I told him I would do my best to give that to him. I also pointed out that it was sometimes hard to give him affection when he was in pain because, in that state, he tended to push me away. Our conversation at this point became strained as we both tried to make ourselves understood, but in the end I was glad we had managed to talk to each other in an open manner. I came out of it hopeful that we could, with a bit of sensitivity, a bit of ingenuity, construct a vocabulary for our relationship that we could both understand.

That day Y had an important work function, one that was going to involve a lot of socialising. I helped him choose an outfit. He did not have a suit, so he wore mine, matched with a shirt of his own. I thought he looked smashing. While he looked in the mirror—his eyes narrowed, his belly sucked in, turning this way and that—he asked me for the fifth or sixth time if I wanted to go to the event. I told him 'no'. I did not give him a reason for not wanting to go because, frankly, I saw no reason for me to be at the function, and, perhaps unfairly, I believed that in a trusting, mutually respectful relationship, when it came to attending social events, a simple 'no' ought to be enough. For me, it was a normal Friday, a work-day, and I wanted it to remain so. *I had better things to do.*

We made a loose arrangement to meet after the function. He did not know what time it would be over, but in the past he and a couple of colleagues had got a taxi to Shoreditch at around nine and gone out in the local area; he presumed this year it would be the same.

'In that case,' I said, 'how about I jump into the taxi with you on your way to Shoreditch. Or you can let me know where you are, and I'll make my own way there. I'll call you anyway during the day, to see how things are going.'

(Oh, the ordinariness of everything. How even the end of a love affair can be so pervaded by the unremarkable.)

At the library, I realised that my phone, an old burner, was on the blink, so in the early afternoon I made a trip to a nearby internet café to make a call to Y on Skype. Y was uncharacteristically rude to me on the phone. At first, I thought he had mistaken me with someone from work, so I said, 'Y, it's me.' To which he responded, 'Yes, tell me.' I said, 'Y, can you hear me? It's Gavin.' To which he said, 'Yes? Tell me!' I was astounded. He was normally extremely warm with me on the phone. (My sense was that he liked to be overheard—by his colleagues, by his friends, by people on the street—speaking gallantly to a man.) Now, though, with a similar relish for the histrionic, he was being outrageously ill-mannered. I asked him how he was. 'I'm talking to my bosses,' he replied. 'Can I call you back?' I told him my phone was not working and that I would call him back in ten minutes. When I did so, he excused himself from the people in his company to speak to me but then refused to answer my queries with anything more than a grunt. He was—it was easy to tell—angry with me about something.

'Would you like to come here?' he asked.

'No, thanks. I'm going to work at the library till nine. Then I'll make my way home. I'll call you from there, to find out where you are, okay?'

I left the library at twenty to nine and got home at twenty past. I called Y on Skype as soon as I got in the door, thinking that he might have been trying to call me on my broken phone. He did not answer. I called another six times. No response. I had a shower, then called again. This time, he answered.

'How are you?' I said.

'—'

'How is your night going?'

'—'

'Are you still at the function?'

'—'

'Are you okay, Y? Has something happened?'

'I'm very drunk.'

'Okay.'

'Are you at home?'

'Yeah, I just got here.'

'Oh. I didn't think you would be at home. I wanted to be alone.'

(What one fears has an impertinent tendency to come about. Since the beginning, I had been fearing the moment when Y would discover that I had, in my heart, turned against him, and when he would, in reaction, turn against me, and the solidification of the air between us—its transformation from a conductor of feelings to an impermeable block— would become irreversible. *I wanted to be alone*: never before had I heard Y express such a desire for solitude, and now that he had, I dreaded the world ahead.)

'Y, I told you I'd call you from home. We were going to meet in Shoreditch, right? Or I was going to jump into your taxi, if you were passing by. Remember?'

'—'

'Are you on the bike? If you're drunk, don't cycle home.'

'I'm downstairs.'

(I dreaded the world but, with equal intensity, I had the self-assurance of a man who no longer wondered at what the world could be.)

'Well, I'm here,' I said. 'So I'll see you in second.'

He struggled to open the door with his key. The first words he said, when he saw me, were: 'I'm drunk.'

'And high,' I said, though I did not know this for certain; I was going by the wild look in his eyes.

'I had a few joints, that's all.'

'Okay.'

'I don't want to go out.'

Another first.

'Oh. We had plans. I showered.'

He lay down on the bed in his clothes. Shoes still on. Limbs rigid. Facing the ceiling.

'I don't want to go out. I want to be alone. I didn't think you'd be here.'

'Where else would I be?'

'I feel totally judged by you for going out and being drunk. This is the first time I've been drunk in ages.'

'I didn't say anything.'

(An untruth: I had said, with condescension, *You're high*, and I had also said, with my looks and gestures, *You're a disappointment, a failure.*)

. I knelt down on the floor to do a couple of things on my laptop, which was on a low sideboard. Nothing was so urgent that it needed my attention at this moment, but I had decided I could not look at Y while I figured out what I was going to do about him: *was I going to leave the room? leave the flat? leave him?*

He came off the bed, pulled off his clothes, leaving them in a pile, and went to the shower room. From there, while sitting on the toilet, he said:

'It's all about you.'

'What's all about me?'

'Everything. There's no space for me.'

I stared into the computer screen: *do I want to get sucked into this?*

Without flushing, he went back to the bed, naked now, and put a pillow over his head: 'You don't—'

'Pardon?'

He took the pillow away: 'You don't listen to me. You only care about yourself.'

Sighing, I left the computer and sat down on the bed. Leaned in. 'Okay, I'm listening now. Tell me.'

(*During our holiday in Spain, in a wine bar in Barcelona, Y had given me some advice:*

'*Give up writing,' he had said. 'Stick to the teaching.'*

'*Why?' I had said, labouring to conceal how his words had stung me.*

'*With a full lecturing salary, added to mine, we could have a good life. We could travel.'*

'*But I wouldn't be happy. Do you want to be with an unhappy person?'*

'*It's terrible to want fame.'*

'*Is that what you think I'm looking for, fame?'*

'*Yes.'*

This wounded me, grievously. Then made me furious. Which probably meant it was true.

'*You're right, in a way,' I said, feigning beneficence, displaying outward calm. 'But I wouldn't call what I want fame. Approval, maybe. The appreciation of my peers. Writing is a pretty niche pursuit these days.'*

'*It has ruined my father's life, you know. His search for recognition as a writer.'*

'*I'm sorry to hear that. But I believe I have talent. I don't want to waste it.'*

He kept his eyes on me as he sipped from his glass, and I realised he was not going to agree with me. About having talent. About the importance of not wasting it.

'*You don't think I'm talented?' I asked, pathetically.*

He shrugged as if to say, What do I know?

'*Well, you didn't like my novel,' I said.*

'*I never said that.'*

'*You got to the end of the first chapter and left it down.'*

'*I haven't had time.'*

'*You had time to read the novella that my friend published recently.'*

'*That was an easy read. Your work requires concentration.'*

'*Right. And? It sounds like you're not willing to—'*

'*Oh God.' He looked over my shoulder and raised his hand to call the waiter. 'Let's change the subject. It's always about you.'*)

'I'm listening now,' I said, moving closer to him on the bed. 'What is this about?'

'You only criticise me, you never criticise yourself.'

'Can you describe precisely what is on your mind?'

'It's all about you! It's all about you!' He had sat up and was now shouting in my face. 'You only think about yourself.'

'Wow,' I said.

'Wow?' he said. 'That's what you say? *Wow?*'

'Do you want to break up with me, is that it?' *Do you want to do what I lack the courage to do, and put us both out of our misery?* 'Do you want to be with me or not? Tell me.'

'Yes and no.'

'Well, I need a clearer answer than that.'

'No, then.'

'Okay.'

A pause: breath meeting breath.

Then he fell back onto the mattress and closed his eyes.

'Y,' I said, 'please tell me what this is all about.'

Suddenly he reared up and put his face close to mine, and said, mockingly, 'Gavin, do you want to know what this is all about?'

'Yes.'

Then he slapped me hard across the face.

(*It was not the first time. In Spain, in a hotel on the Catalonian coast, he had said to me, 'Let's go back to Barcelona,' and I had said, 'No, I want to stay here,' so he went by himself, to go out with his friends, and when he returned to the hotel the next day, he said, 'You're angry with me for going,' and I said, 'I don't care what you do, I had a nice time on my own,' and then he hit me, the same technique, a slap across the face, which did not hurt that much, but which put me in a difficult position. 'You realise I can't stay with you now?' I said to him. 'You realise I have to leave?' And he said, 'Why?' And I said, 'Because you hit me.' And he said, mere seconds after the event, 'I didn't hit you.'*)

I stood up and stepped away. Put a hand to my face.

'I'm going to fucking kill you,' he said.

I made my way towards the door. Following me, still naked, he took hold of my T-shirt and flung me out into the hall. I stumbled. My mind was racing: how was I going to get out? where was I going to go? would I have time to grab my laptop, which was the only thing of importance that I owned?

He dragged me by the arm into the sitting room.

'You have to leave, right now,' he shouted.

'All right,' I said.

I was in my pyjamas, so I asked, requested his permission, to change my clothes.

'You don't get it,' he said. 'This isn't about you. I don't care what you want or need, because it's not about you.' He was in a frenzy. Screaming. Flinging his limbs about. 'All I want is a bit of attention! But it's always about you, isn't it?'

'Okay, I get it, Y.' I was standing behind the coffee table, using it as a bulwark. 'Just let me get dressed and I'll leave.'

'No. Go as you are.'

He went into the room and slammed the door.

And, madly, I went after him.

(*In Allan Gurganus's short story, 'Forced Use', a married man picks up a younger man at a motorway rest stop, and they go into the bushes to have sex. There, after he has ejaculated, the young man beats the married man to a pulp. After which the married man thinks: I wanted that.*

Well, it seemed I wanted it, too.

If the choice was between being hit and being the one who hit—and on some level I believed that, as a gay man, this was my fundamental choice, for there was something inherent in me that inspired violence in others, and which in turn inspired violence in me—I would choose the former. I would take the slaps. Why? Because the alternative felt far worse.

And I should know. Once, on a winter's evening in Rome, after a fight with a boyfriend in which he falsely accused me of infidelity and admitted to reading the messages on my phone, I got out of the car in the middle of traffic, stormed away, my anger rising, rising, rising, until I had entered a state of delirium, which saw me turning on my heels, going back to the car, knocking on the window, and, the way now clear, slapping him across the face. 'You're the only person who has ever hit me,' he later told me. Which put me in the distressing position of being the living verification of two harrowing hypotheses. The first: people who feel oppressed can become more dangerous than the people they fear. The second: people who feel oppressed can become more dangerous than their oppressors—to other oppressed people.)

Y was using his body weight to block the door.

'Y, open the door. Let me get my clothes. Or just my laptop.'

'If you come in here, I'll fucking beat you to death.'

Weirdly composed, I went to sitting room, sat on the sofa, and thought about what to do. *Should I leave the flat in my pyjamas, without my wallet or my key, and hope that someone on the street will help me? Where is the nearest police station? Why had my phone chosen today of all days to pack it in?*

After about ten minutes, he came out of the room, dressed as he had been in the morning, my suit, his shirt, only now more dishevelled.

'Be gone when I get back,' he said, then left the flat.

I rushed into the room, pulled out my suitcase, and began to throw my things into it.

After a couple of minutes, I heard a muffled ringtone: Y had left his phone on the bed, under the duvet. A female colleague of his, whom I knew, was calling. I answered and told her briefly what was happening. She said that Y had insulted her at the function and left in an angry mood.

'What are you going to do?' she said.

'I'm getting out of here.'

I locked the front door. (A little bar in the top right-hand corner that slid across and prevented even a person with a key from getting in. Precisely the sort of lock that I had longed to have on my bedroom door growing up. Using it now, my hands were shaking. I knew he would come back as soon as he realised that he did not have his phone. I did not have a lot of time.)

In the event, I had even less than I thought:

Boom! Boom!

His fists beat on the door.

Boom!

Now he was taking running kicks at it.

Boom! Pause. *Boom!* Pause. *Boom!*

I called through the door: 'Stop, Y! Your phone is here. I just need two minutes to pack my stuff.'

Boom!

I opened the lock and ran into the sitting room.

He stormed in, grabbed his phone, and left again.

Twenty minutes later, I was dragging my suitcase out onto the landing when Y's flatmate came home. She helped me down the stairs.

'Sit with me for a minute,' she said.

She had a bottle of beer in her bag, which we drank on a bench by the canal. I told her everything. When I got to the bit about the HIV, she began to cry. And I cried with her.

'I noticed a change in him recently,' she said. 'There's something dark in him.'

'Now I won't ever know how it happened. How I came to have it. I think I was staying with him to find out. But, honestly, I don't care any more. I just need to get away.'

'Where?'

'Out of England. Back to Spain, maybe.'

I got a taxi to the house of my PhD supervisor. I did not call to warn her, even though it was late. Her daughter's boyfriend answered holding a tennis racket. He had thought I was a prowler.

Her daughter appeared behind him in the hall: 'Gavin? What has happened? Come in.'

Four days later, in my supervisor's kitchen, I received a call from Y.

'We have to talk,' he said.

'That's not going to happen,' I said.

'Okay,' he said, and put down the phone.

We never spoke again.

After a few days, I flew to Spain: I would live off my advance and write my second novel there. Soon after my arrival, I received an email from Y's mother. Y had informed her about what had happened. He seemed to be under the impression that I would go back to him. If he really loved me, she said, he should seek me out and negotiate a mode of coexistence that accorded with both of our needs. As she much as she was critical of him, she continued to believe that he was the most charming person in the world. What he needed was some counselling, which she and her husband were trying to convince him to do. She and her husband were going to be in London the following month. If it did not affect my emotional stability, could we meet, the three of us?

Writing my reply, I grieved for the mother I would never meet. The mother for whom I could have been the good son, *her prince*. I grieved knowing that, if I was to escape from Y, I had to escape from his family as well. Even from serene, wise, beautiful, magnificent Mother. For a fool she was, really. Her admiration for her son built on ignorance and lies. I did not envy Y this attention any more. All this time, I had been searching in the wrong place, for the wrong thing.

I would very much like to meet you in person. It would be painful for me, but maybe would help me to overcome all of this. The problem is, I'm in Spain at the moment. After the break with Y, I came here for some distance and to write in peace. I am hurt, and for this reason tempted to tell you everything that happened with Y, but it would not be fair to do so. I would regret it. I can say only this to you: I am not going to go back to him. I do not want to see or speak to him. I do not want him in my life, not even as a friend. In general, I have good relations with my ex-partners, but I do not want any contact with Y. Maybe this will change in the future, but now, in this moment, I am certain I want to be far away from him.

In my Big Dream, I turn away from the family scene and lie down on a mattress, which I can immediately tell is filled with water. At a certain point, I notice that the water is seeping out of the mattress onto the floor, and that there is a lot of it, far more than the mattress should be able to hold. Bit by bit, the room fills up, and the mattress begins to float on top.

I feel a terrible panic about this, which alerts me to the true nature of the situation: I am urinating. Pissing. Inundating the world with my waste fluids. What is inside of me is coming out, and it is polluting everything. *I am incapable. I am good for nothing. I do not know how to play, and now that I am infected, no one will ever want to play with me. I should hide myself here in the darkness and die in shame.*

A few weeks after my diagnosis, I did a group-therapy session called 'HIV, Shame, and Stigma'. It took place over a weekend in a basement room in a clinic in central London. Ten participants. Eight gay men. One straight man. One straight woman. (*Eight to two:* I figured out the ratio in my head; it seemed to matter.) There were two leaders, a straight white woman who had contracted HIV by using dirty heroin needles. And a bisexual man who had become HIV-positive through penetrative sex with another man.

(It was important for me, at that time, to know how others had got the virus. Specifically, I wanted to understand the nature of their relationship to the person who had transmitted the virus to them, in order to gauge how usual or unusual my own case was. Extremely usual, it turns out. I am learning to embrace that. My usualness.)

Over the course of the weekend, the leaders guided us through exercises designed to help us identify and to break down any feelings of shame we might be feeling about being HIV-positive. On the one hand, we were invited to refrain from blaming others for our becoming HIV-positive and instead to take responsibility for the actions we took that led to our predicament. On the other hand, we were asked to examine the ways in which we might be punishing ourselves, and were encouraged to find forgiveness for ourselves. The virus, we were told, had no morals. It was just a biological entity that, like any other, wanted to replicate itself. It did not care about what you did in bed. It just wanted to access your cells to reproduce itself within them.

(The virus is truly ingenious, I have come to respect it, even though it does not respect its environment: me.)

A lot of the exercises we did were focused on disclosure. When to tell others. How to tell them. And why.

'Think of it this way,' said the female leader. 'Is there shame in having diabetes? For some people there might be. Perhaps they are overweight. Perhaps they had an unhealthy diet for a long time. Is the shame they feel about their condition preventing them from getting the proper support? Is it hindering their ability to look after themselves, physically and psychologically?'

I found that helpful. I decided I would think about my HIV as though it were diabetes. Would I tell my friends I had diabetes? Yes. Would I tell my family? Yes. Would I tell potential partners? Yes. Was there anyone in the world I would hide diabetes from? No.

With this, I was almost there. I just needed one more push. Which came towards the end of the session, when a participant asked the leaders about their experiences of disclosing their HIV status to their families. The questioner presumed, as I think we all did, that anyone who ventured to run a therapy session on shame would have overcome enough of their own shame to be able to make such a disclosure. But it had been wrong to make such a presumption. With visible discomfort, the bisexual man admitted that, despite being a public HIV campaigner in London, he had not yet disclosed his status to his family in Eastern Europe. They had traditional values, he said, and would not understand.

Our eyes then turned to the straight woman: *what about you?*

The woman spoke more confidently than the man, employing an intricately designed rationale to explain why she, a leading figure in the fight against HIV stigma, had decided against telling her parents. Listening to her, I felt cheated. We had just spent two days learning that secrets, by definition, were the product of and produced shame. And that there was no shame in feeling shame. It was natural to hide what is shameful in us. The point was to recognise it, to see it for what it is—an ego trip—and to try to see if we could come to see past it. Were there genuine reasons, other than shame, for keeping our secret? Probably not: at the end of the day, it all came back to shame.

At no point in her explanation, however, did the woman mention her own shame. I would have respected her if she had said, 'I'm still working on my shame in relation to HIV and my family, which is why I can't tell them.' Instead, she went around the world, mentally speaking, to avoid what was so clearly a source of shame for her: her inability to be truly free.

Her example to me was negative: I was *not* going to be like her. I was not going to create a complex web of justifications for imprisoning myself in shame. Was I ashamed? You bet I was. Nothing less than mortified. Disgusted with myself. Crawling in my own skin. And *for this reason* I had to tell my family. I would continue to be ashamed *until* I told them. Telling them, from my place of shame, was nothing less than the way out of that place!

I owe a great debt of gratitude to that ashamed woman for showing me the way. At the next opportunity—suddenly I could not wait—I was going to go home and come out.

Again.

Or perhaps for the first time, properly.

'I've something to tell you, Mum.'

I had come home for a few days and was staying in the spare cell. We had just finished supper and were lingering at the table. My mother was pouring herself a second glass of wine: a half-measure, because she rationed it out, fearing the alcoholism that had gripped her own mother in the years before her death.

'What is it?' she said.

She was sitting directly opposite me. Her face showed concern but not fear.

'I'm HIV-positive,' I said, simply.

My hand was resting on the table, almost halfway between us.

She reached over and put her hand on top of mine.

And what she said next—so plainly, so undaunted—was nothing less, and nothing more, than what I had wanted from her. Proof, it was, that my flight from her to other people, whom I had admired and idealised to avoid my hostile feelings towards her, had really been a means of preserving her—*oh serene, oh wise, oh beautiful, oh magnificent Mother!*—so that

I could return to her, and hear this from her lips, and thereby learn from her how to be free.

Looking at me straight in the eyes, solid, not a single quiver any-where, she said: 'Now tell me what that means.'

INTERLUDE: LONDON, 2015

My publisher organised a tour of some central-London bookshops so that
I could meet the booksellers and sign a few copies of my debut novel,
and I invited my mother, who had flown over to attend the launch that
evening, to come along: at the agreed time, we met my publicist at the
London Review Bookshop, where someone had built a little pyramid
out of my hardbacks on the central table; this was the first time I had
ever seen my work on show, and the effect was not so much moving as
disconcerting: not knowing what to do with myself, I circled around the
pyramid a couple of times and took a picture of it with my phone, then
I began to feel embarrassed by my proximity to it and started browsing
the books on the next table over, where there was a nice-looking volume
about dogs which I picked up and turned over in my hands, 'Oh that's
lovely,' said my mother, taking it from me, 'We'll get this for J,' and once
she had paid for it and I had signed my copies, we left, the three of us
together, and walked through Bloomsbury into Covent Garden, my
publicist and I shoulder to shoulder, my mother two steps behind, 'Are
you all right, Mum?' I called back to her every so often, and she said,
'Yes, go on, don't mind me,' a response which I could tell was sincere,
she could not have been happier walking through Leicester Square,
watching her author son talk to his publicist—she could not hear what
we were saying, but she guessed it must have been about literature, and
she was right—and in Hatchards of Piccadilly, while I was busy signing,
she browsed the ancient bookshelves and decided to take away Elena
Ferrante's *Days of Abandonment*, a novel which I adored but which I had

not thought to recommend to my mother, a fact that struck me as odd, perhaps I thought she must have already read it, and indeed seeing the book in her possession now, it appeared as if it had always belonged to her, as if she had just taken it down from her own bookshelves to dust it off or re-read it or lend it to someone, and it occurred to me— I dare say for the first time—that she, my mother, like Ferrante's character, was an abandoned woman: my father's suicide had also been, in a real sense, an act of abandonment; he had deserted her, broken his vows to her, left her to fend for herself; and in my dealings with her, I was probably not as aware of this as I should have been, it was something I should have reminded myself of more often, especially at those moments when I felt tempted to criticise her inadequacies; yet at the same time, I did wonder whether it is ever accurate to speak of 'abandonment' when one adult person leaves another, be it by walking out the door or checking out of life entirely: *is it not equally true to say that when people leave us they are assuming responsibility for themselves as free beings? does a life in which we feature have more intrinsic worth than a life in which we do not?* these are certainly questions that Ferrante's novel poses, and they were questions over which my mother must have pondered over the years, and to which she must have found some form of resolution, for I had never—not once—heard her say that my father's decision to kill himself was wrong, or that she resented him for doing it, or that she wished he had chosen another course, possibly because she understood that another course might not have been better for him, for her, for anyone; on the contrary, I had only ever heard her speak of his loyalty to his family, his devotion to the identity of male provider, his commitment to a thankless job that was destroying his nerves, his guilt for not being able to give us more, his shame at having to ask his wife to work lowly jobs to survive, his inclination to blame himself for our errors, our failures, our sadness, our madness; and I did not think my mother spoke in these terms about my father because she wanted to create a false mythology about him, she was not blind to his shortcomings, rather she had simply refused to define him according to a single act he had carried out in his middle age, an act which, beyond the right and wrong of it, remained one of the few he ever

undertook by and for himself, an act, moreover, that had had nothing
to do with her and therefore could not be subsumed into her identity
as a wife, a mother, a woman, 'You're going to like that book,' I said to
her when we had left the shop, 'but it might not be easy for you,' and
she gave me a look that said, *When have I ever been interested in easy?*
and now my publicist was leading us along Shaftesbury Avenue and up
Charing Cross Road into Foyles, where my book was on display front-of-
house, alongside the bestsellers and the big names, and this time, yes, I felt
overcome with emotion, which I worked hard to swallow and push down,
I did not know why, what was stopping me from crying or calling out
or standing on a table and bursting into song? why should this moment
not have been celebrated? who on earth would have been offended? but,
fortunately, I was distracted from myself by the task of shaking hands and
making small talk, and I was surprised and genuinely grateful when the
bookseller told me that he had read my book and liked it and chosen it
as one of the store's Books of the Month, and I was enjoying myself now,
I could feel myself beaming, and I was conscious, also, that my publicist
was taking a picture of me to post online, and instinctively I turned my
head away in order to hide how I looked, and I noticed my mother there,
a few metres away, in front of the display of my books, pausing, hesitating,
before taking down a copy and opening it and reading a couple of lines
from the first page, then closing it again and putting it back, then taking
it down a second time and repeating her gestures almost exactly, and I
could see the anxiety on her face, and I knew what she was thinking: she
was thinking, this was the dream, to find something to write, to be able
to write it, to have it read, to be told it is worthy, to be judged good—
to step free from the crowd and to make one's face known—and it was
also the nightmare, to be exposed, to be misjudged, to be subjected to
slights, to be the butt of society's odium; of all the insults and humiliation
I had received in my lifetime, only the public pillorying of my writing
remained for me to experience, and she thought it would be worse than
anything that had come before, and there was nothing that could prepare
me for it; and my heart ached that my mother worried for me in this
way, that she anticipated criticism on my behalf in the belief that this

would protect me from it, for there was no protecting me from what I wanted: my biography was that of a man tortured by dissatisfaction with himself, I was long accustomed to burning myself in my own flame, and it would have been foolish of me to put too much reliance on my own judgement, for it was a sort of blindness to be always alone with the anger of my personal law; at some point, if understanding was what I was after, I had to undress and face outwards, with wide eyes, and offer myself to whoever happened to turn in my direction, and if I felt anything other than humility in the winning of their regard—be it hostile or kind—I would know I was not yet worthy of it.

CELL VII

On the day—at a time like this—I am standing at the kitchen counter peeling broad beans.

'Can I help?' she says.

'All right,' I say, sceptically. I indicate to the two bowls: 'Put the skins in that one, and the beans in that one.'

She perches on a high chair and picks out a bean. Peers at it. Then tears at its skin for a long minute without managing to get it off.

'This is torture.'

'You said you wanted to help.'

'And this is the job you give me? Show me how you do it.'

'Open the skin here,' I say, demonstrating, 'and squeeze the bean out like this.'

Judging from her expression as she watches my demonstration—one intended to inform me that I am mad to be doing this *voluntarily*, that is without being forced by economic circumstances to do it for the minimum wage, in which case, presumably, the work would have, if not sense, then at least some dignity—I can tell she has no intention of following my instructions.

She takes up another bean and wrestles with it according to her own failed method. After about thirty seconds, during which time I have shelled ten or more, she manages to release the bean from its cell. Her success gives her no feeling of satisfaction.

'Look at this one, for goodness sake,' she says, grappling with a third bean. 'It refuses to budge.'

'You have longer nails than me. It should be easier for you.'

'Oh, now, look at that one'—she has risen, on only her *fourth* bean, to exasperation—'this one is too small.'

'Are you going to help or not?'

'And that one, Jesus. How am I supposed to get that one out?'

'Think of it as meditation. *Live in the present*, isn't that what you always say?'

That shuts her up for the space of maybe five beans, before she loses her concentration again.

'Don't put the beans in the skins bowl,' I say.

'What?'

'Skins. Beans.'

'For goodness sake, who in their right mind would buy this amount of beans? Can't you get them frozen?'

'You like the food I cook, don't you? Well, this is how it's made.'

'You shouldn't go out of your way.'

'I don't. I enjoy it. And I'm excited to have these beans. They're tricky to find here.'

'Where did you get them?'

'None of your business.'

'Oh don't tell me. I know where. Don't normal Irish people eat broad beans?'

'You've been Irish for eighty years. You should know.'

'Know what?'

'That *normal* here means driving for an hour on the motorway to get Krispy Kremes.'

'To get what?'

'It doesn't matter.'

We peel in silence for a while. *Has she started to enjoy it?*

'Are they good for you at least?' she says.

'Some people have allergies to them,' I say. 'Like peanuts. If they don't kill you, they're good for you.'

'At least there's a reward at the end of this torment.'

'Death?'

'I expect my skin to be glowing in the coffin.'

'If you open your mind to it, it's nice work.'

'You'll want to put me in the attic next.'

'You've gone soft, you know that? You used to grate carrots for twelve hours at a stretch, at that catering business you worked for.'

'It was hard work, but we had fun.'

'And you did Lough Derg, didn't you?'

'This is *much* worse.'

When all the beans are done—her contribution amounts to no more than fifteen or twenty—I go to the sink to rinse my hands. Turning back, I see her on the way to the bin with the bowl of peeled beans. I yelp and swipe the bowl from her: 'Jesus Christ, the beans!'

'Were those the beans?'

'It's all right, they're saved. Go and sit down. Out of my way, now, come on.'

She does not move. And she will not, it is clear, until she has made the point she now feels called upon to make.

'You should work for a chef,' she says.

'I have a profession, thank you, Mum.'

'You'd have to be the chef, though, giving the orders. You couldn't be lower down. What's the name for that?'

'The *sous*.'

'You wouldn't hack being the *sous*.'

'Luckily, I won't ever have to hack it. Because I have a job.'

She ponders this, as though to transmit to me the question: *Do you, really?*

'The restaurants are in trouble now,' she says then.

'Yeah,' I say.

'Centra, on the other hand, is cleaning up. This morning I got the paper, a coffee, and a protein bar for three-something.'

'That's a mistake.'

'I thought so, too. It's six-something in that organic place in Milltown. Robbers.'

—

In 2019, after four more years in Spain—and just six months before quarantine began—I came back to Ireland to take up a one-year university residency. My stipend was generous relative to the amount of teaching I was required to do, but it did not cover a flat of my own. I could accept the position only because my mother allowed me to stay with her. It was impossible to know in advance if returning to live with my mother was, for me, or indeed any adult male, healthy and good. Nor could I know what sort of impact my presence would have on her, whether it would be destabilising or annoying or cheering or something else. But I did know this. In many aspects, I was still childish. By moving far away, geographically, I had tried to free myself from my childhood, but I had failed. The passage of the years and my headlong rush into, and against, the outside world had left a mass of material behind that had never been dealt with. This material, even though most of the time I could not see it, clung to me and suffused me with infantile feeling. Owing to this, my consciousness remained tied to my mother and could not act entirely independently of her. Now my fear was that, in returning to her, I would succumb to these ancient desires and passions I could not control, precisely because they, in reality, had control over me. I was childish, yes, and I did not want to be, and it would be painful to be reminded (my mother would not have to say or do anything in particular, simply being herself in my presence would be enough) that, at the crucial moments, I had no choice but to be so.

As a protective strategy against this—against my infant self—I assumed a self-consciously adult function: that of the nourisher. I planned the meals. Researched the recipes. Made the shopping lists. Visited several shops and supermarkets to get the ingredients I needed. Carried everything home on my back. I did this in the months before quarantine began, and I do it now, in precisely the same way, during quarantine; my role, before and after, has changed little.

'We have too much food,' she said once while watching me unpack.

'We don't have too much.'

'Are you hoarding?'

'Don't joke, Mum.'

'There's a lot.'

'There's enough. That's different.'

'All these greens. What are you going to do with them?'

'You'll see. Recipes.'

'My goodness.'

'My goodness what? It's food. Just food. That's all.'

'What's wrong with you?'

'Leave me alone.'

'I'm leaving you alone.'

'You're not. You're on top of me.'

As an infant, I had been round-cheeked and plump; presumably, I drank copiously from the breast. But later, when I moved on to solid food, I became what was called a 'picky eater'. *Eat up. Stop being so picky. Think of the starving children in Africa.'* Thinking of all those bloated bellies did not help: my throat would tighten, my stomach would turn, leaving me with the double problem of an unwanted mound of food *and* the feeling that there was something wrong with me (for wanting so much but not wanting *that*). The problem could not have been the quality of the cooking I was being served—in the prevailing regime, such an idea was, if not unthinkable, certainly unsayable—therefore the problem had to be me. I played with the food that was put before me on the table. I tried to hide it on the plate, one thing behind another behind another, because under no circumstances was I allowed to refuse it. Perhaps the most frightening moment of my childhood was the fit of rage my mother had when I told her I was not going to eat the brown-lentil soup she had made. She was outraged. Incandescent. As though I had just told her she was a deficient mother, worthless—which I suspect, thanks to her upbringing, she was regularly close to believing by and of herself; it took the littlest of pushes, a child's hand, to send her all the way there.

As an older child and a teenager, I often felt hungry, not out of poverty, but because my mother was an unreliable provider of food. The fridge was regularly empty, or near to it. A yoghurt or two. A block of cheese. Some coleslaw. A packet of rashers. A jar of mayonnaise. A litre of milk. My father did a big shop on Saturday morning—as soon as the supermarket opened to avoid bumping into the neighbours—but he did so without any real clue as to how one might create a week's worth of meals for a large family. There were dinners, but they did not take place at fixed times, and the food on the plate was uninspiring. Lamb chops toughened under the grill. Flat fish that might have been good had it been introduced to a clove of garlic. Pasta with a bland, sometimes quite inedible, sauce. Quiche, quiche, and more quiche, with the result that I cannot touch the stuff today. Potatoes, likewise. No salt. No herbs. No spices. No imagination. No forethought. No pleasure. No gladness. No willingness to learn. My mother cut out recipes from the Sunday supplements and kept them in a folder, but she rarely tried them out; the collecting was the point, as though the idea of nourishment, of betterment, was more important than the experience of it.

And yet—the delicious contradiction—I have seen few people enjoy their food as much as she does.

'I've got a gut,' she said one day after putting away two helpings of dessert. 'You'll have to stop buying these tarts.'

'You don't have to worry about putting on weight.'

'It's not about putting on weight, I just don't want a gut.' She prodded the flesh above her hips. 'Here and here. I don't want to spread out.'

'There's no danger of you spreading anywhere. You're a stick.'

'Well, I'm not exercising at the moment.'

'Your walks?'

'I mean real exercise. My water aerobics and my swims. I'll be like a barrel by the time the pool opens again. *Roll out the barrel. We'll have a barrel of fun.*'

Later, as my mother got more and more tired of cooking—tired, that is, of having to do something that she never really enjoyed—her dishes got weirder: chopped beetroot and banana and tomatoes and raw peppers and spring onions, presented as a healthy alternative to the traditional fare of cooked meat and carbohydrates. And maybe it *was* healthier. Maybe it added years to our lives. But it was also unsatisfying. This was the period of staring into the fridge, vainly seeking the elixir that would kill the pangs. My normal recourse, it shames me to say, was to binge on breakfast cereals. Sugary flakes. Or plain flakes covered in sugar. With whole milk, often heated on the stove. Several bowls a day. Or brown bread, which was one thing my mother did well: with cheese to start, with marmalade to finish, even though it often gave me heartburn severe enough to keep me awake at night (a sensation I learned to recognise as indigestion only after I had grown up and moved away and entered a relationship with a doctor: *'Did your parents never give you a Rennie?' 'I never told them.' 'Why not?' 'I didn't think it was serious enough.'*)

I was, I mean to say, an unsatisfied child. I felt empty, and I feared this feeling. Out of this fear, an aggressive quality entered my appetite. As soon as I was old enough, I travelled, aggressively, in search of objects which would fill me up. When I lost one person—once I had consumed and excreted him—I cast round for a replacement. Failed ideals I plastered over with novel philosophies. I was easily influenced. I went with whoever had the sugar.

Returning home now, I found myself urgently wishing to have my food accepted. I felt the need to give to my mother, to fill her up. To get under her skin. To be felt within her organs. To prove to her that what I had to offer was good. What to make of this anxious eagerness to satisfy her? Possibly it was merely a disguise for a fear of anxious hunger *in her*; of being consumed *by her*.

If I fill her up, she won't want to eat me.

'Are you saving that for later?' she said, pointing at the remaining food in the pot.

'Do you want some more?'

'No, I don't. Just a half-spoon.'

'So, you *do* want some more.'

'No, just what's on that spoon there.'

'So, yes, you want another helping.'

'No, just...'

———

Before quarantine, I would go to the library to work. My preference would have been to work at home, in private, away from people, but there was no desk in my room, so I did not have a choice, though it was just as well: staying at home would have placed my mother and I within constant reach of each other. The obligation to work outside the flat, coupled with my desire to make proper cooked meals, lent my pre-quarantine days quite a specific structure. I shopped and cooked in the morning, while my mother was out for her walk. I left her portion of lunch on the table and packed my own into boxes. Then, following a similar route to hers, through the leafy local streets and along the nearby river, I walked to the campus, where I ate alone in the common area of the arts block, with hundreds of unknown students milling around me, before heading upstairs to find a desk to sit at. I stayed there all afternoon and into the evening, often until closing time at ten, stopping once or twice to eat again from my supply. Then I walked back home in the dark, getting in after my mother had gone to bed. This way, I saw very little of her: in the morning, briefly, when I was washing or doing my yoga, and sometimes again at night when she got up to go to the toilet, and saw the light on in the main room, and came in to where I was reading the newspaper or a book, and said, 'Don't stay up too late,' or 'You work too hard.'

The situation was not ideal, of course. It would have been preferable to have an office of my own, a flat of my own, a story of my own to tell; at forty-two, I was hardly thrilled to be rooming with my elderly mother. But, for all that, the days and the weeks were reassuringly consistent, and I was enjoying the moments shared with her. We did not fight much. We laughed; or rather, she made us both laugh. She seemed well to me, all in all. Frailer than ten years ago, naturally, but still strong. More active than most people of any age. On account of her bad hearing, she spent most of her time alone, following her own courses and routines, which had made her a touch more eccentric than before. On her walks, she made contact with the other irregular folk of the neighbourhood, and learned about them, and brought home their stories, or made up stories about them—to her, it seemed like everyone else was completely losing their marbles— which I found entertaining, though I noticed that she had taken to repeating herself, and that she got confused about times and dates and places, and had to double-check that she had not said something in error, 'Hold on now, let me think,' which could be trying to listen to, so I was glad I was not there all day long, fielding it; I would have quickly got tired and started to snap at her.

The worry: *What if something happened to prevent me from going to the library? How would I cope if, for some unforeseen reason, I got locked into this cell with her? In such an event, where would I work, what would happen to my mind, how long before I started to bite at her, and she at me?*

The first of February, eight weeks before quarantine, was a cold day but not raining. At four, it was already getting dark. The ceiling lights in the library turned the windows into mirrors, so that the room appeared to extend into the world, and the act of staring out—the attempted escape from the self—was transformed into the unwanted contemplation of the self. *My God, is this how I appear to others? A trapped, starved animal?* At around half past the hour, I sent the final edits of my second novel to my editor. The library was quiet, so I took a stroll around in my socks, shaking the excitement out of my limbs, though there was less of this—fewer emotions—than one might expect. During the writing process, I had been fixated on reaching this moment, this end, it had been all I could think about, and yet the reality of being here was pale in comparison to its many imagined forms. As far as my consciousness was concerned, the novel, although completed mere seconds ago, was already ancient history. *Chewed. Digested. Shat out. Washed away.* And what was left in me was the hunger. The emptiness. The void. *Le néant. El vacío. Il vuoto. Das Nichts.* Terrifying in all the tongues, which was why I now felt the need to run away from it, mentally speaking, and hunt out my next big meal. I stopped in front of a stack of shelves containing books relevant to the subject of my next novel, the third, for which I had already started some preliminary research. *Maybe after three I will be satiated?* I perused these books for a while, making notes of what I had already read and what I had yet to read and what I would have to find elsewhere—*don't stop, keep ingesting, churn and churn and churn and churn*—before wandering back to my desk and checking my email. No reply from my editor. But then, it *was* a Saturday.

I packed my things and left the library at half past five. I exited the campus by its west gate, walked north along a busy suburban thorough-fare, then took a left onto the river path. The way here was narrow. There were no street lights. To the left, over a low wall, was the water, high and fast-running after a season of heavy rain. To the right, tall trees and bushes, which, in the tighter spots, I brushed against, leaving wet patches on my waterproof jacket and tracksuit bottoms. Seeking company in the dark, I made a call to my uncle. Instead of holding the phone to my ear, I used cheap wire headphones to listen to him, while holding the screen in front of my face to speak. This allowed me to use the torch light on the back of the device to help me avoid the puddles on the ground. It also kept me illuminated for the benefit of anyone who should come in my direction: *I am, I hope they see, nothing to be afraid of.*

At a quarter to six, still in conversation with my uncle, I passed by a pub whose back entrance faces the river. The lights from the pub façade and the adjacent car park illuminated the figures of two boys, aged between twelve and fourteen, loitering in the nearby clearing. I crossed in front of these boys, though at quite a distance: no less than twenty metres. They called out to me. I did not know what words they were using, both because I could not quite hear them over my uncle's voice, and because I had learned, from long experience, to ignore the calls of such boys, for there was no answer—none—that would please them, satisfy them, convince them that I could not give them what they were really looking for.

Such boys: as soon as I lay eyes on them, at once, instantly, almost instinctively, I know them to be: such boys.

I continued along the path, which followed the course of the river through the clearing. After about ten steps, I heard the sound of a small object striking my backpack. Then I felt a handful of pebbles hitting my arms and legs. Unfazed, acknowledging events and sensations that were entirely familiar to me, I did not turn around or increase my pace. My gaze fastened on the scene ahead—the upward curve of the path and the silhouettes of the trees and the street lights of the nearby road—I walked exactly as I had been until now: brisk, tall, head held high.

A second, then, and a boy entered my vision on the right side, close to me, about two metres away. He was screaming at the top of his lungs:

'Apologise! Apologise for ignoring me, you faggot!'

I turned; that is, I made a full rotation and looked at him straight in the eyes. I was not afraid of him, because in my life I have attracted the attention of dozens of boys exactly like him, who in my presence have undergone the same paroxysms of feeling, so I was aware that, in these moments of bewitchment, it was me who held the greater power: *the image of me that this boy holds in his mind, what I represent for him internally, is larger, more imposing, more real than any image of himself that he can possibly muster.* Beheld by me—this fearsome figment—he hesitated. Took a step back. Glanced to the second boy, who was a couple of paces behind, and then peered back up the path, where four more boys, whom I had not noticed before, were advancing in a line, shoulder to shoulder, all of them laughing. For the first boy, the sight of his compatriots—exact copies of himself, and he exact copies of them, and they exact copies of other copies, an army of boys lost in a maze of masculine mirrors—was terrifying, so much so that he felt the need to scream: this was what he did now, he screamed, out of fear, so as to hide himself from those he was really frightened of.

'What's your problem, you faggot? Why are you ignoring me?'

He was a child. They were children. None older than fourteen. Fresh tracksuits. Clean trainers. Hoodies. Underdressed for the weather. Pale skin. Short hair. And skinny. So skinny.

Such boys: what they are is ravenous and desperately seeking fullness, and if I were their mother I would pull them into me, envelop them in my flesh and tell them to eat from me, to take as much as they need, to not stop until they had reached my bones, and when at last they were full, lying around rubbing their bloated bellies, I would say to them, 'Now that you are satisfied, now that you know what true fulfilment means, please ask yourselves, for your own sakes, can anyone but me ever give you this?' and they would groan and moan and say, 'Mamma, leave us alone, less of the questions, we're trying to digest,' but eventually, after some more goading, they would answer, loyally, in the negative, for deep down they are good boys, wise boys: such boys.

'What's going on?' came my uncle's voice in the headphones.

'Nothing,' I said. 'Just some kids.'

'You need to get out of there.'

'Don't worry, I'm fine. They're just messing.'

Turning my back on the boys, I set off again, not rushing, feeling alert but calm.

Just before reaching the northern end of the clearing, where the path joins the main road, I was pushed from behind, forcing me to totter forwards for a few steps, which brought me into the light of the street lamps. There, in full view of the passing cars, I was pushed again.

'Faggot!' the one who was pushing me, the ringleader, was saying. 'Faggot! Faggot!'

'Fuck off,' I said to him, simply.

'Where are you exactly?' my uncle said. 'I'm getting into the car and coming to find you.'

'No,' I said, 'don't be silly. Just give me a second.'

I stepped out onto the road and began to flag down the cars.

Seeing me do this, the ringleader ran back to the other boys, who were now emerging from the darkness. I continued to gesticulate. The people in the cars beeped their horns aggressively as they passed me: *get off the road!* None of them stopped.

Spooked, the boys dashed back into clearing.

'They're gone now,' I said to my uncle.

'Are you sure?'

'Yes,' I said, and set off again.

After a hundred metres, the road splits: to the right, the bright road with all the traffic; to the left, a badly lit pedestrian path that cuts through a park and rejoins the river. To get to my mother's flat, I could take either route, but I was used to taking the latter because it is greener and quieter, if not actually shorter. Before turning down onto it, I glanced back: the coast was clear, my pursuers had disappeared.

I cut through the empty park and reunited with the river. A little further along, I passed the waterfall, where the gushing and the swirling of the water made it hard to hear my uncle. 'Hold on,' I said to him, and jogged to the quieter final stretch. 'Okay, I can hear you now.' I was on a tapering path, in some places no wider than an arm span, with branches reaching out and over, and underfoot a track of uneven concrete dotted with puddles and dollops of dog shit. Ahead, I could see car lights moving across a bridge, and the set of steps that would take me up to the road again.

But such boys: they want to be remembered by me, they want me to think of them when I return home, they want me to talk about them tomorrow and the next day, they want me to look back on them when I am old, they want to be immortalised—by me. I am happy to do this for them, it costs me nothing; in fact, at the end of the day, I am the one who gains, I get the credit for these words, I am paid for them, and all the while I am learning from them: learning, that is, how to grow up.

At first, I thought I was being molested, because there were hands— lots of hungry little fingers—on my bottom and waist and thighs. Out of the darkness behind me, these hands were grabbing at me and reaching around me and rubbing me up and down. Finding nothing to dip into or hold on to (my wallet was in a zipped pocket in my jacket, while my penis did not interest them except as a concept: its presumed presence was what permitted them to handle me in this violent manner), they then toughened and stiffened and, in this new form, knocked me to the ground.

The phone flew out of my hand.

'Call the police!' I shouted at it as it spun through the air.

Now—*phump!*—I was on my hands and knees.

I planted one foot on the ground and, rising up, twisted my body round. Right in front of me, extremely close, were three boys. They were deadly silent. I could not even hear them breathe. *Am I holding my own breath, too?*

Then it came.

Weirdly, I felt it before I saw it rush towards me.

A fist smiting my face, on my cheekbone below my right eye, and across my nose.

Which spun me fully around and sent me crashing down onto my front.

(Some people, others, individuals who have never been beaten up—unbelievably, these souls exist—live in fear of this thing that has never happened to them. The possibility of getting pounced on is so scary to them, *If am not careful, it will come*, that it is always happening to them, in their thoughts. Me, because I have been beaten up many times, I am not afraid of it, as a thought. Rather, I am acquainted with it as a reality. It is perhaps for this reason that, in this moment, as I lay prostrate on the wet ground, blood flowing from my nose, I was audience to a series of highly practical ideas. *The river is right there. I can jump into it, if necessary. My laptop is in my backpack, but it's okay if that gets destroyed because I've sent the novel to my ed—*)

Then the kicks came. To my legs and chest and neck. And, momentarily, I was afraid. For it occurred to me that these boys did not know their own strength. They were testing limits, seeing how far they could go, as children do. But also, as children, they did not, could not, should not—*why should they?*—know the difference between a blow that is merely wounding and one that is fatal.

For a split second, I worry for my life.

Then it was over.

And I was scrambling to my feet. Picking up my phone. Trying to unlock it with my fingerprint but prevented from doing so by the blood, the shocking quantity of blood, that had already fallen from my face onto the screen.

I went up the steps to the road.

A couple, a man and a woman, were walking towards me.

'I've just been beaten up,' I said to them, before bending forwards, as though bowing before them, to let the blood run onto the path, rather than onto my clothes.

They crouched beside me.

Comforted me.

Helped me.

—

It was an old tape. A re-run. My initial response was to refuse to allow it—this boring ancient story—to alter in any way the current run of my life. With a swollen and bruised face, I taught my classes and went to the library. After the surgery to get my broken nose moved back into place, I went about my normal business with a large splint from which I leaked fluid all day. But then, at some point—when I understood that I was too tired to leave the house, and had no interest in working, and instead wanted to stay close to my mother and to heal—it dawned on me that this experience was not the same as before. The wonderful thing about visiting something after an absence is that one comes at it older and smarter. I could see things I had not seen in the past. I could discern how I was different and how others were different, too. Which is to say, now I could speak out, which was something I had felt unable to do as a child; and now I was listened to, which was a new gift I did not take for granted.

I paused and looked around at the people who came to visit me at the flat. Who flew in from afar to spend time with me. Who called and sent cards. Who gave me beautiful gifts. Who wrote articles about what happened to me. Who commissioned me to write articles of my own. Who invited me onto their television programmes and their radio shows. *Look—look!—at these people I have managed to gather round me: a community of big hearts and brilliant minds. Their support carries me like a wave. I am in awe of them. And I also know they are a reflection of me.*

Out of love, they asked me questions. *Did you defend yourself?* My answer: What was to defend? What had 'faggot' got to do with me? The word bore no relation to my being. What it actually referred to were the speakers of the word, those who got a thrill from having it in their mouths. If 'faggot' was in these boys' mouths, 'faggot' was on their minds, and what was on their minds in a particular moment—'*faggot-faggot-faggot-faggot*'—was no less than who they were in that moment. So the proper question was, why was 'faggot' on their minds? Why did that word occur to them as something to say to a man who passed them on the street? What did their use of 'faggot' make *them*?

So you did not hit back? Why should I have? The pain of receiving their blows was short-lived, trifling, in comparison to the prolonged suffering that they, as the abusers, were inflicting upon themselves. I had been in their shoes; I knew from vile experience that with every punch, every kick, they were intensifying their own trauma. *And if you had died?* Then they would have been killers, and that, I could be sure, was no way to live. And, anyway, is a child beater something I should really aspire to being? Beating up a child is always going to be abuse, right? Is there a difference between beating a violent child and beating a peaceful one? Thinking there is, thinking that there are beings on this earth who deserve our violence, is the root of the problem, and possibly the only problem.

How did they know you were gay? They did not. Their actions were not based on certainty. The opposite: they needed to make what was ambiguous clear. They were the arbiters of faggotry. They decided who the faggot was. The chosen faggot had no say in the matter. Their attack on me had nothing to do with *my* relationships or *my* sexuality; it had nothing to do with *me* at all. There was nothing inherent in me—a look, an attitude, a persuasion, an orientation—that inspired this violence. I was not the source. The boys used homophobic slurs to justify their own pre-existing desire for violence. They needed 'faggot' to perpetrate that violence, and for some reason that I am not going to spend a second of my valuable time trying to identify—because in fact such a reason does not exist—I fit the bill.

A final one: *How is this still happening?* Change is uneven. The nature of change is that it does not come totally formed. It appears partial and contested. In pockets and networks and islands. As a queer person, proudly walking this earth, I can never be certain that my next step will not land me in a place not yet touched by change. *The next house, the next street, the next city, the next country: will I be welcome there?* (And, truly, there is no point expecting change, in any place, anywhere, if inside myself such change has not been implemented. Like everybody else, I was raised in a homophobic society, to be homophobic: at the time, this was considered good and correct. Correcting this, putting it right within myself, means ending the violence I do to myself in the name of that old, false correctness. The problem is, realising that a previous correctness is now incorrect does not, in itself, make it go away; it persists in our consciousness as a cell in an interconnected and interdependent network of beliefs and assumptions; excising it can take years of intricate mental surgery. A lifetime's work. A task that is possibly even harder for me than for my heterosexual friends who were never that bothered by the correctness or otherwise of their own homophobia—*those were just silly words everyone used*—and who for this reason are able to shed it, easily, like a coat from a previous season, a bothersome cover, unnecessary in the new climate.)

My mother did not ask me such questions. (Probably because she knew there was no answer I could give that did not raise a hundred more questions, and we could go on forever.) Instead, a few days after the attack, she told me straight:

'You're never going to get over this.'

We had just finished eating lunch. I was at my place at the table, on the inside looking out, and she was opposite me. I did not much feel like talking, so I had pulled a folded newspaper closer to me and was scanning through the text of an opinion piece about the housing crisis. *Fuck lot of good these words are doing,* I thought and pushed the paper away.

You're never going to get over this.

'Do you mean this?' I said to her then, pointing at my bruised face. 'This, I'll recover from quite well, I think. It's the old stuff, the things that happened to me as a child, that I won't ever get over.'

'You mean, the school,' she said.

'Yeah, I mean the fucking school,' I said.

Her eyes slid off me as she sipped some wine from her glass. Then they slid back. 'The problem with that place,' she said airily, 'was that they didn't know how to handle boys. Once, after your brother R misbehaved, they put him in a room alone for a week!'

She was speaking jokily, though not quite laughing. We had broached a grave matter, but she was not willing to take it seriously.

'Did you intervene?' I said, refusing to be light.

'I didn't find out till afterwards, and was shocked.'

'You were shocked?'

'I was.'

'So'—I drew out this word, *soooo*—'what did you do about it? Did you complain to the school? Did you talk to my brother, ask him how he ff—?'

But it is useless, there is no answer she can give that will not raise a hundred more questions, and we could go on forever.

I was already out of my seat.

And had left the room.

And was standing, now, in the middle of my cell, under the hanging ceiling light, with nowhere left to go, just four impenetrable walls.

She came in: 'How dare you stand up and walk away like that.'

'I dared,' I said, swinging round, 'and I will dare again, as long as you insist on talking about that school as if you had no part to play in sending us there.'

'You're blaming me again.'

'Well, you *are* the one who sent us there. The buck stops with you.'

'I was doing the best I could.'

'That's right, you were. We all are. But that does not mean avoiding responsibility for what we've done.'

It was her turn to walk out.

I followed her back into the main room:

'It was no place for children. No child would willingly have spent time there. It continues to mystify me that you, an artist, a culture lover, should have sentenced me to five years in such a shithole.'

'I believed in local education. All the children in the community being taught together.'

'Which community? None of the neighbours went to that school. My friends from the estate wouldn't have been seen dead in it.'

'They all went to private schools.'

'That's right.'

'And are they better off now? What kinds of attitudes did they pick up in those places?'

'There were attitudes in my school, too, Mum. There's no escaping attitudes.'

'My own mother, don't ask me how she managed it, paid to send me to the nuns. And I had a terrible time. I didn't learn a thing.' She holds out one hand with the fingers splayed. Uses the other hand to make a sawing action across her knuckles. 'With a metal ruler. Right there. For the slightest infraction. I'd have been better off at the local state school.'

'Come on, Mum. The madhouse or the God-house? That can't have been the only choice for me. Did you even research alternative options?'

She picked up a tea-towel and rubbed around the edges of the sink. 'There was no money. I didn't need to research anything. I knew what the options were.'

'Didn't you stop to ask yourself why I was changing in this way? Why I was so unhappy?'

She rolled the tea-towel up and slotted it into the space between the tap and the wall, where the water splashes up.

'Even just my grades. Didn't you notice that they were dropping? Didn't you ask yourself why?'

She made her way to the table and fiddled with the arrangement of things on it. 'We didn't know. We didn't know what was happening.'

'That's bullshit, Mum. You *knew*.'

'I had a lot on my plate at that time, I was dealing with your father. And your brother.'

I sighed, hating that this was true.

'And, Gavin, you never said anything. You never told us.'

Turning, I took a couple of steps away from her. With my back turned to her, I tried to put my thoughts into an order that might be heard by her.

'You were taken out of school at fourteen, weren't you?' I said, turning back. 'Who was responsible for that?'

'I suppose it was my parents.'

'That's right. Not the Catholic Church. Not Ireland. Your parents. They survived for fourteen years without your wage packet, they could have survived a few years more. But they didn't. They decided to put you to work, and every week they took your hard-earned money away from you. And what's the result?'

She started to clear the table of the lunch things, for she did not want to hear anything about results.

'The result is your anger, Mum. Your fury.'

She thought about this. Then: 'It was just the way it was back then.'

'Yes, things were the way they were, but that does not mean they did not have an impact. Being denied an education and the possibility of choosing a job for yourself, how did it make you feel?'

I could see her test the weight of this question in her mind; it was too heavy for her.

'I must have felt angry. But I just got on with it.'

'Right. You put it all away. Stored it all up. I've seen for myself how you repress your anger. I've seen how the people around you get angry so that you don't have to.'

'My parents—. I mean, it was how I was raised. There was no space for expression.'

'Right. You're not to blame for how you were raised. And neither am I. Remember I, too, have parents, and you're one of them. You learned how to be a parent from your parents, and you raised me that way. I saw how Dad walked out of the room rather than face an argument. I saw you rattling plates at the sink instead of speaking out your frustration and pain. For years, that's how I thought everyone communicated. *Silence is better than confrontation. Confrontation inevitably involves screaming and shouting, nothing can be talked through.* That's what I believed.'

She sighed. Took up a dishcloth. Rung it out. Dropped it back into the sink. She wanted this to be over.

'So you can imagine'—I went on—'how desperate I was when I came to you and asked to change school. How hard it was for me to express something like that. And you dismissed me in the most brutal way. Which confirmed my belief that expressing things gets you nowhere, and that my duty was to accept violence and abuse as my lot in life.'

'You're so angry. You should speak to someone.'

'Counselling?'

'I'll pay half.'

'Don't you see that telling me to get counselling is just a way for you to avoid listening to what I'm saying? I'm not asking you to take away my pain.'

'What do you want, then?'

'I want you to take responsibility. Just once. To say, I did that. And it was wrong.'

'Did what?'

'You chose to send me to that school, and you kept me there even when you knew I was suffering. The treatment I received was not my responsibility. It was yours.'

'Mine?'

'Yours. I was a child. You were a parent. It was your job to protect me. To intervene.'

'I didn't know it was that bad.'

'Oh?'

'We didn't realise what was going on.'

'Don't even try—'

'All right, I failed. We failed. Everyone fails. That's life.'

'Yes, that *is* life. And part of failing, as an adult, is making up for it. In my forty-two years, I have never heard you accept your part.'

'So we failed as parents, is that it?'

'You didn't protect me!' I slammed my fist on the table. 'You didn't help me! I'll be grappling with that fact for the rest of my life.'

I was crying now.

'All right,' she said 'Anyone who went through what you went through would be angry.'

I wiped my face: 'And anyone who went through what *you* went through would be angry, too.'

She did not like this; my turning the tables in this way: 'I can't live with this tension any more.'

'Well, I'm sorry,' I said, 'but I'm no longer willing to hide my feelings about this. From you or from anyone. I don't care what age you are. I don't care how your health is. I don't care if you're the Pope or Mother fucking Teresa. I'm done pretending. I've had enough of silence.'

She moved to the table, where her cotton tote was hanging on the back of a chair. She began to put things into the tote as though preparing to go out for a walk.

'I don't want you to hide anything,' she said.

'I don't care how old you are, do you hear me?'

'I'm well able for it, don't worry. You're my son.'

She put the bag on her shoulder and went to the door.

I retreated to the kettle and filled it, for tea I did not want.

I heard the door open behind me; and then, spoken softly, over the creaking of the hinges, the words: 'Well, look, I'm sorry.'

Then she was gone.

Leaving me alone with her apology.

All I had ever wanted from her.

Yet, at once, I saw that it gave me nothing.

That, in my possession, it was worthless.

That what I had really desired, all this time, was exactly what I had got: like Proust's child narrator, who wishes to prolong the time in which his mother has not come to his room to give him his goodnight kiss, so as to delay the moment when the kiss is over and she leaves him once again; like this boy, whose real desire is that of waiting, of expectation, I had, since childhood, been longing for an apology that I hoped would never come, for I did not want to be obliged to forgive my mother, or even to contemplate the possibility that there was nothing to forgive her for—for what, then, would I do with my anger? where else would I sink it, if not into her flesh?

My Big Dream ends, not with my mother apologising to me, but the other way around, with me apologising to her. Lying down, I notice that the water is leaking from the mattress and filling the room. The sensation of the mattress floating on top of the water provokes in me a terrible panic, and I come to understand, then, that this vast body of liquid is in fact my urine. I am pissing, copiously, endlessly. This knowledge, and the shame that attends it, serves to remind me that I am not alone in the room: the characters of my mother and my younger self (played by my agent and her son) are still present. I look over at them. My mother, up to her knees in my piss, smiles at me comprehendingly. She is trying to show me, I think, that she does not mind that I have inundated the room—her house, the cell—with my excretions; she does not mind that I am destroying everything. Even if she manages to dry the place out, the walls and the floor and the furniture will be stained, damaged, beyond repair, but she forgives me for this.

I want to make my pain her fault. To punish her with it. But it seems she cannot come up with a bad conscience. To her mind, I am the evil-doer, the one who needs forgiveness: hers.

In a state of almost unbearable anxiety, I cave to her unspoken commands and apologise for my misconduct. For my destructive urges. For my being so disgusting. For my having no decency, no self-control. For my persisting in wretchedness and refusing to come to my senses.

I do not use the word 'sorry'. Rather I say, 'Don't worry, nothing will be ruined. The room will absorb everything.' But hot shame is what I feel. Burning heat. I am reprehending an action that has been reprehended for a long time—*what child in history has not wet his bed? what child in history has not wanted to destroy everything, including his mother?*—and, on waking up, nothing remains but cold remorse. Guilt before my deathless god.

'I'm sorry,' I said to her when she got back. 'I shouldn't have lost my temper like that. I'm only beginning to deal with this stuff now, I've never really faced it before. But it's not right to vomit it on you. I'm sorry.'

She accepted my apology with characteristic magnanimity; she was not someone to bear a grudge. We hugged. I could not tell if she remembered her own parting apology or comprehended its significance for me. Either way, she did not reiterate it. She did not want to dwell.

'Most of the time, we get on,' she said.

'Yeah,' I said. And then: 'I love you.'

'All right,' she said.

It was possible that, after this, the atmosphere between us would be cleaner. That the contaminating spell would be lifted and I would be freed of what Adrienne Rich calls *'the unhealed child's fantasies'* of a healing conversation with my mother, in which we could both *'show all our wounds, transcend the pain we have shared...say everything at last'.* Maybe, now, I would be able to be with her *and* leave her be; maybe I would find a way to be her son without imposing any maternal obligations on her. But it could equally be the case that, after one such confrontation, I would want another, and then another after that, for I—or at least the part of me that still felt madly unmothered—would have got the taste for blood, and from now on my inclination would be for hostility, for tearing more and bigger strips out of her, out of both of us.

Unwilling to chance it—*I mean, to chance that my anger will build up to violence as it has so often done in the past, like that time I broke a chair by kicking it down the stairs, or threw plates against the wall, or beat a sweeping brush against the tiles of the kitchen floor until the wood of the handle split, or wrote notes and letters and emails containing the worst of my venom, or walked for hours trying to exhaust myself before returning to the scene of an argument because I was afraid of what I would do fully charged, or screamed until my throat was raw and then opened the windows and doors so that the neighbours could hear my screaming in order to embarrass my adversary into surrender, or paced to and fro for days at a stretch fulminating with murderous feelings, or plotted in my mind terrible acts of revenge, or imagined elaborate scenarios of torture and murder; and in the muscles of my hand I still feel the sensation of making contact with my ex-boyfriend's cheekbone in Rome, and in the tissue of my own cheek I can still feel the impact of my mother's hand when on that one occasion she struck me as a child, and I do not wish to reperform any of that with her, to her, it is enough that I regularly witness the rehearsals in my mind*—so I decided to minimise the danger by going back to working at the library.

My previous routine returned, though I no longer walked home by the river when it was dark, opting instead for the more circuitous route by the main roads. I started to research my third novel in earnest and set a deadline for its completion. My relationship with my mother settled, and it occurred to me—*happily?*—that maybe living with her until the novel was written might not be such a bad idea. And: *hold on, here is another idea, maybe I ought to stay on after that, too, and become her long-term carer. No rent. Good location. Write while she rests in the afternoons. Why not? The more I think about it, the more it makes sense. Is this the solution to the problem of financing my literary career?*

Then—there was plenty of warning, it was hardly sudden, I am exaggerating its irruptive quality—the quarantine was announced. The library closed, along with everything else. The roads emptied out. The machines went quiet. The birds sang. And, as Jung says of one of his visions:

> it seemed to me as if behind the horizon of the cosmos a three-dimensional world had been artificially built up, in which each person sat by himself in a little box...Life and the whole world struck me as a prison, and it bothered me beyond measure that I should again be finding all that quite in order. I had been so glad to shed it all, and now it had come about that I—along with everyone else—would again be hung up in a box by a thread.

And, I, too, *found all that quite in order.* Philosophically speaking, I was at ease with the idea of a closed world whose boundaries I could see and which I could control. Yet it was not long before I, in reality, found myself standing on one side of this *little box*, directly across from where she was seated, and screaming at her·

'Gavin does fucking do it! Why are you telling people that I don't do it!'

For I had overhead her telling her friends on the phone that she was continuing to do her shopping, despite the rule against over-seventies going into shops. 'Well, I mean, I have to get my bits and bobs,' she said to them, and I could hear the voices on the other end of the line objecting, and with good reason: 'But can Gavin not do it?'

Which made me want to explode.

And, predictably, inevitably, I did.

'How do you think the food appears on the table every day? By magic?'

And I thought, *This time I'm not apologising, this time she has gone too far, she clearly has no respect, no feelings for me at all, I have to get away from her, I will die if I spend another minute in her orbit, it is just as Louise Bourgeois says:*

> sometimes I think of a box as an
> agent of refuge withdrawal + peace—
> but of course sometimes children die
> in the womb or are asphyxiated in
> a hiding place

But it transpired that I had no control over what I did in the future, and I ended up needing not to be the wronged one, I could not bear to be the son of a bad mother, so I did what I was always going to: I said sorry to her, again, and thereby made her good.

Six weeks in, her birthday came round.

'Happy birthday,' I said.

'It's not my birthday.'

She had slept late. I had come in to wake her.

'It *is* your birthday, Mum. And your friends are arriving in five minutes with coffee and cake to have outside.'

'Oh my God.'

On the step, after cake, a friend broke the regulations to embrace my mother.

'I just love you so much,' the friend said, as though she were losing my mother, as though my mother were going away forever, and they stood holding each other for a highly illegal span of time, and the friend cried, and all the people watching also cried, and I think my mother did, too.

When her friends left, my mother went for her walk, and I stood in the kitchen, alone, and wept loudly. By chance, at that moment, a friend called from Spain.

'Sorry, I don't know why I'm crying.'

'It's all right, Gavin. You don't have to know. Just fucking cry.'

The doorbell did not stop ringing all day: gifts of plants and flowers and wine and chocolates and cake and homemade brown bread and, of course, books. There were so many cards that a string needed to be hung across the bookshelves to hang them on:

—*Our beloved B.*
—*A dear friend.*
—*You are my inspiration.*
—*You are a beautiful gift to me and so many others.*
—*To one of the most wonderful women to grace the earth.*
—*I think of you with your bright light of curiosity and joy of a ten-year-old.*
—*Your energy and kindness have always inspired me.*
—*Thank you for being you.*

A surprising number of the cards were from people I do not know.

'Who's this from?' I said, holding one of them up.

'Someone I helped,' she said. 'An MS patient.'

'She says some lovely things here.'

'Well, I did work very hard.'

'She's not saying these things because you worked hard, Mum. She's saying them because she loves you.'

She was at the table, making a list of names to send thank-you notes to. When I say she was frantic, I am not hyperbolising. Checking and rechecking who sent what. ('Who sent this?') Circling and recircling each name. Choosing the card from her extensive stash. Preparing the envelopes. Licking the stamps. Arranging the stack, flicking through it, then remaking it. So intense was her fear of appearing unappreciative— the demon instilled in her by her parents—that she would not be able to relax until her heightened expressions of gratitude were disseminated, and probably not even then.

'Did you hear me, Mum?'

'Who sent this?'

By evening, the flat was filled with bouquets. There were no vases left to put them in. The smell was overpowering.

'I find it excruciating.'

'What's excruciating?'

She was kneeling on the hard floor, trimming stems and dividing them into buckets of water.

'People giving me presents.'

'That's not very gracious. You're denying people the joy they're trying to transmit. Let it in, Mum.'

'You either feel it or you don't.'

Later, I put a pair of noise-cancelling headphones over her faulty ears, and the family gathered on Zoom.

'There's K,' she said, pointing at the little boxes on the screen. 'There's M. There's E. Oh, I'm overwhelmed. I can't think of anything to say. I get up at nine, then it's bedtime. I don't know what I'm doing with my life. This is just like Christmas dinner, everyone is talking and no one is listening.'

After supper, I put candles on a cake and lit them. She dutifully blew them out so I could take a photo to send to the others. The photo turned out to be a lovely one. When I showed it to her, she got up unexpectedly and embraced me. I could feel her bones and she could feel mine.

'We are close,' she said. 'Sometimes we clash and get on each other's nerves. But you're the youngest. *My prince.*'

The next day, she was exhausted. Unusually, she did not leave the flat. Between meals, she ate thin slivers of her birthday cake. Sitting on the couch, rather than in her armchair, she switched between staring into space and dipping into one of the books she had been given: Michael Longley's *Ghetto*, a limited-edition collection of poems about Helen Lewis, a choreographer, writer, and Holocaust survivor who lived in Belfast and taught dance there. A beautiful gift, perfectly chosen.

'Have you been to Auschwitz?' she said.

'No.'

'I went there with your brother.'

'I know.'

'It's a place every schoolchild ought to visit.'

'Yes.'

She sighed and turned to look out the window.

'You look pensive,' I say. 'Are you thinking about yesterday?'

'I feel overcome.'

'You are adored, Mum.'

'I'm not *that* good a person.'

'You don't have to be a saint to be adored. Get rid of that idea.'

'I'm lucky to have so many friends.'

'Luck is only part of it.'

'And then there are all the people I hate with a vengeance.'

The following day was my father's birthday (he would have been eighty-two). Six days after that, the twentieth anniversary of his death. A concert had been planned, curated by my opera-singer niece, but this had to be cancelled.

'I'm relieved,' I said to my mother.

'So am I,' she said.

We could not go to the cemetery as it is located in the Dublin mountains, outside the five-kilometre quarantine limit. And, to be honest, I was not sure we would have gone anyway. My mother had only ever been an occasional grave-goer; these days, she did not visit at all. As she was now without a car, she would have been obliged to ask friends or family for a lift, which she refrained from doing, or perhaps forgot to do. 'I must go to the grave,' she said from time to time, but without conviction; saying the words, expressing an intention, seemed to be enough for her (as, for some people, saying 'I must go to Mass' counts as having gone, in the eyes of their god). I had even less interest in making the trip. I had never got anything out of being there. No feelings of closeness. No outpourings of memories or feelings. The cemetery is in a nice location, overlooking the city. And the gravestone, designed by my brother R (a smooth block of granite with a large circular hole drilled through its centre) is impressive. But, on my rare visits, instead of focusing my attention on it—meditating in its direction, as I have seen others do—I would end up strolling up and down the paths, as I would do in cemeteries in foreign cities, perusing the graves of strangers and asking, *What happened to her? What happened to him?*

A few rows south of my father's plot lies the grave of a boy who was in my class in primary school. A boy from a tower block in the working-class estate adjacent to the school. A boy who was always getting into trouble, and who was frequently blamed for misdemeanours, whether he was the culprit or not. A boy who never called me names. A boy who, on the contrary, tended to be soft with me. A boy who asked my opinion about things and was grateful to me when I allowed him to copy my homework.

A few weeks after my father's death, I had, by chance, seen for the first time the carved letters of this boy's name, alongside a mounted photograph of his smiling face—an adolescent face, much older than the one I knew—and it had stopped me in my tracks. Then, yes, I felt something. A deep sadness. I made some inquiries and discovered that he had died by suicide. As unsurprising as this news was, it made a rent in my heart. And I wondered, I really wondered. *Why did he do it?*

The day of the anniversary itself passed without any mention of my father. But a couple of days later, after a glass of wine, my mother brought him up:

'Your father had so much guilt.'

And it occurred to me that, in doing so, she was, in her own way— that is obliquely, not entirely consciously—attempting to answer the question, why did he do it? And I, after twenty years of avoiding this question, of rejecting it as stupid and pointless—*where does such speculation get anyone?*—found myself willing to join her in it.

'His mother adored him, but she herself suffered from her nerves. And his sister went from one breakdown to the next. He was surrounded by it—'

'By what? Sadness?'

'—and couldn't do anything about it, couldn't handle it. He felt guilty about everything.'

My grandmother, my father's mother, had died when I was eight or so. My memories of her cohere around family meals, to which she would arrive wearing a turban and a long coat that smelled musty like old houses. She was very thin and had false teeth that shifted about in her mouth when she spoke. My mother would take her coat and lead her to her place at the table. There, my grandmother would thank my mother for having her and for going to all this trouble, and then she would take to apologising for herself, persistently, until, at some point—sometimes more than once—she would break down in tears. Curious but not wanting to stare, I would chance some glances in her direction, and I would behold there, within touching distance, the strange sight of an old woman openly weeping. I pitied her, as I pitied all people whom I saw crying, but I was also mortified by her, and mystified, too, as to what was happening to make her behave this way. So it came as a relief, then, when my father would say something stern to her—I cannot recall the precise words he used—to make her stop.

My aunt, my father's sister, had a similar routine. She wore bright pink lipstick which would gradually be rubbed off by the contortions of her tongue as she fought to keep her own false teeth in place while she ate. She, too, would make a point of apologising for herself—'It's all right,' my mother would reply, 'just eat up now'—before finally giving way to sobs. At which juncture, my father would convey to her the same frustration, the same impatience as he did to his mother. One affliction, one intervention.

'So,' I asked my mother now, 'do you think mental illness is passed on from one generation to another? That it's inherited, like hair colour?'

Is the mother to blame?

'It's what they say,' she said.

'It *is* what they say,' I said. 'And maybe the statistics bear it out. But is it beneficial for the sufferer to think about his suffering in this way? As something that has been passed on to him and that he will pass on in turn?'

'I don't know.'

'Maybe, on some level, Dad believed that by virtue of the family he was born into, he was doomed to a life of psychological torment. And maybe he could not allow himself to blame his mother or his sister for his problems, so he turned the accusing finger on himself. This way, when the time came, he could also blame himself for how his own children turned out.'

'Maybe.'

There was a moment of silence then, during which I noticed how much I was enjoying talking about my father, and wondered why I did not do it more often. Why did I not feel more for him? Why was I so angry about my mother's perceived abandonment, but not, on the face of it at least, about his?

'Do you think it bothered him that I'm gay?'

'No. Your father didn't care about that.'

'I'm not so sure.'

'He was conservative, but when it came down to it, he didn't give a hoot about what the neighbours or anyone else thought. He just wanted you to be happy.'

'Hmm. And what about N? He definitely saw himself as the cause of N's problems.'

Her features form a pained expression: 'Well, that's true. N broke his heart.'

My father had wanted to see N 'cured'. But what would a cure have looked like? The disappearance of a symptom? An alteration of the underlying personality? If such a thing were achievable, would it be desirable? And where would the curing stop? Where would the line be drawn? Forcing N to confront the truth about himself would require him, N, to accept an immense loss: the confiscation of nothing less than his entire system of belief, decades in the making. What scars would be left after such surgery, if indeed he survived it?

And who would do the curing? My father? Who himself needed the cure?

N, the incurable, had not merely been a problem *for* my father; N had been precisely his own problem reflecting back on him. My father was unable to stop seeing N as a piece of him, of what was wrong with him and could not be fixed. *I made N, and, by being mad myself, I made N*

312

mad. In N's inadequacies, he saw his own, and there was no escape from this noose.

In the months leading up to my father's death, the two things cited by my father as the sources of his stress were his job and N. Which makes me think that they were never properly separate in his mind. The same stress, the same pain. He could not allow himself to hate work or his son (who hated work). The only alternative—the way out—was to hate himself.

The sales process at my father's job was antiquated and unnecessarily labour intensive. Shortly before his suicide, his bosses were planning to introduce a new, computerised system. This terrified my father, even though it would have made his job easier. On a couple of occasions, before the switch, he asked me to come with him to the office to help him clear some order backlogs. This involved punching long lists of serial numbers into a hand-held device for hours on end, a task that today would be done instantly with a scanner.

'This is crazy,' I said when, after only a few minutes of this work, my eyes began to hurt. 'This should be automated. No one needs to be doing this dog's work.'

Which sent my father into a rare fury.

I cannot remember another occasion when he lost his temper with me in this manner. He went red in the face and shouted, which I did not think him capable of. It shocked me. Then filled me with shame, for his colleagues were there to witness it.

He apologised in the car on the way home.

To which I said something like: 'You know, Dad, computers are nothing to be frightened of. They'll train you in how to use them. N can show you the basics on his computer at home. You'll be well able for it.'

But I could tell my words were falling on deaf ears. Such reassurances, from a person much younger and better educated than him, only served to make him more anxious. And what had N's computer ever solved, anyway?

How sorry for him I felt in that moment.

And how sorry I feel for N when I see him nowadays. The feeling is practically, for all intents and purposes, the same.

———

The last time I saw N was just before quarantine, when we went for tacos. Veggie ones for me, meat ones for him. Mine arrived first, in a little basket. Even before I had a chance to thank the waiter, N's filthy, long-nailed hand had picked up my food and brought it to his mouth.

'That's mine,' I said.

'Oh,' he said, and dropped it back into the basket.

When his arrived, he doused it in hot sauce, then wolfed it down, barely chewing.

I ordered him some more.

'It's sort of picky food,' I said when he had finished. 'Are you full?'

He shrugged: 'I need a van.'

'What do you need a van for?'

'To set up my business. Painting and decorating.'

'N, no one is asking you to do that. Why don't you just relax about the work thing.'

His few remaining strands of hair, which emanated from the centre of his otherwise bald pate, he was keeping long. When he dropped his head down to peer at the tabletop, they fell in front of his face, reaching as far as his mouth.

'I'm broke,' he said, brushing them back over his head.

'I know.'

'I never should've left America.'

'You know, N, the government benefits that you get here, you wouldn't get over there. There's no welfare in America.'

He sighed: 'Why are we so poor?'

'We're not that poor. Our sister has a great job. As does R.'

'We should never have sold the house.'

'Our family home? I hated that house. I'm glad it's gone.'

'If we still had that house, I could have used it as a base. For my business.'

'You hated that house, N. And if Mum still owned it, you wouldn't be living in it. You two can't be in the same room for longer than five minutes.'

I did not know why I was reasoning with him in this way. It was not about the house, or the van, or the business. It was about his hunger, which would never, now, be satiated.

'All I need is a van. And a place to stay while I get the business up and running.'

'What about your art?'

'Yeah, that too. I'm going to set up a website and start selling it online. Prints, you know?'

'Oh, that's a good idea. Why don't you focus on that?'

'Yeah. No money in it, though. I might get a taxi licence instead.'

'You don't even have a driving licence.'

'Do you have one?'

'I do. I've never owned a car, though.'

'Well, I need a van. If I had a van, I'd be sorted.'

I gestured to the waiter for the bill.

'And Mum, have you seen her recently?'

He shrugged: 'We should never have sold that house.'

Later, back at the flat, I asked our mother about him, how she thought he was getting on. From what she told me, I got the sense that she did not know much about what his life was like any more. About where he went or what he did. About what state he was in. I had only the scantest idea myself, but my turning away from him had happened a long time ago and had been an act freely undertaken. My mother, for her part, had kept with him, kept at him until physically, chemically, genetically she had no longer been able. Today her knowledge of him seemed not to extend beyond the fact of his sojourns at my sister's.

'I feel terrible that your sister has taken him on.'

At one time, she had been consumed by him. He had occupied a vast space in her psyche and stoked her strongest emotions: usually anger first, then guilt and shame. But, as her memory retreated, so too did her fastening to him. She could no longer hold the great weight of him in her mind. She let him drop. Mentioned him less and less. And when she did, it was with resignation. Sadness.

'When it comes to N, I don't have what it takes any more.'

At some point, N, too, had realised that she had no more to give him, and stopped pestering her so much. She became his last resort. Now, it seemed, he turned to her only on those occasions, rare enough, when my siblings refused to give him more than his agreed weekly allowance (to which I was not, and am not, a contributor). When that happened, he would call her with his demand, that she 'meet him in town', and she would follow the script:

'You mean you want money. How much?'

'Forty or fifty.'

'All right. When?'

He usually insisted they meet that same day.

To which she had taken to saying:

'Remember, N, I am eighty now. I am slower. I will meet you tomorrow.'

When quarantine began, she stopped hearing anything from him, and she did not call him, either. To me, she did not mention him. Until one evening at supper, soon after our confrontation about the school, she said:

'Once I was called into the school because N had misbehaved again. And one of the teachers said to me, *You know, Mrs McCrea, I always liked N.* I will never forget it.'

'Never forget what?' I say.

'Those kind words.'

'You think those words are kind?'

'The kindest I ever heard a teacher use about N.'

I always liked N.

Past tense.

As if his life had just ended.

As if, at fourteen, he was already finished.

A centenarian woman has survived the virus. This is being sold as good news, but my mother is not buying it.

'I don't want to live that long,' she says, pointing to the woman's picture on the front of the newspaper. 'I don't even want to see ninety.'

'I have a feeling you'll get to ninety.'

'Oh God.'

'You'll have to stop being so healthy.'

'You're right. It's not doing me any favours.'

A few days later, a letter appears in the same newspaper, written by a woman from the same neighbourhood I grew up in, about her experience of caring for her demented mother. The letter writer is unknown to me, as are the scenes she describes, though I read her words with a dreadful feeling of recognition, as though peering into a dark puddle that is my future.

Quarantine, she writes, has given her *'a strong sense of déjà vu.'* She has lived in lockdown before, *'for almost six years when I was the sole carer for my late mother who had a stroke and dementia...My mother could not be left unsupervised for even very short periods of time so we did our grocery shopping online and I lost face-to-face contact with my friends as I could not leave the house.'*

I look up from the paper, and for a minute watch my mother sleeping in her chair, her head tilted back against the rest, her arms folded, her belly full of broad beans, the unfinished crossword on her lap, serene, dreaming, in a world of her own. As her condition worsens, she will spend more and more time like this, alone with herself, in her dreams, except, of course, she will be awake. And there will be the question, then, of how much she will know, how much she will feel, when someone else (*I want it to be me, I don't want it to be me, will it be me?*) is changing her and washing her and feeding her. And the question, too, of who I will be, if she no longer knows who I am: what will I love, and what will I hate, about a mother who has forgotten me?

Your rear end I will love. *Your bottom. Your vagina. Your anus. Your shit.* I will adore all of that. It is the exhaustion that I will hate. No, the isolation. No, what I will truly find unbearable is the abandonment:

> Days merged into weeks into months [the letter continues] and
> months into years...We did not sleep in a bed for a single night
> between 2004 and 2007...My mother paced the house all night,

confused and disorientated, and I walked with her. The total and relentless exhaustion was indescribable. The heartbreak was devastating. The isolation and loneliness left me feeling totally alone in the world, abandoned and afraid of what the future would bring.

Fighting difficult feelings, I look again at my beautiful mother at rest. 'If I'm ever attached to a machine,' she likes to say, 'switch it off.'

And I want at all costs to impress her in this regard. To prove to her that I can save her from suffering. But what if there is no machine, nothing to attach her to, and only the four walls of this cell, always returning—*Where am I? You're at home*—and impossible to switch off?

I have lived in rage at my mother for having accepted, too willingly, her lot. I have resented her for having been unable to solve the most important problems of *my* life. Yet I can also see—in lucid moments like this, I can—that what for her has been insoluble, she has outgrown, and, if I am anything like her, I will do the same.

'*The rug was pulled from under me. Therefore I live in the present. I don't trust the future.*'

EPILOGUE: MADRID, 20—

As soon as the quarantine is lifted, I will travel with my mother to Madrid, where we will stay in a rented flat in Lavapiés with two long glass doors giving onto a balcony that catches the morning sun, and after breakfast eaten at a little table perched high over the busy street, we will set out on foot along Calle de Lavapiés, past the Indian restaurants and the Chinese shops and the Africans peddling handbags, to Tirso, where my mother will use the public toilets out of a fear that she will be caught out later, then we will go west along Calle del Duque de Alba to the Mercado de la Cebada, where we will buy some fruit and bottles of water, before heading north again, cutting through Plaza de los Carros and El Jardín del Príncipe de Anglona to the Palacio Real, in front of which, in the Jardines de Lepanto, we will eat our fruit and watch the tourists for a minute, and my mother will rub some more sun cream in to her cheeks, even though she already has a solid layer on, before we continue north to the Templo de Debod, the ancient temple donated by Egypt to Spain, where we will walk under the arch of desert stone, and I will say, 'Does Europe really need—' and she will say, 'Pardon?' and so I will say, louder this time, 'Does Europe really need more African treasures to add to those we've already stolen?' and she will say, 'I know, isn't it gorgeous?' which will put an end to that particular avenue of discussion, even though I will have something further to add (a clever line about Africa being Europe's subconscious), so again we will fall to silence as we make our way to Plaza de España and cross Gran Vía onto Calle de los Reyes, through the streets of Malasaña, taking in Plaza del Dos de Mayo and its memorial to the

1808 rebellion staged by the people of Madrid against the French occupation—immortalised by Goya in his painting *El tres de mayo de 1808 en Madrid*—then we will turn south along the pedestrianised Calle de Fuencarral and east to Plaza de Chueca, where we will sit on a terrace, the fullest I can find, and, while eating our snack of omelette and black-ink rice, we will watch the gay men at the other tables and passing by—the hair and the legs and the sunglasses and the beards—and as much as I will enjoy being here with my mother and playing the gay son, a role which tends to soften me and make me appear more friendly than I am, I will also wonder what the hell I am doing here with her, why I have not come to Madrid on my own, why I am hiding behind her like this instead of asserting my sexuality and actively pursuing an erotic encounter, and then she will say something to annoy me—anything she could say would do that now—and I will snap at her, and she will say, 'What's wrong with you?' and I will say, 'Let's just not talk for a while,' and once she has gone to the toilet again and paid the bill—she will have told me that she is going to pay before sitting down, and I will not have argued with her—we will head east to Retiro, where she will insist we do a full round of the park to work off the food, which will mean another coating of sun cream, for by now it will be late morning and the day will be heating up; the drug dealers hanging around the benches will watch her applying the cream, bemused, and she will feel their gaze and beam back at them, and they will say something like, 'Hey, lady, *chocolate? anfetas? coca?*' in response to which she will wave and say, 'Hello!' for she will not want to appear racist, and I will walk away from her then and pretend not to know her, and it will take her until the Palacio de Cristal to catch up with me, where she will say, 'You're a tyrant, you know that? No one will ever put up with you,' and I will laugh at that without disagreeing, then together we will loop round the Paseo de Fernán Núñez to the Fuente del Ángel Caído, where we will pause to admire the beautiful Lucifer writhing on his slab of rock, a giant snake where his penis should be, and I will say, 'I wonder what Freud would make of that?' and onwards we will go, now, hurrying for the final stretch through the Botanic Gardens to the Museo Nacional del Prado, our destination, where my mother will look at her watch and say, 'We made good time,' and I will check my phone to see how far we have walked—eight kilometres—and we will visit the toilet once more, to piss out all the water we have been drinking, and buy tickets and check in our bags—neither of us will take an audio guide, 'I couldn't bear to go around with that thing to my ear,' my mother will say loudly—then we will pass through the rooms, taking in some of the famous works, disregarding just as many, sometimes less interested in the art than in the people looking at the art, from time to time we will catch snippets of what their audio guides are saying, which will confirm for us the wisdom of not getting one, until we reach Goya's Black Paintings, which will hold us in their thrall for a long time—we will stand in front of *Saturno devorando a su hijo* until our knees begin to ache—but the Goya works I will be most anxious for my mother to see will not be in this room, nor indeed will they be on public display, it will be necessary to get special permission to access them, which I will move heaven and earth to do, for my mother must see them before she dies: I am talking about Goya's drawings, specifically the Dreams series, and especially number six, *Pregón de brujas*, in which an old witch is shown sitting in the gloom reading a book, while at her feet a naked child is doing a handstand in such a way that the candle that has been inserted into his anus can function as the witch's lamp; in the brighter foreground, a younger witch is lifting a second child into the air and using him as a trumpet to make a public announcement, which is to say she is blowing into his mouth and her breath is passing through him and coming out of his bottom, where a penis-shaped butt plug is converting his wind into music; meanwhile, two more children crouch on the ground, vomiting into a basin: it is a disturbing work, yet I will feel compelled to look at it for a long time, exploring and re-exploring its surface in an effort to extract meaning from it, as from a tarot card, returning most often to the children—the objects inserted into their arses, the vomit spilling from their mouths—and it will occur to me how clever it is of Goya to call this picture a 'dream', such a label provides an ideal cover for the obscenity, allowing things to be seen that in everyday discourse would be blacked out by moral mores and legal strictures, and it is interesting to notice that, once the veil of 'dream' has been pulled across my eyes, I accept the depictions of foulness and cruelty, indeed I revel in them, even though I do not believe that their origin is in an actual dream that Goya had; in other words, I give myself permission to scrutinise this horror as if it were dream, all the time knowing that the images portrayed here, far from being a dream, are a product of the waking imagination, or more specifically the anxieties that fuel it, in this case our anxieties about motherhood: *we all of us—*the drawing seems to be saying—*have a vision of our mothers as possessors of a special kind of knowledge, a knowledge proceeding not from male institutions of learning but rather from the natural condition of being a mother, a knowledge applied inside the home in the preparation of recipes and ointments and tonics that nourish us or cure our ailments or pick us up in a way that official medicine cannot; but this vision is accompanied by the suspicion, lurking in the recesses of our mind, that she—the same woman that nurses and sustains us—is also capable of turning on us, using her powers against us, shaming us, speaking through us, abusing us, quite literally poisoning us, making us sick, which is to say, publicly, consciously, we idolise our mothers as sages, while privately, unconsciously, we fear them as witches*: it is this unconscious fear that Goya knowingly captures in his drawing, and I will be curious to know if my mother recognises it, and if so what she thinks about it, how does it feel to be feared in this way? did she have a similar fear of her own mother? has she ever been afraid of herself *as* a mother?—but I am getting ahead of myself now, for there is a good chance that she will not agree to come with me to Madrid, that she will not go along with my desires, that she will refuse the role I have created for her in my daydreams; and it is also likely that, after these months spent in confinement with her, I will not want to be in her company for any significant length of time, either; and there is the possibility, too, that I will not make it to Madrid until after she is dead, in which case I, alone, will stay in a rented flat in Lavapiés with two long glass doors giving onto a balcony that catches the morning sun, and after breakfast eaten at a little table perched high over the busy street, will set out on foot to consult my dreams.

Author's Note

This is a work of nonfiction. My family members appear here as I see them. They had no hand in any of the writing. The judgements I make about them, and about everything else, are purely my own.

For legal reasons, I have changed some small details to protect the identity of non-family members.

Acknowledgements

I am grateful to Breda McCrea, Iñaki Moraza, Niamh McCrea, Barbara Ebert, and Eugene Langan for their love and support; to my agent, Rebecca Carter, and my editor, Molly Slight, for their continued encouragement and copious insights; and to the entire Scribe team, especially Sarah Braybrooke, Adam Howard, and Laura Ali in the UK, Henry Rosenbloom, Bella Li, Laura Thomas, and David Golding in Australia, and Emily Saer Cook in the United States, for their work in producing and promoting this book.

A special thank you to Luke Bird (www.lukebird.co.uk) and Guy Ivison, who designed the covers of my dreams.

Orla Keenan and Tom Vaughan-Lawlor helped to clarify some of my memories about primary school. Ruth Bowie, Rachel Gargan, and Genevieve Blake filled in some of the gaps from the adolescent years. These conversations were not always easy, but I will cherish them, as I cherish the friendships which made them possible.

Most of this book was written during my tenure as writer in residence at the University of Limerick. My thanks to Joseph O'Connor, Sarah Moore Fitzgerald, Donal Ryan, and Rob Doyle for helping to make my time at UL so memorable.

The writing of the remainder of the book was funded by a bursary from An Chomhairle Ealaíon (Irish Arts Council). My thanks to Sarah Bannan and the literature team at the Council for this support.